The Illustrated Guide to the
SUPERNATURAL

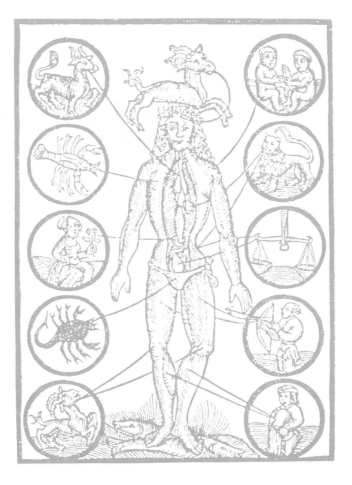

WINDWARD

General Editor: Sarah Litvinoff
Contributors: Vida Adamoli, James Cunningham,
Margaret Hickey, Sarah Litvinoff, Belinda Love,
Philippa May, Oliver Robb, Kate Taylor
Art Editor: Gordon Robertson
Designer: Ross George
Production Controller: Richard Churchill

Published by Windward, an imprint owned by
W. H. Smith & Son Limited
Registered No. 237811 England
Trading as WHS Distributors,
St John's House, East Street, Leicester LE1 6NE

© Marshall Cavendish Limited 1986
ISBN 0 7112 0454 3

Typeset by J & L Composition Ltd, Filey, North Yorkshire
Printed and bound in Spain by Artes Graficas Toledo, S.A.
D. L. TO:1110 -1986

CONTENTS

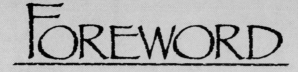

FOREWORD

We live in the third great age of magic in the West. The first was the period of the Roman Empire, when strange cults and mystical ecstasies and psychic experiment swept over the Roman world from the East. The second came during the Renaissance, with the rediscovery of the ancient world's occult lore and the recovery of a man-centred picture of the universe, a view of man as a potential god. The third, in our own time, began in a reaction against 18th-century rationalism and gathered strength with the founding of the Theosophical Society and the Order of the Golden Dawn; to be followed by the appearance on the scene, rising phoenix-like from the unlikely English nursery of Leamington Spa, of the most influential magician of the century, Aleister Crowley.

All three of these periods have characteristics in common. In all of them progress in science goes hand in hand with a decline of traditional, state-supported religion. Peculiar and unorthodox sects flourish. There is a lively interest in witchcraft, ghosts and hauntings, spiritual healing, beings from the outer reaches of the universe, self-development through meditation and altered states of consciousness. There is also a widespread interest in astrology, shared by many educated people.

Behind all this lies, again, a number of common factors: a dissatisfaction with rationalism, science and accepted religion; urbanization, cosmopolitanism, increased physical and social mobility which has cut people off from their roots and traditions, causing uncertainty and anxiety; a demand for a direct, personal relationship with whatever greater reality is hidden behind the surface appearance of things and the events of everyday life.

In our age of spiritual illiteracy, the Christian churches have lost the intellectual dominance they once enjoyed and church-going has ceased to be either a social necessity or an ingrained habit. Science, meanwhile, is too impenetrable for most people to understand and its professional apologists – as seen, for example, in television documentaries – employ a hectoring tone and an air of self-conscious virtue of the kind often found in 19th-century pulpits, but which very few modern clergymen would venture to adopt. So there is a spiritual and intellectual vacuum, and people who need something to believe in search around for a system of ideas to fill the gap.

At the same time, the complexity of life in modern western society creates a feeling of powerlessness and inability to use the conventional ladders to success, power, money and security, which leads people to turn to the occult and the supernatural to get what they want. This is what real medieval witches (real as distinct from the multitudes of completely innocent people who were brutally condemned as witches at the time) were trying to do. The same motive inspires many of the small groups and cults active in the occult underworld today.

It is getting on for twenty years since I first started to put together what eventually emerged as a seven-volume encyclopedia of the supernatural called *Man, Myth and Magic*. Even then there was ample evidence of a rising tide of public interest in magic and witchcraft, paganism, oriental mysticism and spiritual techniques, astrology and the Tarot, alternative medicine, ley lines, flying saucers, meditation and the occult in general. There was a growing appetite for the spiritual and the psychic, and a renewed taste for Gothic horrors like vampires and werewolves. All this was set against the background of a rebellion against rationalism, materialism, science and technology and the world they had made. We were seeing what W. B. Yeats in a telling phrase called 'the revolt of the soul against intellect'.

Today, far from breaking and ebbing, the tide of popular interest has risen higher still, against all surface probability in what is supposed to be (and in many ways is) a materialistic age. At the same time the tide of interest at the scholarly level has also continued to rise. It was scholarly interest in these matters, earlier on, which brought the modern discipline of comparative religion into existence, along with modern psychical research or parapsychology and the attempt to test the hidden powers of the mind and explore objectively such phenomena as poltergeists, out-of-the-body experiences and psychokinesis or 'mind over matter'. Even compared with twenty years ago, the number and quality of serious books and publications dealing with the subjects covered in this volume has very substantially increased.

The book you have in your hands, then, is an introduction, no more, to a huge, rich and fascinating range of topics. They are interlinked and many of them are too large and complex to be dealt with at any great length in a single volume. It follows that in some cases articles can only provide an outline picture of a subject like alchemy or witchcraft. But you will find suggestions for further reading, to lead you deeper into the maze.

The articles are written clearly and avoid technical terms and abstruse language. The illustrations to this book give a dramatic impression of the richness of material involved and the impact which the themes treated here have made on art and ideas over the centuries.

Even in an introductory book, a lot has to be left out. In particular, you will not find much material here on eastern mysticism and magic. The book concentrates mainly on the western tradition, which is the one that will be closest to most of its readers.

Finally, the question of the attitude of a book like this is important. You are not being asked here to believe six impossible things before breakfast, and the more contrary to common sense they are, the better. On the other hand, the determined scepticism, which refuses to let anything new into the charmed circle of what orthodoxy accepts, is equally witless and equally absent from these pages. Neither attitude – credulous or sceptical – has anything to do with evidence, which in each case is hewn and moulded to protect positions that were dug well in advance.

The general attitude of this book is positive rather than negative and sympathetic rather than hostile: though this naturally does not apply to the 'black' side of the subject and to matters like Satanism or malevolent witchcraft. At the same time, however, the contributors have attitudes and beliefs of their own which inevitably shine through what they have written. You are expected to supply your own salt-shaker.

RICHARD CAVENDISH

9

THE AETHERIUS SOCIETY

The Aetherius Society is a world-wide spiritual brotherhood and Church that teaches and practises cosmic wisdom. The founder/president and Metropolitan Archbishop of this educational, scientific and spiritual organization is his eminence Sir George King, a Western master of yoga who in 1954 was contacted for the first time by an interplanetary intelligence. He was instructed to prepare himself to be used as a channel of communication for the words of extraterrestrial beings, vastly our superiors both technologically and spiritually, who wanted to help prepare the world for the new age now dawning. The society has been given a series of teachings that take its spiritual concepts far beyond those of orthodox philosophy. Using an advanced yogic technique Sir George King has received over 600 transmissions from cosmic sources over 32 years, and he is still receiving them. This remarkable claim has been verified by, among other things, his predictions of where UFOs were going to be sighted, which then came to pass.

Sir George has also had other outstanding contacts including one historical event, described in the newly published book *Visit to the Logos of Earth*, in which he had the supreme honour of meeting the three ancient Lords of the Flame and of standing before the Ineffable Flame of the Logos, which is the Life Force of the Goddess Terra herself.

The Society says that metaphysics is the point where science and religion meet, and through its unique programme it proposes to offer a solution to what it calls the most vital crisis on earth — the spiritual crisis.

Its activities include divine services, absent healing and spiritual healing, courses in healing, psychometry and dowsing. Its most ambitious mission is Operation Prayer Power: this is a regular activity which involves ordinary people joining together and storing prayer energy in radionic batteries, which is then released at times of crisis when the earth needs it most.

ALCHEMY

Alchemy is commonly thought of as a medieval pseudo-science and the alchemist as either a charlatan or a deeply deluded human being who claimed that it was possible to turn base metals into gold.

Although alchemy remains mysterious because of the deliberately obscure language and symbolism that its practitioners used, the truth is rather more complicated. What is certainly true is that the alchemists sought gold not for its monetary value but because gold symbolized perfection and that the quest was seen as a spiritual, quite as much as a material, one: the perfection of the self going hand in hand with the perfection of metal.

In the mental universe of the middle ages it was simply impossible to separate what we would call 'pure' science from what we would regard as belonging to the realms of religion or MAGIC. Indeed the training and spiritual preparation of the alchemist are very similar to those of magic users. When medieval Europeans first began to experiment with what we would call chemistry or metallurgy by applying heat to metals and mixing them in their molten state they brought to their experiments ideas and mental atti-

Below: *Using the 'philosopher's stone' the alchemist would contrive to turn base metal into precious gold. (The Alchemist by Adriaen van Ostade, 1610–85)*

tudes that probably go back, like the higher levels of magic, to the Greco-Egyptian world of the last centuries before Christ. Chief among these ideas was the notion that there are secret but discoverable correspondences between all the elements in the universe; that the universe itself has a spiritual as well as a material dimension. All material things are different combinations of an essential material, which the alchemists called First Matter. This is composed of the four basic elements of fire, air, earth and water. These elements are combinations of the four qualities of hot, cold, wet and dry, so that earth for example is cold and dry, air hot and wet, and so on.

The notion of correspondence linked the principal metals with the seven known planets of the ancient world, as follows

GOLD	SUN
SILVER	MOON
MERCURY	MERCURY
COPPER	VENUS
IRON	MARS
TIN	JUPITER
LEAD	SATURN

(Mercury, being both metal and liquid, particulary fascinated the alchemists and was frequently used in their experiments.)

Alchemists believed that it was possible to take humble material and dissolve it to First Matter and then add qualities to it that would turn it into matter of a higher kind, and ultimately into gold. The language used to describe that process could, however, equally apply in the spiritual dimension to the dissolution and transformation of the self.

No one knows whether any alchemist ever succeeded in producing true gold but it may well be that the mysterious writings and richly symbolic pictures of the alchemists conceal secret wisdom of a quite different, and perhaps ultimately a more valuable kind.

Below: *Alchemists believed that the elements of earth, air, fire and water are contained in everything.*

ALIEN ANIMALS

Is the Abominable Snowman a form of Neanderthal man who has survived into the 20th century? And how can toads entombed in rock survive? These and other animal mysteries continue to intrigue the ardent cryptozoologist, who believes that human beings would themselves benefit from a closer study of the anomalous behaviour of animals.

There is a branch of science in which amateurs can still hold their own — they need no elaborate equipment, the language is still easy to comprehend and breakthroughs are as likely to occur to the lone observer as to teams of whitecoats in a laboratory. It is the science of biology. When we examine the fascination which the subject exerts we find that most people are drawn to anomalies, to the inexplicable, and the study of alien animals or animal behaviour, otherwise known as cryptozoology.

From the earliest times the rulers of nations wished to be informed of unusual happenings within the state, and ancient Chinese and Babylonian records exist, chronicling disturbances in the normal course of nature. Unrest among animals, for instance, was interpreted as indicating a possible earthquake, a phenomenon which scientists are currently researching — a little slow on the uptake!

Cryptozoology is the word coined by Dr Bernard Heuvelmans, who has interested himself in the mysterious aspects of the animal kingdom. The 19th century saw a pitched battle between rational scientists and 'amateurs' who refused to be trammelled by notions of what was acceptable or not. Naturally, self-styled 'rational scientists' looked down on those who reported weird monsters, showers of fishes and frogs, ape-men, and other bizarre phenomena, but the public has put its weight behind those honest souls who risk ridicule to record the evidence of their own senses.

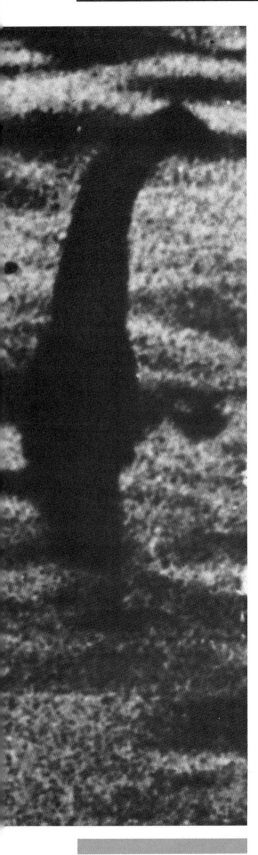

Above: *Is it possible that a huge aquatic serpent lives in the depths of Loch Ness?*

Famous Animal Mysteries

One of the world's favourite mysteries must be that of Nessie — the supposed Loch Ness Monster. It may be that there is a perfectly simple explanation for the many sightings there have been, but in over 50 years no one has managed to dispel the aura of mystery surrounding the creature — if creature there be. The earliest reports date back to 1933 and, interestingly, in the same year there was a series of reports from Vancouver Island about another aquatic monster. It was on Scotland, however, that the world's attention focused. Later it was discovered that there were earlier reports — one dating back to the 6th century, when St Columba, the Irish monk, drove back a great serpent.

In 1962 an investigative body was set up by Tim Dinsdale, whose photographs of Nessie had survived sophisticated computerized analysis, and several full-scale investigations have been carried out since, but to no avail — Nessie continues to elude us. It seems, at all events, that he or she has brothers and sisters all over the world, for apart from the Vancouver Island sightings, there are numerous reports of other Canadian aquatic monsters, a very clear photograph of a giant creature in America's Lake Champlain was taken in 1977, and other reports have come in from the USSR and also from the Japanese island of Hokkaido.

Perhaps as celebrated as that of Nessie is the case of the Yeti, or Abominable Snowman. This is one of many ape-men said to lurk in the more deserted parts of the earth. Stories have come in from the Himalayas (the Yeti), Borneo, Malaysia, South Asia, Australia, the western states of the US and Canada, Kenya and other parts of Africa.

Thought-form and Teleportation Theories

It is possible that some form of Neanderthal man has survived into the 20th century, but none of the reports has been backed by any evidence — we have casts of footprints but not a single bone. The physical evidence for these elusive creatures is as non-existent as it is for UFOs, and this has led to suggestions that they may be 'thought-forms', seemingly solid substance, conjured up by images in the human mind. Consciously or not, perhaps we can harness mental powers to create what we desire to see.

This latter theory may throw some light on a compelling branch of crypto-zoology — the phenomenon of animals being spotted where they ought never to have been. The British Isles has given a home to many imported fauna and even sheltered exotic zoo animals which have escaped and turned feral, such as the Peak District wallabies. Rational explanations can be found for most misplaced animals, but some stubbornly refuse to be accounted for.

The most widespread anomalous creature is the British big cat. After a spate of sightings, a puma was captured in 1980 by an Inverness farmer, at the other end of the country from Surrey where frequent reports of a puma-like creature had been made over the years. A strange animal, thought at first to be a puma, was seen in Kent, but pawprints and hairs proved that the beast was a spotted African hyena! If these are not thought-forms, nor escapees from private zoos and the like, there may be another explanation — that they were brought by teleportation. This theory has it that some force simply lifts a creature and transports it maybe hundreds of miles. It also accounts for the vast numbers of wingless creatures transported through the air, and the mysterious rains of beasts, particularly frogs, toads and fishes. This latter phenomenon is so widespread that scientists have had to find an explanation for it, since it cannot be denied. The current thinking is that whirlwinds and waterspouts suck up creatures that lie in their path and then deposit them as they gradually lose energy. But this theory does not, as it were, hold water. Only rarely do several species rain down together — frogs, fish, mud and weeds would all come down if the contents of a pond had been sucked up. So what has filtered out everything except, say, the frogs, and why is it that so often the animals fall to earth alive and unhurt? Some more adequate explanation will have to be found for a mystery which Pliny set down as far back as AD77.

Learning from Animal Behaviour

Besides falling from the sky, toads present another improbable yet well-attested phenomenon, but this time in the other direction, for many are the cases of workmen digging and splitting open a rock to find a toad inside it. Sometimes the toad is mummified, but often it emerges alive, and this has led to several experiments being carried out to test whether a toad, deliberately immured, can survive over a period of years. In one experiment, begun in 1771, two toads emerged alive in 1774, having had no air, water or food in that time.

It seems evident that closer scrutiny of animals, their behaviour and abilities, could lead to enormous benefits for human beings. Bats, to give just one example, had evolved an unerring radar system when humankind was still primitive.

The abilities of animals to cross thousands of miles of unknown territory must surely merit investigation. We know that some animals, such as pigeons, have a great instinct for homing. They may have some, as yet undiscovered, ability to find magnetic north and so orient themselves in the direction of their homes, but the distances covered can be enormous.

One story tells of an Alsatian bitch which travelled across the Southern Arizona desert, across the Grand Canyon, over mountain ranges in Nevada and Oregon to get back to her home in the state of Washington, over 2000 miles away. What guided her? And what is infinitely more puzzling is how some animals cover long distances to reunite themselves with their owners in places they have never been to before. A case authenticated by the RSPCA tells of how an Irish terrier, Prince, left his home in Staffordshire in the winter of 1914 and somehow got across the Channel and made his way to the trenches in France; he had come to join his master in the war. No human being would be capable of such a feat. Dumb animals?

Everyone is able to observe some creatures close at hand, from the family pet to animals in the wild, and the most sceptical of people would admit that there are still mysteries to be solved. The whole field of cryptozoology is wide open to all comers, and each of us can contribute by remaining alive to the teeming world around us with its sometimes irrational-seeming phenomena. Nothing is barred except a closed mind.

Above: *This is a cast of a mammoth footprint found in the Russian mountains in 1979, apparently a trace of the huge 'Russian snowman'.*

ALL HALLOWS' EVE

All Hallows' Eve or Hallowe'en is the evening of 31 October, the night before the Christian feast of All Saints or All Hallows. Since that is a particularly holy day in the Christian calendar the night preceding it has long been seen as one on which evil creatures, demons and witches especially, were likely to be active.

However, All Hallows' Eve coincides with a festival much older than Christianity, a pagan festival of fire and of the dead. The Celts of northern Europe called this celebration Samhain and it is likely that the bonfires that are now lit in Britain on Guy Fawkes Night derive from the ritual fires of those ancient Celts.

The onset of the cold and dark of winter, the bringing of the cattle into shelter, the feebleness of the sun, must all have suggested the vital importance of fire, and the lighting of bonfires may have been a form of IMITATIVE MAGIC to assist the ailing sun and assure its eventual return to full vigour. But the bitterness of the season just beginning must also have induced a desire to welcome into the warmth of the household the wandering souls of the dead. The gifts that children demand as they go from house to house on Hallowe'en

almost certainly recall the food and drink that were left for the ancestral ghosts in pagan times.

Hallowe'en is also a night on which one is particularly likely to encounter the trooping FAIRIES.

See also WITCHCRAFT

Above: *Hallowe'en – a children's festival now, which still echoes its earlier connection with witches.*

ANGELS

The word 'angel' comes from a Greek word meaning messenger and most of the early Bible references are to angels conveying messages from God to Man, such as the angel who spoke to Abraham when he was about to sacrifice Isaac, and the angel who announced to Mary that she was about to bear the Son of God.

They are also seen, however, as the host of spiritual beings who surround the throne of God and who have ranks and functions and even leaders, such as Michael who led the heavenly host against Satan, and Gabriel, the angel of the Annunciation. In medieval Christianity the angelic functions became highly specific, each nation and each individual having its own guardian angel. The lower ranks of angels, who inhabited the lower heavens, looked after human affairs, while the higher ranks were Angels of the Presence, surrounding God Himself. The supreme angelic figures were the seven archangels, who now included Michael and Gabriel and sometimes even Christ, and who were associated with the seven planets then known.

Although angels are almost invariably described as perfect spiritual beings, Christian beliefs also contained the apparently contradictory idea of a War in Heaven in the course of which the proud angel Lucifer and his army were defeated, to become Satan and his fellow-devils. Matters of this kind were the subject of much debate among medieval theologians, who have been mocked in later ages for their discussions on such questions as the number of angels that might dance on the head of a pin.

See also DEVILS AND DEMONS

Below: *The world of angels was intensely imagined by great artists. Fra Angelico saw it as a pastoral paradise for angels and saints.* (Heaven *by Giovanni Fra Angelico*)

AQUARIUS

Aquarius the Water-carrier, the 11th sign of the Zodiac, is an Air sign, ruling those born between 20 January and 18 February.

Aquarians are highly individual. They are inventive, creative and ever fascinated by new ideas. They read widely. The ancients believed Aquarians had the mythical psychic 'third eye', which could explain a tendency towards visionary ideas, flashes of intuition and brilliant invention.

Often Aquarians are misunderstood. Although gregarious, they may seem slow or shy to others. The truth is that they are dreamers, idealists, for ever seeking Utopia in their minds. They can appear absent-minded and even lazy at work.

Some Aquarians are over-influenced by the stern planet Saturn, which means that they tend to take life and their work rather seriously. They are sensitive to the opinions of others and are unable to shrug off criticism lightly. Sometimes they exaggerate problems in a bout of gloomy pessimism.

Yet when the planet Uranus prevails, it brings out the characteristically unconventional, rebellious streak in Aquarians. Then they feel no timidity, no compulsion to conform to other people's ideas of how they should act.

Science and technology often attract Aquarians, who are well starred to take up careers in radio, TV, computers or aviation. Charles Darwin was a typically Aquarian genius, with a flair for logical thinking and a relentlessly probing scientific mind. His revolutionary theory of evolution, *The Origin of the Species*, rocked the foundations of Christian teaching in the last century.

A strong imagination and a gift for insight are both typically Aquarian traits. These lead them to excellence in journalism, acting or writing. Germaine Greer, for instance, feminist author of *The Female Eunuch*, uses her talent for communication to argue for the rights of women in an unequal society. She is a truly Aquarian humanitarian.

Symbolized by the Water-carrier, they enjoy looking after other people. The 'caring' professions often draw them, as does religion. They may devote themselves to a cause in life. Aquarians are sympathetic, gentle and patient with other people. They dislike snobbery and pretentiousness, abhorring class differences and racial prejudice. No social climbers, Aquarians would hate to be thought better than they are, because truth is all-important to them. At their best Aquarians embody many of the finest of human qualities.

In relationships, however, their shyness can be a serious drawback. Friends are never certain whether an Aquarian likes them or not, for Aquarians imagine that their feelings are obvious. Lovers may interpret such undemonstrativeness as coldness or indifference. Yet Aquarians have deep emotions and can suffer from extreme jealousy. Loyalty is one of their best qualities and they are compatible with those born under LIBRA and GEMINI.

Physically Aquarians tend to be tall and well made, with pale skin. They may have a high forehead, a prominent chin and light brown hair. Aquarians are prone to damage in their calves and ankles, and should also watch out for blood disorders such as bad circulation and varicose veins.

See also ASTROLOGY

Below: *Mia Farrow, an Aquarian famed for sensitive acting.*

ARIES

Aries, the Ram, is the first sign of the Zodiac, a Fire sign, ruling those born between 21 March and 19 April.

This is the sign of renewal, leadership and energy. Ariens did not get where they are today (the top) by sitting around thinking things out. They did it with drive, determination, immense confidence and enthusiasm. Impulsively they always act first and think later. Self-doubt is almost unknown in Ariens, who inspire others with their firm, unwavering beliefs.

Ariens lead by example, fearlessly tackling the most daunting challenges. Physically courageous, they make strong military leaders. Politics also attracts a great many Ariens, notably Lenin and Hitler.

Although he is an extreme example, Adolf Hitler illustrates some of the typically Arien faults rather dramatically. They can be pigheaded, ruthless, impatient, short-tempered, greedy, uncompromising and power-mad. They may ignore the rights and wishes of other people in their single-minded pursuit of a goal. Yet, right or wrong, Ariens have the charisma to inspire others to follow them. Luckily most Ariens settle for realistic personal goals rather than world domination, channelling their energy and ambitions in positively beneficial directions.

Another famous Arien was Charlie Chaplin. As a film director, Chaplin was so sure that his way was right that he would often act a scene himself to show the actors how he wanted it. Now he is often acclaimed as a genius, but his typically Arien methods must have exasperated many an actor.

Ariens make good executives in many fields. Their independence, ingenuity, self-reliance and aggression give them a formidable edge in business. It is good to have an Arien on your side for they drive a hard bargain. In negotiations of any kind, Ariens are likely to state their position clearly and firmly, reiterating their viewpoint forcefully as often as is necessary to persuade the other side to give in. They will never compromise if they can help it.

Ariens also have successful careers in the fields of sport, exploration, travelling, engineering, mechanics, the medical profession and the police and fire services. Metal or fire are likely to feature in the work.

Compatible with Ariens are those born under LEO and SAGITTARIUS. In relationships, Ariens may be too domineering to be easy partners, but at least their energy and enthusiasm ensure that they are never dull. They will have many admirers. To be successful in marriage Ariens need to notice their partners more, making an effort to consider someone else's wishes for a change.

Physically Ariens tend to be lean and wiry, moving quickly. They seem to have boundless reserves of energy, which can give them an impatient air. They may have round faces, with snub noses, full chins, hazel or grey eyes and brown-to-red curly or wiry hair.

They should watch out for health problems related to the head. Eye difficulties or headaches warrant investigation. Head wounds, toothache and fevers such as influenza are likely.

Below: Adolf Hitler had many of the negative qualities associated with this fire sign.

See also ASTROLOGY

ASTRAL BODY

The astral body, also known as the body of light, is a replica of your physical body in every way, except that it has no solidity. Most people are unaware of their own astral bodies, existing as they do inside us and inhabiting both the physical and the astral plane. But some people can, by effort of will, project their astral bodies and travel in them for short periods of time.

During astral travel you retain all your normal senses. You can see your physical body where you left it — usually lying on the bed. You can travel, ghost-like, through solid objects and remember all that you saw and heard after you return to your normal body. You are visible to anyone you meet, but although you look solid, your appearance is more luminous than normal. People can hear, as well as see, you.

Part of the pleasure of astral travel is the feeling of buoyancy and the ability to float and fly at will. It only feels unpleasant if you are frightened by your success in leaving your physical body and panic about returning.

Some people, when very ill or extremely exhausted, spontaneously find themselves in their astral bodies looking down at their physical selves, although these experiences are usually much briefer than conscious astral projection.

Aleister CROWLEY in his book *Magick in Theory and Practice* warns that if you do not properly reunite your two bodies after astral travel, 'your body of light may wander away uncontrolled and be attacked and obsessed. You will become aware of this through the occurrence of headache, bad dreams, or even more serious signs such as hysteria, fainting fits, possibly madness.'

Astral travel is practised by ordinary people as well as magicians. Sylvan Muldoon, an American writer, believes it is possible for anyone to do this. Like other astral travellers he places great importance on being able to regulate your breathing — and even your heart-beat — as well as creating a strong mental image of your astral body and building an intense desire to inhabit it.

Dr Francis Lefèbure, was a doctor in an Algerian prisoner-of-war camp during the Second World War. He practised astral travel regularly, which he partially accomplished through Yoga breathing exercises. He was considered a joke by the other officers, until the night his astral body went walking and met the lieutenant. The lieutenant greeted him, and the doctor answered, 'It's not me, it's my double,' and promptly disappeared.

The lieutenant, who had not touched a drop of drink all day, rushed back to the camp and found that the doctor was in bed, and had never left his quarters.

From then on, it was acknowledged that the doctor had strange powers, and the phrase 'It's not me, it's my double' became a catchphrase in the town.

See also OUT-OF-BODY EXPERIENCES

Below: *Astral travel as interpreted by an artist. 1) The astral body leaves the recumbent form, attached by a 'silver cord'. 2) The astral body drifts upwards. 3) The astral body is now free to travel. 4) It must return, or harm may come to the physical body.*

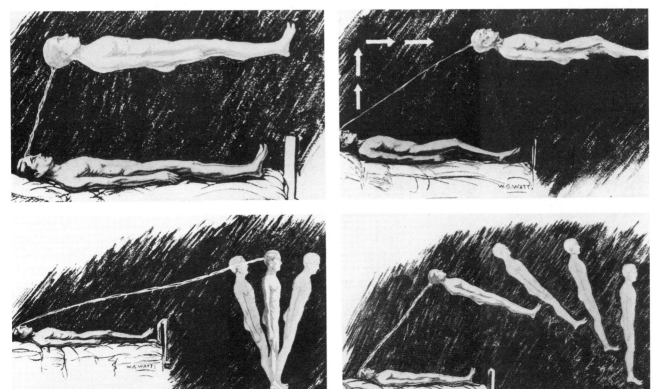

ASTROLOGY

Astrologers believe that our personalities, relationships, careers, fortunes — in fact our whole lives — are influenced by the planets. Is the traditional Zodiac out of date? And will the coming Age of Aquarius be one of peace and harmony or an age of winter?

Astrologers have long believed that our characters are shaped by the movements of the planets in the solar system. Astrology is the ancient art of foretelling and interpreting the influence of planets on human lives.

Modern astrology is the result of an amalgamation of many ideas. Theories from ancient Babylon, plus astronomy (the scientific study of planetary movements) mixed with psychology and intuition make up the science/art of astrology. As the sum of human knowledge has increased, astrology has evolved too.

Early astrologers were respected astronomers, mathematicians and scientists who were determined to make sense of the universe. They devised the HOROSCOPE to relate the fragments of information they had gleaned from their observation of the planets and stars. This was simply a geocentric (Earth-centred) map of the heavens. To this day, a horoscope is drawn as a circle to represent the known solar system, with Earth placed in the centre and the relative positions of the Sun, Moon and planets charted around it. The planets are Mercury, Venus, Mars, Jupiter, Saturn, Uranus, Neptune and Pluto.

The other dimensions needed to draw up an accurate horoscope are time and location. With someone's birth date, time and place, a birth chart may be drawn up to analyse their character and likely fortunes. All the planetary positions on the chart are calculated scientifically in relation to the time and location, expressed in degrees and minutes of latitude (north or south of the equator) and longitude (east or west of the meridian of Greenwich). In the past these calculations were so complicated that only the best mathematicians attempted them. Now astrologers can buy tables called ephemerides which list the daily noon positions of the Sun, Moon and the planets, and which simplify calculations considerably.

The resulting horoscope maps out relationships between planetary movements and the individual. It is an objective scientific chart — but it is meaningless to the untrained eye. At this point science alone is insufficient to interpret the chart. Here the controversial and fascinating art of astrology steps into the realm of intuition, psychology and the results of thousands of years of human experience. The key used to unlock the secret significance in each horoscope is the ZODIAC.

The Twelve Houses of the Zodiac

The idea of a zodiac dates back to Babylonian times. As with the horoscope, astrologers took the circle of sky representing the Sun's annual pathway through the stars, then they divided it into 12 sectors, each measuring 30 degrees. Each sector is named after a fixed star constellation, forming one of the twelve houses of the zodiac.

The most important factor in someone's birth chart (after their 'star sign', Aries, etc.) is their ascendant. The sun rises in the east and sets in the west every day, reaching its highest point in the sky at noon and disappearing below the western horizon at night. According to the astrologer's zodiac each of the twelve houses takes up 30 degrees of a circle. This means that at every moment in each day a different one of the 360 degrees in the zodiac is rising on the eastern horizon. Every two hours a new sign is in the ascendant.

To find someone's ascendant the astrologer must first discover the mid-heaven, using the tables in the ephemer-

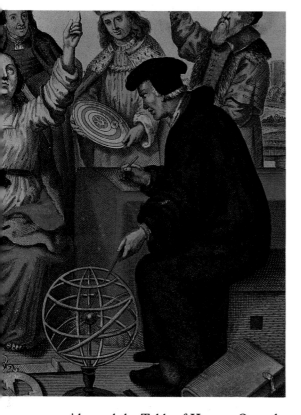

lies, weakness and psychic powers. Pluto stands for power and dictatorship.

If a planet is close to an angle, especially the ascendant or midheaven, it will have a particularly strong influence on character. Sometimes one planet may appear exactly opposite another on the chart (180° away), or in conjunction (0°), which could be good or bad, depending on the planets involved. Trines (120°) and sextiles (60°) are good aspects. Squares (90°) and semi-squares (45°) are difficult aspects.

The planets also take on some of the attributes of the zodiacal sign in which they fall, so that Saturn in Aquarius is not the same as Saturn in Taurus.

The signs, which appear in symbolized form on the chart, have these main meanings:

ARIES stands for courage, energy and recklessness.

TAURUS stands for patience, stubbornness and tenacity.

GEMINI stands for cleverness, a lack of stability, and progress.

CANCER stands for sensitivity, elusiveness and inspiration.

LEO stands for power, pride, dignity and open-mindedness.

VIRGO stands for logic, reason, studiousness and perfectionism.

LIBRA stands for harmony, judgment and pettiness.

SCORPIO stands for depth, persistence and force.

SAGITTARIUS stands for justice, morality and empty rhetoric.

CAPRICORN stands for independence, obstinacy, dreams and visions.

AQUARIUS stands for delusion, conviction, and spirituality.

PISCES stands for laziness, compassion and endurance.

The houses, numbered anti-clockwise from the ascendant sign, affect the following aspects of life:

1. The ascendant rules childhood, personality, physical growth, surroundings.
2. Money and goods.
3. Communication and relationships.
4. Hereditary traits, family home.
5. Sex, risk, fun and fertility.
6. Health.
7. Marriage, partnerships, enemies, society.
8. Death, inheritance, accidents.
9. Beliefs, travel.
10. Career, public image.
11. Friendships, hopes and dreams.
12. Unforeseen problems, isolation, unexpected enemies.

Left: Astrology is one of the few ancient sciences that has survived to the modern day without diminishing in popularity. Most ancient cultures have studied the heavens: the zodiac is based on Egyptian and Babylonian sky maps.

ides and the Table of Houses. Once the midheaven has been worked out, the degree of the ascendant can be looked up in the tables. Then the angles of the ascendant are drawn on to the chart.

Now the twelve houses can be superimposed on the chart, drawn in anticlockwise from the ascendant, which is this person's first house. To interpret the results of the birth chart, the astrologer lists the planets, including the Sun and Moon, and writes by each one the angle of the house in which it appears. For instance, the Sun might be 20° 10′ Taurus. From the resulting list of planetary angles, the astrologer can discover much about the person's character. Each planet is said to represent certain aspects of human life.

The Sun stands for life itself, psychic energy, the body, male principles.

The Moon stands for the soul, fantasy, emotion and change (it governs the months and the tides).

Mercury stands for movement, communication, intelligence and reason.

Venus stands for love, sex, art and sentiment.

Mars stands for energy, aggression, libido and action.

Jupiter stands for health, humour, riches and expansion.

Saturn stands for inhibition, loss, limitation and concentration.

Uranus stands for violence, creativity, the occult and revolution.

Neptune stands for romance, fantasy,

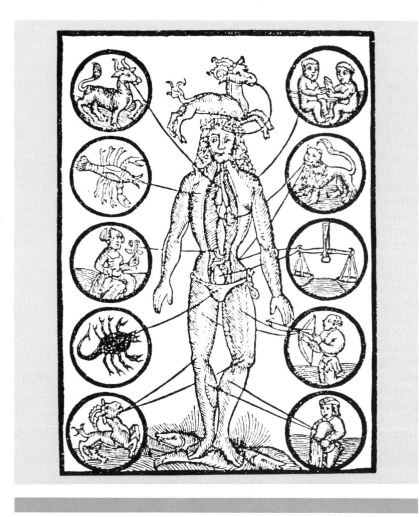

However some astrologers feel that the traditional zodiac is now out of date, due to the precession of the equinoxes. When traditional astrology places the sun in Virgo, for instance, it is actually in the house of Cancer, according to the real or 'sidereal' positions of the constellations today.

The spring and autumn equinoxes are the two periods each year when the days and nights are of equal length. Each equinox brings a change of season, when the Sun seems to cross over from one hemisphere to the other.

The Sun was in Aries at the time of the spring equinox 4000 years ago. Since the 3rd century AD the Sun has been in Pisces at the spring equinox. We are now in the last phase of the Piscean Age, which was heralded as the Age of Christianity. From the 24th century the Sun will be in Aquarius at the spring equinox. The Age of Aquarius, some astrologers say, will be an age of peace, harmony and gentleness; others fear it as the coming of an age of winter.

Astrology and the Psychologist

During a strong revival of interest in astrology in Germany between the Wars, C G Jung, the pioneering psychologist, used astrology in his work. He analysed the birth charts of some of his most interesting patients, believing that this would provide additional information about their characters. He suspected that it could also show that some people are more prone to neurosis than others. This has since been borne out by the studies of a group of British doctors. They analysed the signs of psychiatric patients in their care and found that many of the schizophrenics and manic depressives were born early in the year.

Another interesting link between the stars and character types was proved by psychologist Hans Eysenck and astrologer Jeff Mayo in the late 1970s. Using Eysenck's standard personality test for introversion and extroversion, they found that introverts usually belonged to even-numbered signs — Taurus, Cancer, Virgo, Scorpio, Capricorn and Pisces. Extroverts usually came from odd-numbered signs — Aries, Gemini, Leo, Libra, Sagittarius and Aquarius.

Who knows what further scientific discoveries await to prove or disprove astrology? Whatever the outcome, it will be hard for sceptics to completely dismiss the findings of the most ancient science of all.

Above: *This 17th century woodcut shows the parts of the body and the signs of the zodiac to which they are linked; these associations are still accepted.*

The meanings of these aspects can be found in astrological text-books, but the best astrologers will use their instinct and experience to come up with the most important clues to a person's character. This is often amazingly accurate, even if they haven't met the person.

Yet even without an individual birth chart, it is interesting to see if any of the broadly typical characteristics attributed to your 'star sign' apply to you (see individual entries).

According to traditional calculations, these are the birth dates relating to each of the Houses: Aries the Ram, 21 March to 20 April; Taurus the Bull, 21 April to 21 May; Gemini the Heavenly Twins, 22 May to 21 June; Cancer the Crab, 22 June to 23 July; Leo the Lion, 23 July to 22 August; Virgo the Virgin, 23 August to 22 September; Libra the Scales, 23 September to 23 October; Scorpio the Scorpion, 23 October to 21 November; Sagittarius the Archer, 22 November to 21 December; Capricorn the Sea-goat, 22 December to 20 January; Aquarius the Water-carrier, 20 January to 18 February; Pisces the Two Fishes, 19 February to 20 March.

AURA

The aura is an emanation of radiant light surrounding the physical body like a cloud. Although visible only to clairvoyants and the psychically gifted, auras, especially in the form of haloes, have been depicted in the religious art of every culture throughout the ages. One theory of the aura is that it is the manifest phenomena of the thoughts, aspirations, emotions and memories that accompany a person through life. Another that it is simply an energy mantle generated by the physiological process of living. The mystic explanation also says that the human being has several non-physical bodies of which the aura is only one.

In 1858 Baron Karl von Reichenbach, an industrial chemist, embarked on a series of experiments to find out more about the subject. Selected individuals of high sensitivity were left in darkened rooms to concentrate on plants, crystals, magnets and mammals in the hope they would see the radiation. The tests were successful. The North Pole aura of a magnet, for example, was revealed to be blue in colour and cool to the touch, the aura of the South Pole was orange and warm. Tests on the human body showed that the right side had a cool blue glow while the left side was a warm orange. Von Reichenbach called this radiation Od, Odyle or Odic force.

In 1911 another investigation was undertaken by W R Kilner. He placed his subjects against a black backdrop and observed them through a diluted solution of the *dicyanin* dye. What he saw was the physical body surrounded by a bluish-grey radiation divided into an irregularly shaped outer aura marked with small parallel lines and an inner aura resembling an empty hole. W R Kilner's belief was that physical illness radically changed the appearance of the aura and that the ability to study it would enormously benefit diagnosis. His view is shared by all who 'read' their patient's aura for the cause and necessary treatment. The headway made by science means that nowadays the aura can be captured on film.

See also KIRLIAN PHOTOGRAPHY.

Below: *The halo has always been associated with holiness. Discovery of the aura suggests that a form of halo does exist, which can reveal spiritual and physical health. (The Last Supper by Franciabigio, 1482–1525)*

AUTOMATIC ART/ WRITING/MUSIC

Beethoven and Brahms, Chopin and Liszt continued to compose their music beyond the grave ... the spirits of Dürer, Goya and Picasso controlled the brush of a medium to produce yet more paintings — these are some of the claims made by mediums of automatic work.

The 'automatic' production of words, pictures or musical scores is particularly fascinating to the student of the paranormal. The MEDIUM, in trance or semi-trance, produces work on paper without any conscious effort at all. This can then be analysed at leisure, in the way few other paranormal happenings can.

The best results are really remarkable. For instance Rosemary Brown is a medium who purports to transcribe music dictated to her by the great composers. She has had a little music training, but while conscious she is unable to compose for herself. Beethoven, Brahms, Debussy, Liszt, Chopin, Schubert and Stravinsky have all channelled music through her, and each piece is in the distinctive style of the composer. Some of the pieces are written for a full orchestra, and though none of them reaches the standard of the composers' music in their prime of life, they are all good enough to have drawn serious attention from the music world.

Another extraordinary example is the work of Frederick L Thompson, a goldsmith who had no evidence of paranormal abilities and had certainly never acted as a medium. In 1905 he began to experience compelling hallucinations of images that he felt impelled to reproduce as paintings. Thompson was always fully conscious of what he was doing, and never sank into trance, but always felt that the painting of these landscapes was something he 'had' to do. A year after he started to produce the pictures he went to see a retrospective of the late Robert Swain Gifford's paintings. Not only were they similar to his own but again he was overcome by a hallucination — this time a voice that said, 'You see what I have done. Can you not take up and finish my work?'

Thompson continued to paint furiously the scenes he hallucinated so persistently, and when people became interested in his work it turned out that these were no dream landscapes. All the pictures were of landscapes known and dear to Gifford

in his lifetime, which he had never got round to painting himself. They were places that Thompson had never visited nor, so far as he was consciously aware, had he even seen photographs of them.

Many mediums produce automatic writing during a sitting, much of it apparently from ordinary people attempting to convey messages from the other side to friends and relations still living. These are, of course, hard to verify, and many psychic researchers would say they could be the result of telepathic communication between sitter and medium — though many sitters are convinced that the messages are genuine.

Cross Correspondences

More interesting to students of the paranormal are the automatic scripts known as 'cross correspondences' — fragments of messages received by a number of mediums, which make no sense when read in isolation but when put together have a larger message that cannot be explained by telepathy.

The most impressive of these was a series of automatic writings received by a group of highly respectable, well-educated, middle-aged ladies at the turn of the century, only one of whom was a professional medium. The messages apparently came from three dead men, all prominent psychical researchers in their time: F W H Myers (the author of *The Human Personality and its Survival After Death*), Edmund Gurney and Professor Henry Sidgewick.

These dictations continued for about 30 years, producing around 2000 scripts which were compared, combined and published. Although one of the women was a classicist, most of the others knew no Latin or Greek, but most of the scripts are peppered with words and sentences from these languages.

Another extraordinary case was that of the Brazilian medium Chico Xavier, who was receiving entire chapters of a book that seemed to have no continuity. Then his spirit guide told him to get in touch with a Dr Waldo Weira. When the two men met it turned out that Dr Weira had also been receiving discontinuous chapters, and when the chapters were put together they made a coherent whole.

Methods of Working

People who produce automatic work do it in varying ways. It is almost always true to say, however, that it takes time before they produce work of any worth.

Most mediums find they have to be in

trance or semi-trance before the messages begin to flow, and some have no idea what they have produced until they 'wake'. Some mediums, however, remain fully conscious and are aware of what their hands are doing.

Many of the theories of SPIRITUALISM are based on automatic writings, a lot of which concern themselves with the afterlife. Although the descriptions vary to some degree, it has been estimated that roughly half of the 'religious' writings agree to a remarkable extent. These 'spirit teachings' are similar in style and tone to each other, as if dictated by one person alone. Many of them have been published in book form, such as *Spirit Teachings*, by W Stainton Moses.

Psychic Art

Psychic art, which is different from automatic work, is also practised by certain mediums. These mediums, who have artistic gifts, attempt to reproduce in pictures visions that they have received. The main difference is that they are aware of making conscious efforts to do this as William Blake did.

Many researchers have tried to find explanations for automatic work, which include fraud, chance (when there are correspondences between the work of two mediums), telepathy between the living — or messages from the dead. In the best researched work, however, only the last explanation seems possible.

Above: *Automatic artists recognize that a talent outside themselves helps them produce their work. William Blake was reluctant to take credit for his work.*

THE BERMUDA TRIANGLE

The Bermuda Triangle is a geographic area in the North Atlantic Ocean lying between the coasts of Bermuda in the north, Puerto Rico in the south and Florida in the west. Its name was first coined by a writer, Vincent Gaddis, in the mid 1960s and has since been widely used to define a part of the world which has been the site of a large number of disappearances of boats and aeroplanes, from great sailing schooners to small private aircraft. The reason these disappearances have long been the focus of international interest is because many occurred in bizarre and mysterious circumstances which have never been fully explained. While there have been many theories put forward to explain the baffling disappearances of various craft in the Bermuda Triangle, there remains a strong suggestion that there are, in fact, supernatural forces involved in the events which are particular to that zone.

Columbus himself, when exploring America, was first to note some of the unique and unusual phenomena in the Triangle. He encountered the great Sargasso Sea there — a huge patch of ocean characterized by massive, freakish growths of floating seaweed and, between the latitudes of 30 and 35, an almost unnatural absence of wind which could becalm a sailing ship for weeks. Columbus, and other crew members, also saw mysterious night lights before sighting land in 1492 and, 10 years later, he lost 500 men and some 20 of his ships disappeared during a storm in the Bermuda Triangle area. These ships became the first recorded casualties of that part of the North Atlantic; the list of disappeared craft now runs to over 200.

Perhaps the weirdest early examples of disappearance on the ocean are the cases of the ships *Seabird* and the *Rosalie* — vessels which were found, in the 18th and 19th centuries respectively, drifting completely crewless. In the case of the *Seabird*, there was no evident explanation at all for the absence of people on board. A half-eaten meal was found along with some pet animals, but no sign whatsoever of emergency or catastrophe.

As the transatlantic shipping trade became much busier in the latter half of the 19th century, so the list of major casualties grew. In 1854 the *City of Glasgow* went down taking 480 people and, four weeks later, the *Bella* was lost on its

way from Brazil to Jamaica. The *City of Boston* with 200 people on board disappeared in 1870. Little trace was ever found of these sailing ships, except for bits of widely scattered wreckage which gave few clues as to the cause of disaster.

Before the century was out the number of derelict ships found aimlessly floating in the Bermuda Triangle had grown, too, including the *James B Chester*, the famous *Marie Celeste*, discovered off the Azores in 1872, and another unnamed ship found in 1881.

One of the largest ships to disappear in the Triangle was the 17,560-ton coal ship *Cyclops* which vanished in 1918 after calling in at Barbados. And, with the growth of commercial aviation, aircraft, too, began succumbing to the region's mysterious destructive forces. The first known victim was a monoplane flown by a very experienced pilot which disappeared over the ocean off Florida in 1931. During the Second World War, many American bombers went missing in the Triangle, including the well-documented 'Flight 19' — five TBM Avenger torpedo bombers which completely vanished while on a routine flight in 1945, along with another plane which was despatched to look for them.

In the case of aeroplanes, disaster has often struck in similar circumstances. It has occurred many times on a calm night when the craft has been less than 100km offshore. The pilot radios one last message indicating that the flight is on schedule, then silence follows.

Along with the disappearances, eyewitnesses have reported seeing strange, anomalous phenomena which may have some connection. These include a ball of light, rotating compasses, unnatural turbulence, a strange glowing on the horizon and bizarre upwellings of water on the ocean's surface.

Many theories have been put forward to explain the mysteries of the Bermuda Triangle. Some disappearances have been attributed to the extremely volatile weather conditions in the area including a hurricane season from June to October, which make it one of the stormiest places in the world. Electromagnetic peculiarities, pirates, disease, giant sea creatures, human error and meteors have all been suggested as possible explanations for Bermuda Triangle disappearances; there is also a popular belief that ships and planes in the area have been abducted by extraterrestrial beings, although there has been little evidence to support this theory.

Above: *Disappearances in the Bermuda Triangle have puzzled military experts such as Rear Admiral Richard Byrd. 'Logical' explanations never quite seem to suffice.*

24

BLACK MAGIC

Magic is found at all levels, from the country wise-woman making herbal potions and practising simple forms of IMITATIVE MAGIC to the adept of RITUAL MAGIC who seeks to capture and use godlike powers. At the higher levels magic tends to transcend questions of good and evil, but a distinction is normally made between WHITE MAGIC, which seeks to help and heal, and black magic, which seeks to harm and destroy. Black magic is therefore associated with SATANISM in Christian cultures. As with satanism, it exults in such qualities as hardness, cruelty, hatred, unqualified self-interest, uninhibited sexuality. It detests the gentle virtues of humility, kindness, altruism and continence. In its symbolism it will tend to use left-handed or inverted signs, such as the inverted cross or PENTAGRAM. It deliberately cultivates behaviour, especially in sexual matters, that is normally seen as perverse, indecent or even disgusting.

Rituals for summoning up demons in order to acquire their powers are described in detail in the medieval magic textbooks known as grimoires and these have a specifically European character, but in other respects black magic practices have many similarities in all cultures. The CURSE, the INCANTATION and the SPELL, all of them conveying the idea of concentrated malice in verbal form, are universal phenomena. So also is the form of imitative magic which involves making an image or doll representing the intended victim and inflicting injury upon it. In black magic of that kind the victim might well be reinforced by using something associated with that person: hair or nail clippings, a piece of clothing, or even simply the repetition of the victim's name, as in a famous Scottish case when the witches of North Berwick were alleged to have tried to kill King James VI by making a doll and burning it, having first of all passed it among them saying, 'This is King James the Sixth'.

Whether the black magician uses dolls or potions or verbal formulas, or has summoned up demons for the purpose, it is probably the magician's own psychic powers, the ability to concentrate and direct his personal malevolence, that enables him or her to cause injury and even death. There are many indications that black magic does indeed occasionally work, perhaps especially if the intended victim is aware that it is being directed against him or her. If there is such a phenomenon as extra-sensory perception then it is not impossible that it can convey harmful forces between the sender and the recipient in ways we have not yet begun to understand.

Below: *To release the evil power of black magic requires complex rituals and often exhausting ceremonies. Each of these objects is invested with its own distinct power, which aids the conjuring up of demons and the working of spells. The pentagram is a symbol of special significance.*

Above: *This Book of the Dead, the Papyrus of Ani, dates from around 1250 BC. It shows the mummy being escorted to the necropolis.*

BOOK OF THE DEAD, THE

In the second millennium BC the ancient Egyptians began the practice of placing in the tombs of the dead papyrus copies of texts designed to aid the deceased in the journey from death to the afterlife. These texts constitute what Egyptologists call the Egyptian Book of the Dead, which itself represents a relatively late stage of a much older tradition, going back to the beginnings of Egyptian civilization.

In the previous millennium the priests of Heliopolis, responsible for the cult of Atum-Re, the Sun God, had inscribed similar texts on the walls of certain royal pyramids. These Pyramid texts are designed solely for the guidance of the dead pharaoh and they give priority to the Sun God over the more traditional figure of Osiris, the god most strongly associated with the idea of resurrection and the afterlife.

Later the nobility began to have texts of this kind painted on the sides of their wooden coffins. These were likewise designed to enable the dead to pass safely through all the perils of the journey to a happy afterlife, to supply the dead person with provisions and to express ritually the terror of the judgement to come.

From about 1500 BC selections from these texts began to be written on papyrus and placed in the tombs of humbler people, the names of the deceased being inscribed in spaces left for the purpose. Only the rich could afford the complete Book of the Dead, the finest surviving version of which is probably the Papyrus of Ani, made for a royal scribe of that name, and now in the British Museum. Like other expensive versions, this is richly illustrated in colour and is an illuminating source for the funerary rites of the ancient Egyptians and for their ideas about death and the afterlife.

BROOMSTICK

In popular belief witches are closely associated with broomsticks and in the WITCHCRAFT trials of the 15th, 16th and 17th centuries a number of women did confess to having flown on a broom. The trial records and the writings of witch-hunters sometimes suggest that the stick was annointed or coated in a special grease.

As a familiar domestic implement, the broomstick is a symbol of womanhood and perhaps also of the oppression of women. Turning it into an instrument of magic, of magical freedom of movement, may well be indicative of the extent to which witchcraft in northern Europe was a reaction to oppression. The act of placing the broomstick between the legs, whether in flying or in the ritual dancing of the European witches, has obvious sexual connotations, emphasized by the reports of annointing or greasing. One French witch of the 15th century described at her trial how the devil had given her a stick and a jar of ointment. Having greased the stick, she would place it between her legs and cry, 'Go, in the Devil's name, go!' and would immediately be carried into the air. It is likely that behind these confessions lie hallucinatory experiences, induced perhaps by the intense ecstatic experience of the witchcraft rituals.

See also WITCHCRAFT

CABALA

The word Cabala (also sometimes spelt Qabbalah or Kabbalah) is the name now generally given to a body of mystical doctrines that emerged among the Jews of Provence and northern Spain in the 12th and 13th centuries AD.

It belongs, however, to a much older tradition of Jewish mysticism concerned with the nature of God, with the geography of the universe (which was linked closely with the geography of heaven), and with the ranks and functions of ANGELS. These questions became mingled with other religious and philosophical ideas in the Mediterranean world of late antiquity and took on an esoteric and magical aspect. The main text of the Cabala is the *Zohar*, written by a Spanish Jew called Moses de Leon towards the end of the 13th century.

The central study of cabalists is the secret nature of the Divine Being, so inaccessible that it is not openly revealed in the scriptures, and the process by which God 'comes into being'. The Divine Being is seen as consisting of ten aspects or manifestations, known as the ten *sefiroth*. The universe itself is seen as an ordered series of 'emanations' from the divine, which is at once absolute Nothingness and ultimate reality.

In its purest state the Cabala was the possession of an elite who devoted their lives to its study. With the expulsion of the Jews from Spain in 1492 cabalistic ideas spread throughout Europe and began to be taken up by Christian students of the occult. Corrupted by translation, the Cabala began to degenerate and to merge with European MAGIC, for which it was a rich source of mysterious language and symbolism. In Cabalistic magic the adept seeks to climb up through the tree of the sefiroth until he reaches knowledge of or oneness with God. Cabalistic ideas have greatly influenced modern magicians, such as Aleister CROWLEY.

Below: *The Princess of Wales displays the typically Cancerian love of home and children.*

CANCER

Cancer, the Crab, fourth sign of the Zodiac, is a Water sign, governing those born between 22 June and 23 July.

Home-loving, sympathetic Cancerians devote themselves to their families. Loyal, faithful, motherly, sentimental and kind, they hate excessive change. After a holiday, or even a hard day's work, they love nothing better than coming home to a good meal and a comfortable armchair.

They hold on to old friends, but are suspicious of outsiders. To the cautious Cancerian, any stranger is a potential threat. No one must be allowed to disrupt the routine, or chaos could result. New ideas also worry Cancerians, who will argue for traditional values without considering the new ideas at all. The status quo must be preserved. Conservative in their tastes, Cancerians are often patriotic, believing their country to be the best in the world. If they do travel, they often refuse to attempt the native language and may even seek familiar food rather than risk anything too foreign. Yet they are humorous, modest, intuitive, calm, imaginative, sensitive and very romantic people.

Despite this soft side to their natures, Cancerians often do very well in busi-

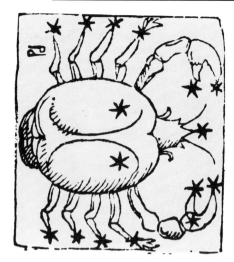

ness. They are shrewd, methodical and independent, with good judgement and the staying-power to see a job through to the end.

Yet Cancerians must beware of leading an insular life. They can be almost too protective towards their family, who may want to branch out in more adventurous directions than a Cancerian would think wise. They can be moody, timid, dreamy, unreliable and lethargic. At other times they may be over-confident that they are right. Self-pity, pride and a touch of morbidness can also afflict members of this sensitive Crab sign, who are at their best when they can be coaxed out of their shell.

Idealism often leads Cancerians to become part of the established church, though their cautious natures prevent them from joining any wild religious sects. Those born under this Water sign often find work related to liquids in some way. They may become pub managers, hoteliers, restaurateurs, brewers or even sewage workers. The call of the sea is strongest of all, and many Cancerians

Below: David Bowie is a true Capricorn artist, combining economy of musical style with the wit also associated with this sign.

join the navy or become involved in marine studies.

Compatible with those born under the signs of PISCES and SCORPIO, Cancerians make loyal, faithful, receptive lovers. Though emotional, they can be reserved at times and their feelings are easily hurt. As parents they excel in creating a stable, tightly-knit family.

Physically Cancerians are often short and plump, with a kind yet timid air. They often have straight, light brown hair, pointed chins and noses, plump hands and feet and round faces. They tend to have pale skin, with large hazel or grey eyes.

Cancerian trouble spots are the female reproductive organs, particularly the ovaries and the womb. The lymph glands are also prone to difficulties. They should beware of over-indulging in food and drink as they are also prone to diseases of the stomach and liver, pancreas and digestion. Stomach ulcers, wind and indigestion are common problems.

See also ASTROLOGY

CAPRICORN

Capricorn, the Sea-goat, the tenth sign of the Zodiac, is an Earth sign, governing those born between 22 December and 20 January.

The most hard-working, ambitious people tend to be Capricorns. They are cautious, self-disciplined, meticulous and economical, largely because the sign is ruled by Saturn, the sternest and oldest of all the planets. Saturn also gives Capricorns a link with Father Time, so they may live to a ripe old age.

They are exceptionally kind people, who are extremely loyal. They like to keep old friends, also enjoying traditional customs and celebrations, because they dislike change. This can lead them to live in the past, a limitation they should resist.

Capricorns would like to be rich and many of them will work hard and patiently all their lives trying to accumulate wealth. If they achieve it in the end, they've usually earned it, for no one could accuse them of being irresponsible or work-shy. Those who fail to reap the rewards of their hard work, however, may become bitter and full of envy. Capricorns are terrible worriers, always expecting the worst. This pessimism,

plus excessive caution can hold some Capricorns back in any career.

Tactful and diplomatic, they make good politicians, for they are unlikely to say the wrong thing out of carelessness or forgetfulness. Their powers of concentration and their perseverance are great. An authoritative manner and a tendency to take work seriously helps them to do well in their chosen career. Sometimes, however, they can become self-important and may seem to 'use' people who can help them get on.

Capricorns are very effective as public speakers, because they are economical in all things. Their speeches get straight to the point, without a hint of repetition.

Journalism attracts many Capricorns, whose economical, sometimes witty, writing style is much appreciated. Francis Bacon was a notably concise writer born under this sign.

In music Capricorns also excel. From Mozart to David Bowie, Schubert to Elvis Presley, Capricorns have often delighted the public. Mozart's compositions are clean, economical and lovely to hear. No self-indulgent repetition spoils his work. David Bowie's lyric writing style tends to the brevity of poetry. Rich in imagery, his words evoke ideas and atmospheres without the need for dull explanation.

Capricorns also do well in clerical work, estate agencies, farming, building, engineering, the army, police or mining. The influence of the earth is strong.

Compatible with those born under TAURUS and VIRGO, Capricorns make faithful lovers, though they can be moody. They are self-critical and need reassurance.

Physically Capricorns tend to be tall, even lanky, yet with a slight build. They may have a narrow chin, a lantern jaw, a large straight nose and dry, sallow skin. They often have blue eyes and fair hair.

Health problems to watch out for may be centred on the knees, joints, hair and skin. Dislocated bones, rheumatism, cramp, broken bones, syphilis, eczema, rashes and toothache are common problems.

See also ASTROLOGY

CARD READING

Fortune tellers the world over use cards to help them see into the past, present and future of their clients. An ordinary pack of 52 playing cards will do, though the TAROT pack of 78 is considered the ultimate clairvoyant aid by those who tell fortunes professionally.

Card-reading methods vary. Although anyone can learn the significance of each card in the pack according to the position in which it is placed, interpretation makes all the difference to a reading. The most remarkable card readers always have extra psychic power or intuition which makes the reading highly personal and relevant to each client.

There are elements that are standard to all readings: first the fortune teller shuffles the pack. This neutralizes the

Below: *The eight indicates prosperity, the ace love, the Queen a strong woman: what will the reader predict?*

teller designates areas which will reveal particular things, among them your past, present and future, and the cards that fall in those places are read in that light. Alternatively the cards are shuffled and laid out three times in all: once for the present, once for the past and finally for the future.

Usually the readings are far more detailed than simply a summary of your life so far and a prediction of the future. Influences as well as incidents are divined, and fate as well as fortune explained.

In a standard pack of playing cards the four suits — hearts, clubs, diamonds and spades — have particular associations. The 'picture cards' — King, Queen and Knave — represent people with certain qualities. Crudely, spades and clubs represent dark people, hearts and diamonds people with fair colouring. But certain personality characteristics are also represented.

Each numbered card also carries its own significance, and the meaning changes according to its suit. Five of hearts for instance, is usually taken to mean a legacy; five of diamonds denotes a meeting; if it is clubs it means a legal battle, whereas five of spades can indicate a funeral.

The tarot pack is a more sophisticated fortune-telling tool. It has 22 'picture cards' known as the major arcana, and the meanings ascribed to these are extremely subtle. Really gifted card readers study their subject deeply, for they must know not only the basic meaning of each card but how that meaning varies according to whether the card is presented upright or upside-down and where it comes in sequence, as well as how the meaning shifts according to which card it is placed beside.

See also TAROT

Above: *The Tarot cards formed into a wheel of fortune, from which the card reader can give uncannily precise information.*

cards so that no influences from a previous reading remain. Next the client must shuffle the cards. This is the single most important moment, for it is believed that there are no coincidences in this apparently random process. In the process of shuffling, the cards are moving into the positions that will uniquely throw light on the life and prospects of the person handling them.

After the cards have been shuffled they are cut by the client and laid out by the fortune teller in a prearranged pattern. This varies from card reader to card reader, but may take the form of a circle, a tree or a symbolic geometric pattern.

Whatever the pattern, the fortune

CLAIRVOYANCE

Clairvoyance, literally meaning 'clear sight', is the ability to perceive things beyond the natural range of sight. Possessors of this mysterious talent receive images of objects, people, and even events that might be taking place hundreds of miles away.

Precognitive clairvoyance is the vision of events still in the future.

See also SPIRITUALISM, TAROT

COLOUR THERAPY

The effect of different colours on the human mind has been widely appreciated by different cultures, both ancient and modern. It has been reflected, for example, in the brilliant colours of Egyptian and Greek temples and in India and Tibet, where colour has long been an integral aspect of the meditation process.

Rudolf Steiner, through a series of lectures he delivered in 1921, triggered a renewed interest in the therapeutic value of colour. Today, the sensory reaction to environmental colour has been closely studied, and colour healing, whereby specific parts of the light's spectrum are used to cure particular ailments, has become an established form of alternative medicine.

Research has shown that the physiological reaction to colours, ranging from low-frequency red through orange, yellow, green, blue and violet at the highest frequency, is quite pronounced. Experiments at Cambridge University in the UK, for example, documented responses showing that large fields of red light induced the symptoms of emotional arousal, such as the speeding up of the pulse rate, changes in skin resistance and electrical fluctuations in the brain. Some mental hospitals in fact avoid red or orange colour schemes because it is believed these can exacerbate some conditions. A Norwegian study revealed that people in a blue room felt cooler than at the same temperature in a red room. Other research has shown that exposure to different parts of the spectrum affects people's capacity to concentrate and remember, as well as their perception of time. Dr Max Lüscher also pioneered work in the 1940s into the connexion between people's personalities and their perception of colour. He devised a test using colour cards from which he was able to do a profound psychological analysis of a patient.

Some colour healers work on the principle of the 'psychic anatomy', whereby they read the 'AURA' which surrounds a patient using psychic powers. This 'aura' is believed to be the emanation of various energies which all forms of life give off. It has been related to the results of KIRLIAN PHOTOGRAPHY which reveals a multicoloured shroud of patterns around the human body. The psychic diagnosis connects colours to specific states. For example, grey means fear, malaise or anger, pink can mean intuition and white enlightenment. The healer often sees a multi-faceted and confused aura around a diseased person. By psychic transfer of energy, often involving religious prayer and meditation or massage and manipulation of pressure points, the practitioner aims to reach the psychosomatic source of what may be a physical problem.

The eight colours of the spectrum are often seen by colour healers to relate to the 24 vertebrae in the back bone and the 12 bones which make up the sacrum and skull. And some practitioners have also found that particular colours are useful in the treatment of illnesses all over the body. For example magenta has been applied to some heart conditions, violet to help childbirth and to cure sciatica, blue for skin problems and yellow for liver and stomach ailments.

There is considerable variety, however, in the approach to actual treatment. In most cases, the healer becomes closely acquainted with the patient's condition, initially on a physical level and perhaps on a deeper, spiritual level, too. Usually treatment involves exposing the patient physically to the colour, or combination of colours, in the form of lamps, illumination, filtered light projectors, painted walls and fabrics of particular hues; it can also be done by mental image-making or even counselling.

Because particular colours are widely regarded in therapy as having harmony with other forms, treatment is often carried out linking, for instance, blue to horizontal forms and spheres, and red with vertical or cube shapes.

Below: *Colours can affect mood and physical health. Colour therapists can treat a range of problems.*

Above: *Crowley dedicated himself to the study and practice of black magic.*

CROWLEY, ALEISTER

In the 1930s and 40s British newspapers carried sensational reports about the activities of Aleister Crowley (1875–1947), who called himself 'The Beast 666'. Sensational and scandalous though his life undoubtedly was, he is probably most usefully seen as only one of the more recent figures in a long line of men and women who have become fascinated by the idea of acquiring power through esoteric wisdom and who have either possessed miraculous powers or been able to convince others that they possess them.

The son of a wealthy and deeply religious brewer, Crowley was brought up in the Christian faith but while still a child found himself drawn to the arcane mysteries of the Book of the Revelation of St John, in which 'the Beast whose number is 666' and 'the Scarlet Woman' figure prominently.

As a young man Crowley joined the magical society known as the Hermetic Order of the Golden Dawn, whose main teachings were centred on the CABALA and on ceremonial magic. As a member he took the name Perdurabo (I shall endure to the end), one of the many names and titles that he adopted in the course of his life. Deeply ambitious, he set out to rival and surpass the leader of the order, the magician MacGregor Mathers, who claimed to be receiving guidance from superior beings known as the Secret Chiefs. Expelled from the Golden Dawn, Crowley travelled the world in search of a revelation that would make him the supreme magician of his day. He found it, by his own account, in Cairo, where he received a visitation from his Holy Guardian Angel who dictated to him the revelations known as *The Book of the Law*.

Central to these revelations and to Crowley's work for the remainder of his life are two ideas. The first is that until the time of the revelations there had been two aeons in the history of mankind: the age of Isis, the age of the domination of woman; and the age of Osiris, the age of the domination of the male principle — of the ideas of Christianity, Judaism, Buddhism and Islam. What had been announced to him was the beginning of a new aeon, that of Horus, the child. The key idea of that aeon would be self-will, *thelema*, 'Do what thou wilt'.

The second idea or discovery of Crowley's was the power of sex in ritual magic, an idea almost certainly derived from the Tantric mysteries of oriental religion and put into practice by Crowley in both heterosexual and homosexual forms.

To develop and spread these ideas Crowley set up his own magical order, calling himself a Magus and calling his mistress the Scarlet Woman. After the end of the First World War he went to Cefalu in Sicily where he consecrated a temple to the new aeon, painting on its door the words 'DO WHAT THOU WILT'. His life's work is summed up in his magnum opus, *Magick in Theory and Practice*.

See also MAGIC, RITUAL MAGIC

Right: *Crowley channelled his artistic talent into the black magic field. This was his design for the*

devil card in the Tarot pack.

CRYSTAL BALL

A crystal ball is normally a piece of rock-crystal carved into a smooth or faceted sphere in which future or remote events may reveal themselves as images. Crystal-gazing is the most familiar form of SCRYING.

See also SCRYING

Left: *The psychic may see clear images and scenes in the crystal ball, or less distinct cloudy forms.*

CRYSTALS

Crystals are those beautiful, geometrically shaped, mineral formations found in the seams and hollows of rocks. There are literally hundreds of different types and the variety of colour, size and form is quite staggering. But however different they might look, they all share basic characteristics. They are solid minerals with flat intersecting surfaces and an internal structure of atoms, ions or molecules. Quartz is the mineral with the greatest variety of crystals, including famous examples such as rock crystal, amethyst, agate and onyx.

Crystals are a particularly powerful source of energy and it is an energy that is perfectly balanced and harmonized. Some people believe that these special stones have the ability to harmonize, transform and focus our energy too.

Crystals are used for many purposes. They can be buried in the earth to revitalize an ill plant, slept on at night to aid the creative workings of the unconscious mind, or simply be given the task of harmonizing the home environment. Their two major uses, though, are in healing and meditation. In this sort of healing the healer perceives a disturbance in the energy of the patient's AURA, which manifests as pain or illness in the physical body. Treatment consists of the healer focussing thought and energy through the crystal. Sometimes it is just the healer who holds a crystal, on other occasions greater harmony and balance is created if both healer and patient have crystals. In meditation, too, the crystal is used as a focus and harmonizer of energy. It can either be held in the hand or placed near the person on the floor. In group meditation it is common for a large crystal to be placed in the centre of the circle for all to concentrate on.

Before a newly acquired crystal can be used for a specific purpose it has to be cleansed. This process leaves its natural energies intact, removing those absorbed during past handling. Techniques for doing this vary but there are several that have proved especially effective. They are rinsing the crystal under flowing water, exposing it to the purifying rays of the sun, and visualizing the crystal being swept with positive energy. After cleaning, the crystal is ready to be programmed for whatever specific purpose you have in mind. Programming means to imprint it, by means of exact thought, with those instructions which you want it to retain. If a crystal is to be used for the healing of more than one person, however, it must be cleaned and reprogrammed after each healing session.

Crystal energy is as unique and individual as that of a human being. There is also a 'right' crystal for different uses and different times of life. This is very important to remember when you come to choosing one. The first thing is to forget anything you have ever heard about matching a particular birth sign to a particular stone. It is only your sensitivity and intuition that can tell you which is the right crystal for you. To choose a crystal first close your eyes and relax your mind. On reopening them pick the first one your hand is drawn to. Another method is to close your eyes, induce the relaxed state, then pass your hand back and forth over the crystals without touching them. People testify to experiencing pulsating heat or a magnet-like attraction pulling them to a certain stone. Sometimes you simply have to look at a selection of crystals to see one that seems to be doing everything but jump into your hand to attract your attention. When this happens, the fact you were meant for each other is immediately obvious. Or, one might say, crystal clear.

Above: *Crystals contain their own form of energy which can be 'programmed' for a purpose.*

CULT OF THE DEAD

Although beliefs about the nature of the afterlife vary from culture to culture there is probably no human society that does not solemnize death and take steps to commemorate the dead. Behind the human impulse to mark death with ceremonies and the building of tombs, lies a natural desire to ritualize grief and to ensure remembrance of the dead by the living; but there is also a belief that the dead in some sense continue to exist and can influence the lives of the kinsfolk who survive them.

Some of the earliest surviving human remains, dating back as many as 500,000 years, show evidence that the dead were not merely discarded but treated with reverence or perhaps also with fear. In some cases the bodies are trussed in a particular position or laid in a particular orientation; sometimes they are surrounded by ritual objects; sometimes there are indications that parts of them may have been eaten, perhaps in the belief that their surviving kinsfolk could thereby acquire something of their strength and wisdom. Neanderthal people seem to have treated the dead with tenderness, burying them near the hearth with tools and meat to help them in the afterlife and at least in one case strewing them with flowers.

The practice of burying the dead with grave-goods, which appears in very early times, seems to reflect a belief that the afterlife resembles the world of the living but that the dead need to take at least some of their worldly treasures with them if they are to enjoy the same status as they had while alive. As long ago as the third millennium BC this practice had become extremely elaborate. Men of rank were not only buried with rich weapons, jewelry and utensils but also with the corpses of courtiers, concubines, soldiers and retainers, who had been killed so that they could accompany their master into the afterlife.

The ancient Egyptians, whose complex beliefs about life after death are illustrated in the BOOK OF THE DEAD, filled the tombs of their kings with treasures of exquisite beauty, but do not seem to have practised ritual murder of this kind. Something very like it however continued in the Hindu practice of *suttee* until the 19th century.

With the colossal pyramids they erected over the mummified bodies of their

People have always revered their dead, but few with such extravagance as the ancient Egyptians. Above: *The gold mask of Tutankhamun, found in his tomb.* Right: *Wall paintings in an Egyptian tomb show the dead being tended with care by servants.*

pharaohs, the Egyptians took to an extreme the practice of tomb-building. However, there are parallels in the megalithic tombs of Britain and western Europe, some of them of considerable size and built of stones so large that archaeologists still do not clearly understand how they were transported. The sheer weight of such monuments sug-

CURSE

Cursing may simply mean swearing or blaspheming but it can also refer to the act of calling on supernatural powers to bring misfortune, suffering or death to the person or persons named. The ancient Greeks and Romans were in the habit of inscribing curses on lead or pottery. As many as 200 curse-tablets of that kind were found on the site of a single Roman temple in Gloucestershire. In Bath, excavators found a lead sheet bearing the following inscription: 'May he who carried off Vilbia from me become liquid as the water; May she who so obscenely ate her lose the power of speech; whether the culprit be Velvinna, Exsupereus, Severinus, Augustalis, Comitianus, Catusminianus, Germinilla or Jovina.' Another Roman British plaque bears the words: 'Tacita is cursed by this and declared putrified like rotting blood.'

As well as individuals whole families may be the victims of a curse, such as the house of Atreus in ancient Greece.

Cursing may be merely the product of superstition, but it is possible that the act of concentrated malevolence that lies behind it may represent a mysterious kind of power. Certainly the many stories of people in Africa dying as the result of curses are strangely convincing, as are the stories of men cursed for violating the tombs of ancient Egypt. If a person lives in a society that believes in hostile magic and has been conditioned to believe in it also, and if that person then becomes the victim of sorcery, the effect can be devastating. Death becomes a certainty in everyone's minds; family and friends will treat the victim as if he or she were already dead. The combination of fear and rejection can indeed prove fatal. The Christian form of the curse is excommunication, in which an offender is ritually excluded from the knowledge and love of God. Perhaps one of the most famous of all curses is the one chosen by William Shakespeare as the epitaph for his tomb at Stratford, which follows in an ancient tradition, designed to protect graves from the attentions of grave-robbers:

Good friend, for Jesu's sake forbear
To dig the dust enclosed here.
Blest be the man that spares these stones
And curst be he that moves my bones.

gests a desire, conscious or unconscious, to keep the dead in the earth where they belong.

The building of tombs and shrines for the dead has stimulated people to produce some of the most dramatic monuments. Probably the most beautiful of all is the Taj Mahal, built to preserve the memory of the wife of a Mughal king.

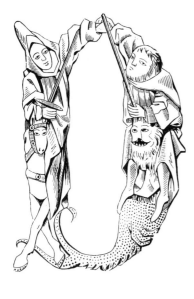

Below: *John Dee was noted for his abilities as a scientist and astrologer.* Above right: *Dee also dabbled in magic and some said he used necromancy to make predictions.*

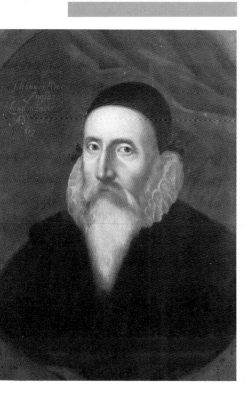

DEE, JOHN

John Dee (1527–1608), the Elizabethan scholar and magician was reviled by many of his contemporaries as an imposter and a sorcerer. The truth about his life will probably never be known, but he was certainly a man of very considerable gifts, a scientist in advance of his time who also became Astrologer Royal to Elizabeth I.

Born at Mortlake near London, he went to Cambridge at the age of 15 and became Under-Reader of Greek four years later. After leaving Cambridge he met the great Flemish cartographer Mercator and began to acquire advanced knowledge and techniques in the fields of astronomy and navigation which were to be of supreme importance in the Age of Exploration. At about the same time he began his studies in natural or 'white' magic, which at that time was seen as perfectly compatible with scientific research. As an astrologer he soon attracted the attention of Queen Mary, for whom he cast horoscopes, but he also developed an association with Princess Elizabeth, which nearly cost him his life after he was accused of treason. As it was he spent some time in prison.

When Elizabeth acceded to the throne in 1558 Dee continued to serve her, and it is quite likely that about this time he also began to work as a spy in the service of Sir William Cecil and of Sir Francis Walsingham, Elizabeth's sinister spy-master.

Sometime in 1581 Dee developed an interest in crystal-gazing or SCRYING in association with a somewhat dubious character known as Edward Kelley. He also claimed to be in communication with angels who appeared to him in visions, and many of his records of these 'angelic conversations' have been preserved. With Kelley he visited the King of Poland and the Emperor Rudolph II and at one point he was offered a vast salary and many honours if he would enter the service of the Czar of Russia. These monarchs were clearly interested in his gifts as a seer, but it is quite possible that the questions they asked him to put to his 'angels' were also valuable intelligence about their political and strategic aims. Although Dee undoubtedly passed reports to Walsingham he does not seem to have prospered in his career as a spy, perhaps because the Queen could not afford to be associated publicly with a man who might be dabbling in the black arts. He was rewarded with a minor academic post and died at Mortlake, his birthplace.

DEVILS AND DEMONS

In traditional Christian belief the Devil is the embodiment of absolute EVIL, the arch-enemy, the Prince of Darkness, also known as Satan, Lucifer and Belial among other names. Curiously, Satan as a proper name appears in the Old Testament only once, in 1 Chronicles.

These names reflect the way in which the idea of the Devil came into being. In much of the Old Testament the 'satan' is the prosecutor at the court of God, utterly sceptical about the worth of humankind; it is he for example who persuades God to heap misfortune on the head of Job in order to test the sincerity of his righteousness.

Lucifer was the great archangel who rebelled against God because of his pride, was defeated in the war in heaven and was cast down with his rebel angels to live and rule in Hell until the day appointed by God to bring all things to an end.

The idea of an utterly evil angel, the eternal enemy of God, called sometimes Beliar or Belial, probably emerged sometime between the 6th and 4th centuries BC when the Jews came under the influence of Persian Zoroastrianism, which believed in two rival gods, of good and evil. As the idea of a single god, omnipotent and good, established itself firmly in the religion of the Jews the need arose to explain the existence of evil in the world. It is probably for that reason that the prosecuting angel became the utterly evil ruler of this world and of Hell, tolerated by God in his inscrutable plan but ultimately doomed.

This is the figure that appears in Christian teachings as the Prince of Darkness, constantly seeking to tempt mortals to sin but also the ruler of the Hell where sinners are punished. His physical appearance and the horrors of his infernal dominions are graphically depicted in medieval painting and sculpture, in sermons and in such works as Dante's *Inferno*. Although these lurid descriptions were designed to terrorize men and women away from sin, to certain minds they had a certain perverse appeal that led to the Devil-worship of SATANISM and WITCHCRAFT. The fact that the Devil is so often depicted in animal or semi-animal form, often with a horned head and goat's legs, probably reflects some survival of the appearance of pagan or prehistoric deities, but the view that the Devil-worship of the witches is actually a conscious survival of a pre-Christian religion has been largely discredited.

Satan shares Hell with a multitude of demons, of whom the best known are Beelzebub, Asmodeus, Astaroth and Beherit, most of their names reflecting those of the heathen deities whom the Jews encountered in the surrounding countries of the Near East. One of the supreme achievements of MAGIC and particularly of RITUAL MAGIC is the summoning up of demons in order to command them and use their power. The 20th century magician Aleister CROWLEY, for example, sought to invoke Beelzebub, the Lord of the Flies, and 49 other demons.

See also RITUAL MAGIC,
SATANISM, WITCHCRAFT

Above and left: *Demons came in all sorts of forms, often part animal, part human – and their power to corrupt was feared.*

37

DIVINATION

Divination is the act of foretelling the future by magical or supernatural means, something that people have attempted since the dawn of Time. The methods used are extremely varied, but all seem to rely on the principle that God or the gods have declared their future intentions in a coded form that can be read by anyone who is properly instructed; they include the reading of the marks on animal bones; the reading of animal entrails, especially the liver; the I Ching; astrology, both Chinese and western; crystal-gazing or scrying; fortune-telling by means of cards, especially the Tarot; the riddling prophecies of oracles, and many others.

See also CARD READING, ASTROLOGY, DOWSING, MEDIUMS, OBJECT-READING, PALMISTRY, SCRYING, TEA-LEAF READING, I CHING, TAROT

DOWSING

Once connected with the occult and black magic, dowsing is today recognized as a valid occupation with a respected place in the world of science.

No organization could have a more down-to-earth and hard-headed image than such giant multinational companies as DuPont and the RCA Company, and yet they have both employed dowsers to find adequate water supplies for them on company land.

Dowsers have been called in to assist the police, medical practitioners, the US Marine Corps and the government of British Columbia among other bodies, and this degree of official recognition is unique among activities which can be thought of as 'paranormal'. The reason is evident: the results of this activity can be tested empirically — the proof is in the digging.

Dowsing may be defined as using some implement, often a forked stick, to locate underground sources of water, oil or minerals. It may even be that the rod is dispensable, for Australian Aborigines can locate water in the desert without any instrument.

The History of Dowsing

Be that as it may, the history of dowsing stretches back thousands of years. There are several references to it in the Old Testament, from Jacob, who found water in Canaan, to Moses, whose dowsing is mentioned in Exodus 17.5–6 and again in Numbers 20.10–11: 'And Moses and Aaron gathered the assembly together before the rock, and he said unto them, Hear now, ye rebels; shall we bring you forth water out of this rock? And Moses lifted up his hand, and smote the rock with his rod twice: and water came forth abundantly, and the congregation drank and their cattle.'

In the Caves of Tassili in the Atlas Mountains there is a picture of a dowser painted at least 8000 years ago, and there is similar evidence of its frequent practice among the ancient Egyptians, and a record of its exercise during the reign of the Chinese Emperor Yu in 2200 BC. There is a curious lack of reference to it in Roman times, but it re-emerges during the 11th century, and was in

Right: The traditional forked hazel stick has largely been replaced by nylon divining rods or metal wires.

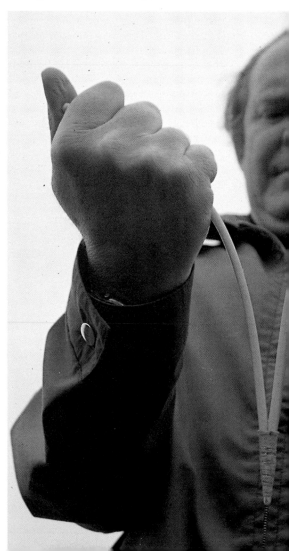

common practice by the 16th century.

Dowsing was frequently used by German miners seeking out underground seams, and it is strange that Martin Luther felt compelled to condemn it as a form of black magic, for his own father was a miner who must have seen it practised regularly. The influx of German miners who came to rediscover lost tin mines in Cornwall during the reign of Elizabeth I meant that dowsing was well established in Britain, and from then on it grew in influence until by the 19th century societies existed on both sides of the Atlantic to promote its principles and practices.

The old association of the dowser with supernatural or occult forces was reinforced by the use of a rod made of hazel, rowan or ash — all magical woods, so it was thought — and the fact that only certain people seemed to be sensitive to these unseen forces. But the modern dowser uses a whole variety of implements from a metal wire to a pendulum on a thread, and many dowsers can be just as effective by performing at a table, pinpointing the desired object on a map. It would seem that distance does not lessen the dowser's powers.

An instance of dowsing in action might be helpful. During the US conflict in Vietnam, the then Secretary of Defence, Robert McNamara, invited suggestions as to how land mines, ammunition dumps and other military phenomena might be located. The US Marine Corps, under Major Manley, resolved to test out 'radiesthesia' in the field and were astonished at the high degree of success they had in locating underground tunnels, buried communication lines and the like. These findings were passed on to General Westmoreland by the civilian dowser, Louis Matacia, at whose instigation the programme had been started, and the *New York Times* filed a story about 'combat dowsing' in 1967.

The Theory of Radiesthesia

Why is it that some people and not others are able to 'sense' the presence of hidden objects? Is there an element of extrasensory perception in the phenomenon? And, allied to this, what is the significance of the fact that the dowser Guy Underwood, the author of *The Pattern of the Past*, was able to pick up strong sources of subterranean energy, such as 'blind springs', geological faults and underground streams, at sites of standing stones, stone circles and other artefacts of prehistoric construction?

The most widely accepted account of how dowsers operate is that which goes by the name of 'radiesthesia', and the capital city of this theory is Paris, where there are hundreds of practitioners. Its believers hold that water, oil and minerals, indeed all matter, give off 'radiations' which the dowser 'picks up', often by means of a pendulum. The location of prehistoric sacred sites on areas of strong terrestrial energy argues powerful dowsing abilities among early peoples.

Whether dowsers are physically gifted or are simply in touch with a power that is within us all — the instinct that animals exercise when travelling home from unknown territory — is as yet unknown, but Colin Wilson states that, in his experience, nine out of ten people can dowse, and the tenth cannot because he or she is set against it.

In conclusion, it is noteworthy that Albert Einstein is reported to have found the concept of dowsing intriguing, and believed that the answer would be found in studies of electro-magnetism, while the French Nobel Prize winner, Charles Richet announced flatly, 'Dowsing is a fact we must accept.'

Above: *This renaissance woodcut shows German prospectors dowsing for precious metals. Sensitives, such as Uri Geller, still do this – for a handsome retainer.*

DREAMS

From ancient times people have recognized the importance of dreams: in the Old Testament Joseph became second-in-command to Pharaoh because of two dreams; and a dream might have changed the history of Christianity if only Pontius Pilate had listened to his wife.

Anyone who claims not to dream is mistaken — we all dream, and scientists have been able to prove this since the 1950s, showing that REMs, or Rapid Eye Movements, signal the phases of sleep in which we dream. The French researcher Dr Jouvet set up experiments in which people were deprived of dreams, and his subjects displayed such alarming

symptoms that the experiments had to be stopped. Animals subjected to the same conditions actually died, so we may conclude that dreaming provides a function which is as essential (not only to human beings, but to all animals) as the beating of the heart.

Since the beginning of the century there has been a resurgence of interest in dreams in the West, but as far back as records exist people have been fascinated by them. In certain cultures the entire family sits around in the morning, each member recounting the dream he or she had that night, and children are encouraged to remember their dreams. It seems that the dreams of primitive humans were instrumental in developing their awareness of themselves as something more than just flesh and blood, in helping them to recognize their spiritual natures.

Before 1000 BC there were Hindu writings about dreams distinguishing the dreaming and non-dreaming phases of sleep, and records exist of the dreams of the ancient Egyptian Pharaohs, the most dramatic being an account of a prophetic dream carved on a tablet between the paws of the Great Sphinx of

Below and right: Some dream images are universal, as revealed by Freud and Jung, but many have only personal relevance to the dreamer.

Giza. Predating these examples is a set of dream interpretations in the Chester Beatty Library, which date back to 2000 BC. All of these testify to ancient people's intense and abiding fascination with dreams, and they show that they were interested in the physiology of dreaming, in the prophetic capacity of dreams and in the importance of interpreting dreams — all three are lines of enquiry which intrigue modern scientists and philosophers.

The prophetic powers of dreams are particularly emphasized in the Bible. One of the best-known instances of prophetic dreams and an ensuing interpretation of the dreams is Joseph's explanation to the Pharaoh of the significance of two dreams he had had of seven fat cattle and seven fat ears of corn. Joseph forecast that seven years of plenty in Egypt would be followed by seven years of famine, and the Pharaoh was so grateful for this warning that he set Joseph up second only to himself throughout the land.

In the New Testament dreams are often a means through which God communicates with people. Instances of this include the time when Joseph was told in

a dream that he should marry Mary, and, again, was warned that he must escape with his family to Egypt, for Herod was a threat. At the end of Jesus's life when he was brought before Pilate to be condemned, a message was carried to Pilate from his wife, begging him to have 'nothing to do with that just man, for I have suffered many things this day in a dream because of him'. We know that Pilate ignored this warning.

In the ancient Greek world dreams were given great prominence. In Plato's *Republic*, Socrates is reported to have maintained that the dreams of a righteous soul are pure and prophetic, and the practice of incubation, that is, sleeping in a shrine in the hope that the god would visit the sleeper with advice as to how to obtain a cure, was widespread. The famous oracle at Delphi, the shrine of Apollo, is an example where the hopeful would go to sleep with the aim of seeing a dream which was divinely inspired, rather than a dream for a medical cure, but the most common prayer was that some physical ailment would be relieved.

With the two greatest 20th-century interpreters of dreams, Freud and Jung, we have a very different concept of the dream-cure. Both saw dreams as giving valuable insights into the individual's unconscious, although their paths diverged, as we shall see.

Freud's Interpretation

Freud published his great work *The Interpretation of Dreams* in 1900 and his maxim, 'The interpretation of dreams is the royal road to a knowledge of the unconscious activities of the mind', expresses a view he held throughout his life. He believed that the dreamer manages to fulfil in the secrecy of a dream a wish he or she has had, a persistent wish, which, if unsatisfied, would interfere with sleep. Dreams, he asserted, are the 'guardians of sleep'. One dream he interpreted reads as follows: A still-young woman, married for many years, is at the theatre with her husband. One side of the stalls is empty. Her husband tells her that Elise L and her fiancé had wanted to go too, but had only been able to get bad seats — three for 1 florin 50 kreuzers — and, of course, they could not take those.

Freud first isolated real-life happenings which had been distorted into elements of the dream. The young woman had wanted to go to a certain play and bought the tickets well in advance only to find half the stalls empty. The sum of

Above: *Dreams may reflect the events of the day or may recur, dealing with important preoccupations of the dreamer.*

Above: *The dream world is unpredictable – sometimes offering comfort, at other times producing warnings from the subconscious.*

has exorcized the pangs of envy she feels at hearing of her friend's engagement 'an old triumph was put in the place of her recent defeat'. The dream is a good example of how people 'censor' thoughts and desires they do not wish to recognize and, as almost always with Freud, the all-invasive influence of sex is stressed.

Jung's Ideas

Turning to Jung, Freud's junior by 19 years, we find a different attitude to the meaning and function of dreams, and although the relationship between the two men was close for a time, their eventual split stems from the fact that they held incompatible views about human nature. As they developed, Jung's ideas turned away from an insistence on the individual mind and more towards an appreciation of the unifying experience of religion, and a development of his idea of a collective unconscious, something which is already locked in our minds from birth. Towards the end of his life Freud seemed to be persuaded that Jung had revealed a truth, for he wrote, 'Dreams bring to light material which cannot have originated either from the dreamer's adult life, or from his forgotten childhood. We are obliged to regard it as part of the archaic heritage which a child brings with him into the world.'

Jung looked to the 'archetypal' images which constantly crop up in dreams to provide a key to the 'other' in us, that which puts us in touch with our past and may also give us insights into the future. He himself often painted his own visions and dreams and he encouraged his patients to do likewise — his was a more creative approach, drawing on mythology and a study of world religions, and his archetypes, such as The Princess and The Priestess, The Tramp and The Trickster can be found in the dreams of all people and all ages.

Dress Rehearsals

Dreams have been seen in various ways. They have been described as a 'dress rehearsal' for life, as a means by which supernatural messages are transmitted to human beings, as capable of prophecy, as a way of keeping the conscious healthy, as an instrument through which a physical cure might be achieved, as a door leading into a common unconscious, and as an inexplicable but indispensable physical necessity for all animals. All these are open to question, but what is beyond doubt is that you and I are going to dream when we go to sleep tonight.

1 florin 50 kreuzers was clearly linked to a present of 150 florins which her sister-in-law had been given by her husband and which she had rushed off to exchange for a piece of jewellery; and the day before the dream her husband had told her that Elise L, her friend, had just become engaged.

Having considered these associations, Freud was struck by the number of things which were done too early or too late or in a hurry, and came to the conclusion that the young dreamer was regretting having married too soon. If she had followed her friend's example she might have found a better man, and the sum of money in the dream indicates that she could have used her dowry to more advantage. The problem of interpreting why Elise L and her fiance had wanted to buy three tickets remained, and Freud fell back on associating 'three' with a man or husband. Going to the theatre to see a play, however, was, he claimed, a metaphor for entering into marriage and being thus allowed to witness sexual secrets. Elise, not yet married, has not come to the theatre and so the dreamer has one up on her. By means of the dream the young woman

ECTOPLASM

Ectoplasm is a whitish substance that allegedly issues from the bodily orifices or breast of a medium in trance. The volume can range from barely visible wisps as insubstantial as smoke to dense, fully formed and clothed bodies. On some occasions ectoplasm has been likened to a thick liquid or jelly that by degrees assumes a physical shape. Many photographs of ectoplasmic outpourings exist.

See also MEDIUMS

ELEMENTS AND ELEMENTALS

One of the main pillars of medieval science and medicine was the belief, inherited from the ancient Greeks, that everything in nature is composed in different proportions of the four elements of earth, air, fire and water. This belief was fundamental to ALCHEMY but also to medicine, since the four elements were linked with the four 'humours' of the body: earth with black bile; air with blood; fire with yellow bile; and water with phlegm. A healthy and well-balanced person would have the four humours in a condition approximating to perfect balance; a serious imbalance would cause disease or a particular kind of unhappy or unpleasant temperament.

Medicine and elementals

The medieval doctor, therefore, sought to restore the balance, for example by bleeding a patient thought to suffer from having too much blood. (Such words as bilious, sanguine and choleric derive from the theory of elements and humours.)

However, the belief in the four elements extended beyond the realm of medicine into ideas about the nature of the universe and of the human psyche. It also led to the notion of the Elementals, creatures whose natures are wholly determined by one or other of the four elements. Gnomes are identified with earth, Sylphs with air, Salamanders with fire, and Nereids with water. According to the 16th-century mystical philosopher Paracelsus, the elementals live their own distinct lives, moving freely in their own elements. The Gnomes, for example, can move and see through earth as freely as human beings move and see through air; Salamanders live and breathe freely in fire, Nereids (sometimes also known as Undines) in water.

Despite their very different natures and forms, it was believed that Elementals could assume human shape if they wished and interact successfully with human beings. Some marriages were said to take place, though if an Elemental became offended it would choose to return to its natural element.

As creatures identified by medieval science, Elementals are quite distinct from FAIRIES.

Below: *An earth elemental was said to move and breathe as freely in earth as humans do in air.*

ESP

Extrasensory perception is the name given to the ability to obtain information about the environment without using the normal sensory channels. Serious investigation of this ability, with testing under controlled conditions, grew out of the intense interest in spiritualism and mediums in the 19th century. So far three types of ESP have been identified and these were known long before the actual term was coined in 1934. These are CLAIRVOYANCE, PRECOGNITION and TELEPATHY. For many years research into the subject was hampered by the idea that the various categories had to be kept rigidly separate. Now, however, together with PSYCHOKINESIS, they are classed as manifestations of a single ability, PSI.

The way ESP expresses itself within these categories is very diverse. Premonitory dreams in which a person 'sees' an event, usually a tragic one, before it has taken place, is a commonly reported experience. Telepathy also surfaces in the dream state. Psychologists have noted various cases where patients with a close emotional link have shared identical dream symbols. A man reported a dream of walking across a wide empty plain towards a huge and ominous-looking windmill on the horizon. On the same night his wife dreamt that while she was pushing their toddler across a large field, the toy windmill he was holding grew so big that it seemed to fill up the whole sky.

Another phenomenon displayed with regularity is sudden intuitive conviction that something is wrong, or about to happen, to a friend or loved one. This unfocused sense of danger was responsible for a woman leaving a bingo game and rushing home to find her invalid father had fallen asleep with a lighted cigarette and set himself on fire. Another woman in the middle of a dinner party was overwhelmed by an urgent desire to phone her sister hundreds of miles away in Scotland. Her call was answered by her tearful nephew who said his mother had just suffered a heart attack and been taken to hospital. Was it just clairvoyance or had the woman telepathically picked up her sister's cry of agony? Although much less common, there have been cases where a person alerted telepathically to a particular condition of a loved one, suffers the same physical symptoms. This may involve going through the labour of childbirth or the agony of a fatal fall.

Nowadays there is little doubt in anyone's mind as to the importance of these puzzling human experiences. They highlight how little we still know about energy, magnetism, the brain and its potential. It used to be thought that psi ability was possessed by a few select individuals. While there is no doubt that some of us are much more talented than others, the view held now is that psi ability is a latent potential possessed by us all. Whether it is developed or inhibited depends on attitude and interest more than anything. Recent large scale tests in America and Holland have corroborated this theory. Results seem to show that ESP and other psi abilities are an integral part of our natural inheritance.

See also CLAIRVOYANCE, TELE-PATHY

The most chilling kind of ESP experience is premonition, for it is usually of a disaster.
Right: *Jeanne Dixon foresaw the assassination of Kennedy in November 1963, but was powerless to avert it.*

EVIL

The question of the origin of evil, identified with the apparent inevitability of suffering and death as well as with sin, has troubled people's minds since the beginning of time. A variety of answers have emerged in the world's great religions.

In the religions of the ancient Near East, evil as well as good is seen as being ordained by the gods or, in the case of early Judaism, by God. Later Judaism, influenced by Persian Zoroastrianism, attributed evil to Satan, who is locked in struggle with a wholly good God but ultimately doomed to defeat.

Evil and Christianity

Christianity took over this idea but gives more importance in its theology to a third idea, that of the essential sinfulness of man, stemming from the fall of Adam. This doctrine of original sin, from which people are saved only through Christ, was formulated by St Paul: 'Sin came into the world through one man and death through sin, and so death spread to all men because all men sinned.'

Evil, as the idea of absolute wickedness, the absolute negation of good, has become foreign to the European mind of the 20th century, which tends to take a more relativistic view. The idea was, however, real to the medieval mind, who thought of it as embodied not only in the very real person of the Devil but in a host of demons, who shared with him the work of tempting men and women to sin and torturing them in hell.

The variety of devils is indicated in a 14th century miracle play:

'Smooth Devils, Horned Devils, Sullen Devils, Playful Devils, Shorn Devils, Hairy Devils, Foolish Devils'.

The fact that evil did undoubtedly exist in the world, that it seemed all too often to triumph over good, led some people to the view that perhaps after all the real power in the world lay with the Prince of Darkness, that in the dualistic cosmic struggle between the goodness of God and the evil of Satan, it was Satan who would finally prevail, if indeed he had not prevailed already. Such ideas led at least some men and women to SATANISM and WITCHCRAFT.

See also DEVILS AND DEMONS, INCUBUS AND SUCCUBUS, SATANISM, WITCHCRAFT

Above: *The world was innocent and a paradise before evil first showed its power in the corruption of Adam and Eve. Since then people have used many means to try to protect themselves from its effects, such as this American Indian box* (left), *whose eyes were believed to ward off evil.*

EXORCISM

Can innocent people truly be possessed by an invading demon? The Roman Catholic Church as well as some members of the medical profession believe in the curing powers of the exorcist.

The word 'exorcism' comes from the Greek 'exousia', meaning 'to dismiss', and it refers to the ceremony during which a demon or evil spirit is 'dismissed' or banished from a person or place. Although the ritual was portrayed in a highly sensational manner in the film *The Exorcist*, thereby making modern religious leaders the more reluctant to discuss it, exorcism is found in the most sophisticated as well as in the so-called primitive religions, and has a very ancient history. Solomon, for example, is believed to have been given the power of exorcism by God.

Religious Attitudes

While exorcism is widespread today among tribal religions, it is interesting to examine how its practice has declined in both Judaism and Islam. Jesus's references (Matthew 12.27 and Luke 11.14–20) to the practice of casting out devils make it clear that it was an established fact among the Jews of his day, and cabalistic sources testify to a belief in dybbukim, or demons, whose prince is Samael, the serpent that seduced Eve. The Jewish historian Josephus, who was born during the reign of Caligula, describes the exorcism of a dybbuk by a certain Elcazar, and such practices have continued throughout the centuries, although Jewish authorities claim that none is performed in Britain today.

Similarly, in Islamic tradition djinn, or demons created out of smokeless fire, were believed to be capable of possessing people, but because of the crude and even dangerous nature of some of the rites the practices are discouraged; if a Muslim is believed to be possessed, the imâm recited two surahs from the *Qur'an* over that person, invoking 'the Most Gracious ... the Sustainer of men' to give refuge to the victim.

Matters are more complicated in the Christian community. In the Church of England, the current Archbishop of Canterbury, Dr Runcie, seems to be inclined against the ritual, and wishes all questions surrounding exorcisms to be

referred to him personally, but a former Archbishop of Canterbury, the Most Reverend Michael Ramsey, has said, 'I believe there is a genuine demonic possession and a genuine exorcism, but the genuine element is probably in the minority.'

Methodist and Baptist ministers are held to be free to make their own basic decisions, although the Methodist Conference of 1976 laid down certain guidelines.

The Roman Catholic Church, however, has always believed that physical possession of a person or place by the forces of evil is an undeniable fact. Pope Paul VI affirmed in 1972, 'We know that this dark and disturbing spirit exists and that he still acts with treacherous cunning.' Over the years there has been established a set of Rules, approved by the Vatican, which specify the conditions under which an exorcism may be performed, and which urge great caution on the part of the priest. This is especially important since 'Sometimes the devil will leave the possessed person in peace and even allow him to receive the holy Eucharist, to make it appear that he has departed ... For this reason the exorcist must be on his guard not to fall into his trap.'

What is 'Possession'?

It is important to consider how it is that the devil comes to take possession of a person or a place. Aquinas, the 13th century theologian, argued that the human's intellect and will were bulwarks against possession, and therefore

Below: *Madness was believed to be the work of demons, and exorcists worked to free the afflicted from their power. This woman was possessed by many demons, all of whom had to be banished.*

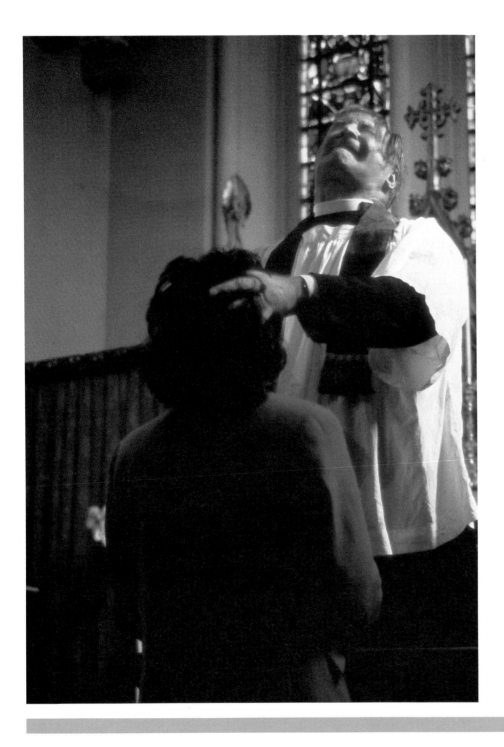

those who were possessed had brought it upon themselves, and another manifestation of this view is those who dabble in the occult or investigate black magic are particularly susceptible. It does appear, however, that some people are innocent victims of an invading demon, and that some places are the haunts of evil spirits, although care must be taken not to confuse them with sites of poltergeist activity.

With the frontiers being ever pushed back, it is possible to identify many so-called cases of possession as cases of neurosis or psychotic illness, but there are members of the medical profession who believe that in a small number of cases the only possible explanation is that the patient is in need of exorcism.

Even if possession by spirits is one day disproved, there is no denying that throughout history exorcisms have taken place and countless distraught and unhappy people have been brought back to living a normal life by the prayers and rituals of the exorcist.

See also GHOSTS, HAUNTED HOUSES

Above left and right: *The exorcist may be attacked psychically and physically by the demons so he must prepare carefully for the solemn rite of exorcism.*

Below: *Fairies are by no means always benign: this is the demonic 13th fairy who cursed Sleeping Beauty*. Bottom: *The fairy ring – an area of strong enchantment.*

FAIRIES

The word 'fairy' was originally 'fai-erie', a state of enchantment brought about by supernatural creatures who were described by serious writers of the 17th century as being midway between angels and human beings. Later it came to be used for the country of those creatures, but people who believed in them rarely used the word. Often they are given euphemistic names like 'the wee folk' or 'the good neighbours' or even simply 'them'.

There are literally hundreds of different fairy types in the British Isles but they can be grouped under a small number of major classes according to their size, appearance, character and habits.

The aristocracy of the trooping fairies are the heroic fairies, of whom the best-known are the Daoine Sidhe (Dana o'Shee) of Ireland. These are of human size, strikingly beautiful in appearance, and their life-style is that of the aristocracy of the Celtic world, devoted to fighting, riding and hunting.

The humbler fairies are generally smaller, varying in height from a few inches to that of a small child. Some of them live in small communities but most of them are solitaries, such as the Irish fairy shoemaker, the leprechaun. Many of these smaller fairies are attached to particular places, families or homes. The banshees of Ireland and the Scottish Highlands are responsible for a particular family or clan and will be heard weeping just before the death of a member of it. Brownies, lobs, hobs and hobgoblins are domestic fairies, ugly in appearance but generally well-disposed to human beings and willing to perform various domestic chores.

A third class consists of goblins and bogey beasts, which range from the merely mischievous to the truly evil and which appear under a huge variety of names. The glaistigs of the Scottish Highlands for example appeared to unwary travellers like beautiful women but were, in fact, vampires. Creatures of that kind frequently took on animal or at least non-human form, like the water kelpies who took the form of horses in order to carry their victims into the water, where they would devour them.

Fairies are associated with certain general beliefs, such as their tendency to kidnap human babies and replace them with their own, known as changelings. Time spent with them does not pass in the normal way; many stories tell of men who have feasted with the fairies for a single night, only to find that a hundred years have passed.

There are various theories about the origins of fairy beliefs. The most convincing suggest that most represent memories of the gods, local deities and demons of the pre-Christian world, the Daoine Sidhe for example being the old gods of Ireland, while some may recall memories of an earlier race who literally went underground when the stronger and more warlike Celts arrived. This latter view is reinforced by the traditional belief that fairies are terrified of iron, for it was almost certainly the Celts who introduced iron weapons into Britain.

See also LITTLE PEOPLE

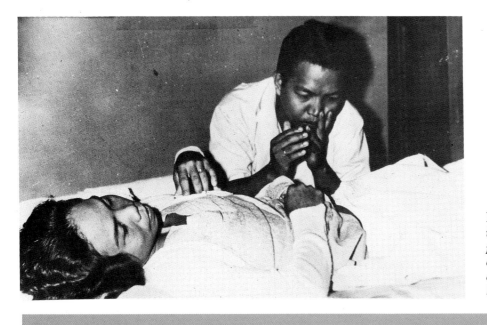

Left: *The healer must put himself in the right frame of mind by prayer or meditation and concentrate his powers on the afflicted site to enable healing to happen.*

FAITH HEALING

Former sceptics are now reconsidering with interest the results of recovery through belief — a form of healing practised since the time of the ancient Egyptians.

Faith healing usually describes cures that have happened without the use of medicine or surgery, which are inexplicable by traditional practitioners of modern medicine. The 'faith' may be of a religious nature, or may simply lie in the patient's belief in the powers of the faith healer. Some healers claim that no actual faith is needed except their own, and that purely by the laying on of hands, or concentrated thought about absent patients, they can effect a cure.

Now that thinking about the nature of illness and disease is changing, people who previously dismissed the idea of faith healing are reconsidering the question. Doctors are coming round to the holistic view of health — that the mind and body cannot be separated in matters of health and sickness. This means that not only 'psychosomatic' disorders (where the sufferer exhibits symptoms without there being real physical cause) are attributed to the power of the mind over the body. Nowadays it is recognized that acute stress (such as the death of a spouse) is often followed within a year or so by actual physical illness — in other words, emotional damage can be a major factor in physical damage. Also, a positive mental attitude seems to have beneficial effects. For this reason certain

alternative forms of cancer-treatment involve teaching people to mobilize what the doctors call 'patients' inner resources for self-healing', which include visualizing the body's immune system attacking cancerous cells.

With all this being so, many people believe that the apparently non-scientific practice of faith healing has to be looked at again.

Faith healers work in different ways, but there are certain fundamental similarities within the different methods. Important to all of them, for instance, is for the faith healers to experience a kind of empathy with the person they are trying to heal. When healing, most report that they can feel what the other is feeling — emotional and physical pain. All healers agree that the sufferers must truly want to get well, even if they have little real belief in the healer's powers. This is because some ill people seem actually to draw comfort from their unhealthy state and may not want strongly enough to be cured. The desire to get well, on the other hand, creates a kind of energy (mobilizing the inner resources for self-healing).

The healer must feel in tune with the patient, usually calling up his or her own resources through prayer, incantation or concentration of thought, and while doing this directing 'power' towards the site of the problem. Then, if healing is taking place, it is believed that an energy passes between the two, which starts the healing process. Some people experience this physically as a sensation of great heat. If the desire to heal and the desire to be healed is there, it is said that this process can even happen at a distance.

Above: *Faith must be felt by the healer or the subject – not necessarily both. Jesus was probably the greatest healer ever.*

Practice Through the Ages

Many of Jesus's miracles, of course, are also based on faith healing. Some involved direct touch, as with the man whose amputated ear grew again after Jesus had touched it. Others involved simple faith: for example, the woman who touched the hem of Jesus's robe without his knowledge and was cured. At shrines such as Lourdes many spontaneous cures are attributed to the intercession of the Virgin Mary and the power of prayer and faith of the sufferer.

All apparent cures from Lourdes are studied fully by the Catholic Church before they are accepted. There are seven requirements that have to be fulfilled. Firstly the illness should be serious and seen to be either impossible — or very difficult — to cure by conventional methods. Secondly the illness should not be on the decline or be in a state where it could naturally improve. Thirdly no treatment should have been given, or it should have been shown to be useless. Fourthly the cure should be sudden. Fifthly the cure should be complete. Sixthly it should be provable that there was no possibility of the cure happening by natural causes. Lastly the illness should not recur.

Christian Scientists are a sect that believe that faith healing is the only true form of healing — that sickness and health are both in God's gift — and many of them refuse to consult doctors when they are ill.

By far the largest single group of faith healers belong to the Spiritualist movement. These healers believe that their own healing powers are augmented by the help of spirit doctors and guides, who are able, from the other side, to guide the healing power to the correct site, and aid in diagnosis.

One of the most famous Spiritualist healers, Harry Edwards, was born in Britain in 1893. He discovered his healing powers when he was in his late 30s, and set up what he called a healing 'sanctuary' in Surrey. In the four years 1954–1958 alone, Edwards claimed to have cured 10,000 people, many of them classified as incurable. Much of Edwards' healing was done at distance, and at the height of his powers he was dealing with thousands of letters a week. He claimed an 85–90% success rate, whether using absent healing or the direct laying on of hands.

Today's Unorthodoxy — Tomorrow's Convention

Faith healers believe that healing should take its place alongside other more conventional healing methods. The problem here is that 'proof' is so hard to obtain. Most doctors will agree that 'inexplicable, almost miraculous healings occasionally occur in the average medical practice'. So believing in spontaneous cures is an excuse for those who wish to refute the evidence of some of the amazing cures that healers point to as proof. The one proof it is impossible to obtain is that the cure would not have happened anyway without the healer's intervention. However in 1983 the British Medical Association set up an inquiry into the workings of alternative medicine, faith healing included. As its president, the Prince of Wales, was quoted as saying, 'What is taken for today's unorthodoxy is probably going to be tomorrow's convention.'

FAKIR

In common parlance the word 'fakir' is most often applied to Indian holy men who are more properly called *sadhus*. The sadhus practise lives of extreme poverty and asceticism, seeking out discomfort and sometimes even self-mutilation. Lying on beds of nails is the method of mortification best known in the West, but sadhus will also immerse themselves in water or in hot ashes for prolonged periods, sit or lie in one place for years on end, or keep their hands permanently clenched so that their nails grow into the flesh.

Many, but not all, sadhus beg for their living, others practise magic or fortune-telling or make and sell charms. Many undoubtedly are charlatans exploiting the credulity of a deeply religious people; many others are equally certainly true seekers after spiritual enlightenment and divine merit.

In the Arabic or Islamic sense of the word the fakir is someone who has renounced the world and its wealth and put his trust in Allah to bring life or death, good or ill, while he pursues the life of a holy beggar. There are many sects, differing in the extent to which they practise extremes of asceticism.

Below: *Fakirs practise a form of mind-over-matter. They are able to endure lying on a bed of nails without apparent discomfort.*

FAMILIARS

A witch's familiar is an imp or minor devil in the form of an animal living in association with her.

The black cat is the form of familiar best-known to the popular imagination, but many other kinds of small animal are found, such as birds (especially blackbirds and crows), and frogs and toads. The popularity of the cat may stem from two factors: the quite separate tradition in which the witch turns herself into a cat at night; and the practice, during periods of anti-witchcraft hysteria, of turning on old women living in isolation with only their cats for company.

The familiar is never an incarnation of the Devil himself, but may be a gift from him to the witch who serves him. To confuse matters further, the Devil was commonly believed to visit his witches in animal form, often as a cat or a dog. In a great many cases from all over Europe the witch is reported as suckling the familiar at her breast, as in the case of the Somerset witch who stated that 'her Familiar doth commonly suck her right Breast about seven at night, in the shape of a little cat of dunnish colour ... and when she is suckt, she is in a kind of Trance.' The suggestion was of course that the familiar was being rewarded in this way for the evil services it performed.

As well as milk, familiars were quite often fed on blood, like the cat called Sathan inherited by the Chelmsford witch Elizabeth Francis from her grandmother. Sathan also had the ability to turn itself into a toad whenever the Pater Noster was recited in Latin. A further

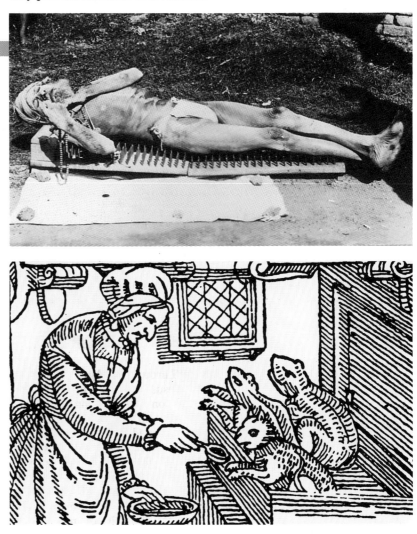

belief was that familiars were suckled on the special extra teat which witches were believed to have 'in the secretest part' of their bodies, the finding of which was infallible proof of a witch.

Familiars were frequently given names (often suggested by the Devil), that suggested their devilish nature.

Above: *A witch feeding her familiars. Some witches were said to suckle their familiars with a secret teat.*

See also WITCHCRAFT

Above: *Mithras, a mythological controller of fate.*

FATE

In battle, people come face to face most dramatically with the notion of fate, and in the First World War there was a common belief that whatever you did, you would only be killed if a 'bullet had your name on it'. But even convinced fatalists accept that one can take steps to avert an evil fate and few people step out blind into the traffic, trusting to the power of destiny.

If, then, the modern person has an ambiguous attitude to fate, what of our ancestors? Study of early mythology reveals a strong belief in gods and goddesses, who allotted joy and pain alike to humankind, and who governed birth, life and death. The most well-known of these are Clotho, who spins the thread of destiny, Lachesis, who weaves the tissue of fortune, and Atropos with her scissors,

who cuts the thread of life at some unforseen moment.

If the idea of predestination is correct, why should we not be utterly self-seeking? What point is there in righteousness? The early Greeks felt that too strong an assertion of one's will led to hubris, pride, inciting the wrath of the gods, but by Epicurus's day there was an acceptance that people could exert free will.

The notion of free will has always been strongly affirmed by the Roman Catholic Church, in defiance of Calvinist doctrines of predestination, the idea that only an elite of true believers will enter heaven. Hinduism embraces the idea of KARMA, and while Muslims may bow to Kismet, the will of Allah, they are urged to righteousness within the constraints of their lives.

We may decide that we are 'as flies to the gods', but human dignity demands that we consider the possibility that we are masters of our own fate.

Above: *Fertility rites on earth apparently mimicked the actions*
52 *of the gods.*

FERTILITY RITES

Until the present century, and even today for the majority of people living in the world, the natural condition of the human race has been a struggle for existence. Fertility — the ability of women to bear children who will grow up to continue one's labours, the fertility of crops and of animals — has been for most people and for most of time an immediate, life-and-death issue.

For primitive people it was and is an issue that is inseparable from a belief in the supernatural world, the world of gods and spirits that control for good or ill the everyday life of humankind. From the very earliest times therefore, we find evidence of people's efforts to propitiate if not control this world. Even the cycle of the seasons, of seedtime and harvest, wet season and dry, depended on the will of the rulers of the spirit world, and many of the festivals that survive in Western Europe today hark back to a time when they had an urgent purpose: to ensure that the sun would return in winter or that the rains would come in time to nourish the crops.

Fertility and magic
The measures that primitive people took to win the favour of the spirit world reflect a kind of associative thinking or IMITATIVE MAGIC. We see it in the

famous Old Stone Age cave paintings of Spain and France, where the beautiful depictions of successful hunting almost certainly have the magical purpose of ensuring such success.

Earth as woman
The fact that these paintings were made in caves suggest the association of fertility with the earth from which it was believed to spring, and the caves may have been perceived as the 'wombs' of earth. Certainly by the time people had begun to practise agriculture the earth had been personified as a woman. Some of the earliest-known cultural artefacts are the so-called 'Venus' or 'Earth-goddess' figurines, which strongly emphasize female sexual and maternal characteristics. Human sexuality and the fertility of crops and cattle were identified very closely in the primitive mind and many fertility rites involve actual or symbolic sexual intercourse in the belief that human sex can stimulate natural fertility.

In the religions of the ancient Near East the king, representing the male principle, would enter into an annual sacred marriage with the priestess of the goddess in order to ensure fertility for his land and his people for another year. The association of fertility with the interaction of male and female permeates religious belief in the ancient world and in modern tribal societies, as does the identification of male gods with the sun and the sky and female goddesses with the earth. This identification is not universal (the ancient Egyptians worshipped a sky goddess for example) but the mating of pairs of male and female deities is found in almost all the religions of the world: Osiris and Isis in ancient Egypt, Zeus and Hera in Greece, Frey and Freya in pagan Scandinavia. In the primitive forms of these religions we find again a strong emphasis on sexual characteristics, the goddesses either pregnant or with exaggerated breasts and pudenda, the gods with enlarged and erect phalluses.

Hints of such beliefs remain in many customs that survive in Western Europe and are now seen as merely charming: for example in the practice of dancing around the phallic symbol of the maypole, a custom that was once so closely associated with sexual licence that the Puritans banned it.

FETISH

In African religious or magical belief a fetish is a charm or cult-object, protecting its owner from harm (like a TALISMAN), or able to perform specific magical benefits.

In fetishistic religion fetishes may take either a domestic or a wider social form.

In the domestic form they are common natural objects (such as a tooth), ritually prepared for their owners by the medicine-man and capable of both protecting and curing.

In the wider social form they are seen as the embodiments of particular spirits with particular powers. Important fetishes of this latter kind are served by fetish-doctors, who are protected by them and are able to use their powers for the good of the community. A member of the community with a particular problem or need, whether it be the desire for success in hunting or a safe pregnancy or the detection of an enemy, will resort to the appropriate fetish-doctor who will supply him with the necessary charm.

Fetishistic beliefs went to America with the slaves and long survived there in black communities.

FLYING SAUCERS

On 24 June 1947 an Idaho businessman, Kenneth Arnold, was flying his private aircraft over Mount Rainier in the state of Washington, USA, when he saw an inexplicable series of discs in the sky. He told newsmen 'they were like saucers skipping over water' and this description is the origin of the phrase 'flying saucer' which is given to phenomena known to purists as Unidentified Flying Objects, or UFOs.

FORTUNE TELLING

The basis of fortune telling is the belief that the universe works according to an underlying pattern, that the future has been predetermined and, through the study of seemingly irrelevant and arbitrary factors, can be predicted. Of the innumerable methods used astrology, palmistry and card reading are the most common.

See also CARD READING, ASTROLOGY, DOWSING, MEDIUMS, OBJECT-READING, PALMISTRY, SCRYING, TEA-LEAF READING

Below: *A clear photograph of flying saucers over Conisborough, taken by Steven Pratt – but would it be accepted as genuine after laboratory tests?*

GELLER, URI

The world's most famous psychic is undoubtedly Uri Geller (born in Israel in 1947), whose metal-bending and telepathic feats provided British and American television audiences with so much fascination in the 1970s.

There is no doubt that this man has extraordinary powers; he is most famous for causing metal to wilt just by stroking it, or mending watches and clocks damaged beyond normal methods of repair, and reproducing drawings of others by obviously telepathic means. Around him machinery goes crazy — often without conscious effort on his part — objects appear and disappear, jump or change shape. His recorded feats range from the apparently trivial (but nonetheless 'impossible'), such as causing the giblets from a rock-solid frozen turkey to appear on the table by its side, to the downright frightening, such as stopping a ship's engine by the power of thought alone — at precisely the minute he had predicted. But

Below: *Uri Geller's strange metal-bending powers mean that at a touch keys will start to warp — and continue to do so even after he has left the room.*

perhaps his most lasting claim to fame will prove to be his ability to inspire similar paranormal abilities in a huge number of ordinary people, just by appearing on television in their homes.

Whenever he gives any kind of public demonstration of his powers he seems to set off a psychic contagion, especially among children. In his wake are small armies of what researchers term *Gellerini*: children or teenagers to whom bending metal is as natural as breathing — and often just as boring! In laboratories all over the western world metal benders are still being put through extraordinarily stringent tests. By now the phenomenon has been proved genuine beyond all doubt, but the major question thrown up by this work is 'What does it all mean? Is spoon-bending the beginning and the end of an admittedly strange talent?' Apparently not. Geller-inspired metal-benders have been discovered to possess other psychic abilities, such as healing, which is undoubtedly of more use to the world.

Geller first came to fame in Britain on 23 November 1973 on BBC television's *David Dimbleby Talk-in*. Within half an hour the pattern of his life for the next few years was firmly established. He bent spoons, caused watches to stop and go — and the BBC's switchboard was jammed with callers with not a functional fork in the house. He exuded a certain brash charm, won over a great many sceptics and made a lot of enemies.

The Anglo-Saxon world has always been suspicious of flamboyance. Geller is a natural showman and his mentor of those early days, American inventor Dr Andrija Puharich, had created an image for Geller that was to prove a difficult act to follow. Strange stories began to be circulated — both by Puharich and Geller himself — about how it all started. Extraterrestrial beings, it was claimed,

had bestowed the powers on the Israeli as a boy. Geller's extraordinary partnership with Dr Puharich is over, and the space beings are no longer mentioned.

His enemies are mainly culled from the ranks of the scientific establishment and stage magicians, notably America's James ('The Amazing) Randi and Britain's Paul Daniels. The history of psychical research is littered with character assassinations. The 'impossible' is very difficult to accept gracefully. Those adept in sleight of hand maintain that Geller must be a fraud because they can reproduce his feats fraudulently. These accusations overlook the facts: Randi, for example, needs preparation time for his metal bending, Geller does not. Randi is obviously always aware of his effects — things just happen around Geller, frequently without his knowledge and often without his physical presence. Author Brian Inglis tells how a key that Geller touched — and bent — *continued to bend* after he had left the room. Needless to say, Randi and his fellow artistes cannot even attempt this.

Today a more mature, self-possessed Uri Geller lives in London with his wife and family. He no longer feels the need to 'perform' to try to impress the scep-

tics. He makes a considerable living by 'map dowsing' for mining firms (he just points to a place on a map where valuable commodities will be found — they always are) and, perhaps sinisterly, by using his powers for military research. As he says, 'Just imagine if you had 15 or so trained minds like mine . . .'

Above: *Author Colin Wilson championed Geller in the face of scepticism – but dismissed his tales of extra-terrestrials.*

GEMINI

Gemini, the Heavenly Twins, the third sign of the Zodiac, is an Air sign, ruling those born between 22 May and 21 June.

Geminis have thoughts of quicksilver, ruled as they are by the planet Mercury, the winged messenger of mythology. They can solve problems in their heads with lightning speed and unerring logic. They enjoy working with facts and figures, making good mathematicians, accountants, astronomers and salesmen. Their love of logic also makes them good musicians and physicians.

With their butterfly minds they gain knowledge in many areas, though they seldom delve too deeply in any one subject. As teachers they excel, for they find so many subjects interesting that their enthusiasm is bound to rub off. They also have a natural affinity with children, for their ruling planet Mercury is the smallest planet, never straying far from the paternalistic pull of the sun. This can give Geminis a childish streak, lasting well into adult life. They are the original Peter Pan characters, unwilling

to leave the carefree Never-Never Land.

Life is one long party as far as bright, frivolous Geminis are concerned. They hate being alone, preferring to shine in company. Charming, witty, vivacious, generous and polite, they are clever conversationalists, victorious in debate.

Yet sometimes their cleverness makes them egotistical and selfish. They can be deceitful, disloyal and over-extravagant. Their lack of concentration and staying-power means that they are easily bored, leaving half-a-dozen hobbies and projects unfinished. Sometimes unreliable, superficial, immoral and undisciplined, they may become sly, believing that crime is wrong only if you are caught.

Symbolized by the Heavenly Twins, Geminis are sometimes said to have two sides to their nature. Certainly it is true that they are extremely versatile and adaptable. They may well take up more than one career in a lifetime and some change their jobs frequently out of boredom. They seldom take their own status too seriously, however, and this endearing characteristic means that they have no qualms about leaving one promising career to start from scratch in another

Above: *Despite Queen Victoria's often quoted phrase 'We are not amused' she shared the sense of fun common to Geminis.*

completely different type of business.

A love of language makes Geminis good writers, translators, journalists or secretaries. They also love to travel and enjoy taking risks. This can lead to heroism, for they refuse to believe in danger.

Attractive, sociable Geminis have no trouble making friends or finding love. They are most compatible with those born under LIBRA and AQUARIUS. Yet in relationships some Geminis are apt to grow tired of their lovers, leaving a trail of broken hearts behind them. With the right partner, however, Geminis achieve the stability they need to fulfil their potential.

Physically Geminis are often lightly built though fairly tall, with straight backs. They have a quick manner, with lively brown or hazel eyes, aquiline noses, broad shoulders and dark hair.

Typical health problems affect arms, shoulders, hands, bones, muscles, lungs, voice, nerves and senses. Geminis are prone to colds, bronchitis, pleurisy, asthma and nervous problems. They are resilient and usually recover swiftly from illness and trauma.

See also ASTROLOGY

GENIE

The English word 'genie' is derived from the Arabic word *jinn* or *djinn*. In the Koran and in popular belief the genies are a class of creatures who resemble the demons of Christendom but also the more malevolent of the FAIRIES; some of the jinn also resemble the fallen ANGELS. They are seen as mortal and as capable of reproduction, but longer-lived. Unlike some Western demons and fairies they are not seen as having individual existences but they do have sub-types, notably the malevolent *ghul* ('ghoul' in English) which behaves rather like the Western Will-o'-the-wisp.

Human individuals are believed to have genies associated with them, which are trying constantly to lead them astray, but genies are also linked with particular places, especially lonely places far from human habitation.

There are various methods for protecting oneself from the malevolence of the genie. They fear iron and salt and can be driven away by recitation of words from the Koran or by the wearing of an

Right: *A genie may be large and malevolent, even demonic, but he can be stupid too – traditional tales tell of him being tricked to enter a bottle.*

amulet or talisman. Occasionally, with the right kind of persuasion or flattery, they can be induced to help rather than harm.

GHOSTS

Are ghosts the product of telepathic minds — or psychic particles which remain in the form of some traumatic scene? And why do dogs react with such fear in an area known to be haunted?

Ghosts are manifestations of the dead. They may appear as solid and real, transparent and insubstantial — or in some barely recognizable form, such as wisps of smoke, strange smells, ghoulish sounds or spooky atmospheres.

But becoming a ghost is not a natural consequence of dying. Survival of the personality and a wish to adhere to life on this earth is rare. Those that become ghosts are maladjusted, unable or unwilling to leave this existence entirely, because of traumatic events in their lives — or at their deaths. Other ghosts are motivated to return continually to warn the living of future events, or have a malevolent desire to stay to cause evil.

Another category of ghost makes only one or two appearances, around the time of his or her physical body's death, appearing sometimes thousands of miles away, to family or friends.

Very rarely, many ghosts continually replay events from their lives together, caught in some ghastly time warp. One story tells of a company director driving through the countryside at night, when he saw an encampment of Roman soldiers. He presumed that they were extras in a film, and slowed to watch. But it immediately became evident that they were nothing of the kind. There was no lighting crew, sound people or director, and as he strained his eyes to look, the driver could see the shape of the trees clearly through the soldiers' bodies.

The Search for Evidence
Ever since scientists have applied themselves to researching the paranormal, a sub-group have attempted to capture evidence of these elusive apparitions.

Where known ghosts walk, for instance, researchers set up hidden cameras, powder to catch foot or handprints, machines to register changes in temperature, and tape recorders to catch the ghostly voice. Very little concrete evidence has emerged from these scientific traps, although photographs claimed to be of ghosts do exist. The most well-documented 'evidence' is of temperature change — usually a drastic drop when a ghost is about.

Matthew Manning, the great British psychic, who has collaborated to great effect with parapsychologists, lived his young adolescent life in a house that positively teemed with ghostly activity. One former resident appeared often to Matthew and all his family, and would even bring and leave objects from his time. One room in the house became covered with the signatures of neighbours from this period, and from a slightly later time. None of this, however, can be taken as irrefutable fact — Matthew, or those around him, could have lied or faked evidence. It is his unbesmirched reputation as a quiet unassuming, genuine psychic, that lends weight to his strange and exciting stories.

Certainly, all those who, like Matthew Manning, have experienced ghostly activity are in no doubt of the cause, even if they cannot produce evidence that would stand up in a court of law.

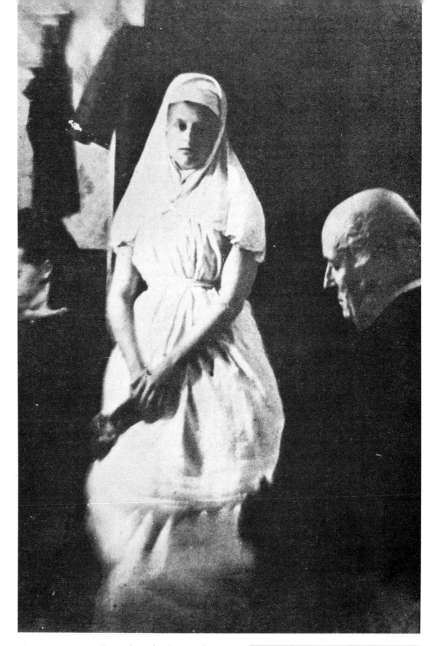

Above: *Ghosts come in different forms. Perhaps the most frightening is the solid apparition that looks completely life-like.*

Ghost Theories

Stories and legends of ghosts have been found in all cultures throughout history. In certain tribes ghosts become 'gods', able when dead to protect or harm, according to how they felt. The goodwill of the ghosts was won by offerings and rituals of praise.

Other ancient cultures developed a view of ghosts that coincided more closely with our own — that those spirits that still manifested themselves in some way to the living were unhappy or maladjusted for some reason. The land of the dead, whatever it was called — the happy hunting ground, the Elysian Fields, Valhalla, etc. — was denied to them as a punishment or through accident, such as improper burial. Ghosts were spirits trapped between this life and the next, craving one or both and denied either.

In our time many attempts have been made to explain ghostly phenomena, made more difficult by the variety of manifestations.

What does the ghost who manifested himself all too solidly in a 19th-century Bristol vicarage — stout, moustachioed, regularly shaking the beds to awaken the occupants — have in common with the ghostly lights of Borley Rectory? These lights were seen flickering from the windows whenever the place was uninhabited, giving substance to the thought that ghosts can manifest as forms of light rather than solid creations. Theories that the Borley Rectory lights could have a human explanation are somewhat shaken when the reactions of dogs in the vicinity are taken into account. They show obvious terror, even in broad daylight when people with them see, feel or hear nothing.

Similarly, can you say that these two ghostly manifestations have anything in common: the floating head that chased away any potential inhabitants of a house in Hamburg in 1953, and the 'cloud of smoke' that one year later lured a sentry from his post at the Tower of London, changing its shape but never dispersing until it vanished suddenly?

Some poltergeist phenomena have been traced to the disturbed brain activity of an adolescent child, but some have no such explanation. The poltergeist at the Bank of England, who sometimes knocks the weapons from the hands of the guards, is one such example.

Despite the bewildering variety of ghostly manifestations — of which these have just been a tiny selection of examples — many people have attempted to rationalize and classify them.

Different experts have drawn different conclusions. The sceptics say that people who see or experience the presence of ghosts are having a form of personal hallucination or temporary derangement.

William James, the American psychologist, believes that ghosts could be formed by the telepathic conjunction of two minds, unconsciously producing an objective hallucination. F W H Myers believed, similarly, that telepathy between two or more people could somehow alter what they were looking at to produce the hallucination.

Those who believe that ghosts are real give different interpretations of how they continue to exist. One theory has it that a ghost is an ASTRAL BODY, that has somehow remained when the physical body has died. Another explanation is that living creatures emit 'psychons'. These are actual psychic particles which remain in a house, for instance, sometimes in the shape of a traumatic scene which can be picked up by certain people in certain circumstances.

Some of these explanations conflict, and some are complementary. Because of the variety of ghostly phenomena it is quite likely that there is more than one explanation — and that until we know what really happens after death we are a long way from understanding the subject.

Right: Ghosts can be faked, as in this 18th century cartoon, but false ghosts tend to be produced by imagination rather than fraud.

GLASTONBURY

What is it that links prehistoric Druids with St Patrick, King Arthur with Joseph of Arimathea? The Holy Grail with a heathen ritual maze? The answer is Glastonbury and its several levels of great significance in widely differing religious and philosophical worlds make it unique.

What is beyond dispute is that it is a small market town in Somerset in the west of England, and that its outstanding physical feature is Glastonbury Tor, a single hill which juts up 500 feet above sea level, topped by the remains of a church dedicated to Michael the Archangel. John Michell has demonstrated convincingly the existence of a LEY LINE, the St Michael Line, which passes through this chapel, and we may accept that the Christian foundation at Glastonbury was built on a far more ancient site of supernatural significance.

Geoffrey Ashe has expanded on an

Below: *The legend of King Arthur links him to Glastonbury, also known as the Isle of Avalon, where the king was taken after being wounded in battle.*

Above: *This is the Chalice Well, thought to have been a meeting place for the Celtic Magi of legend, to whom Glastonbury was a holy place, as it then remained.*

idea put forward by Geoffrey Russell that the terraces around the Tor are the remains of an early ritual maze, while Katharine Maltwood argues that the town and its surrounding area form a gigantic natural diagram of the signs of the Zodiac, and both theories deserve consideration.

Whatever the truth of Glastonbury's earliest history, there is evidence, even if hedged around by confusion, that there was a monastery built by British Christians prior to the Saxon invasion, possibly under the guidance of St Patrick, and a Christian settlement may date back to the 1st century AD, giving support to the stories that Joseph of Arimathea came to Britain. Linked to this story is the Holy Thorn which may be seen at Glastonbury. It is claimed that it sprang from the staff which Joseph planted in the ground when he landed, and it is also claimed that he brought with him the Holy Grail.

This Holy Grail legend then arises in the Arthurian tradition, for its followers see Glastonbury as being the same place as Avalon, and recent excavations at Cadbury Castle, thought to be Camelot, reinforce the identification of Arthur's Avalon with Glastonbury. The Abbey monks claimed to have unearthed Arthur's grave in 1191, and in 1957 the archeologist Ralegh Radford put forward an argument supporting the feasibility of that claim.

Legends, myths and confusions abound, for even the name is open to question, but we do know that by the 12th century it was thought of as the 'glass island', associated with mystical properties. Early Welsh legend has Glastonbury Tor as an entrance to Annwn, the underworld, and the belief persists today that there is some kind of chamber hidden inside the hill.

From the great tangle of fact, conjecture, myth and tradition, one certainty may be picked out: Glastonbury, Britain's first native Christian foundation, has an 'otherness', a spiritual character, which attracts Christians and non-Christians alike, all of whom are able to see it as the 'holiest earth' in all the land.

Right: *The site of King Arthur's tomb at Glastonbury. His grave was reputedly discovered in 1191 by monks. The coffin was a hollowed-out log and bore the remains of a woman too.*

GUARDIAN SPIRITS

Both in the world of ancient Greece and in modern tribal societies we find a belief in spirits who look after particular places or particular individuals. The Greeks called such a spirit a *daimon*, the Romans a *genius*, the *genius loci* or spirit of a particular place having some relationship with the belief in Elementals (see ELEMENTS AND ELEMENTALS). The Christian equivalent is the guardian angel and very similar ideas are found in tribal Africa and in the totemic beliefs of the Australian Aborigines and of many American Indian tribes. In the latter case the spirit will very often appear in the form of an animal.

In an early version of the Christian belief in guardian angels we find the view that each person has two, a good one who directs towards righteousness and an evil one who leads into temptation and wickedness. In Muslim belief a person has four guardian angels, two for the day and two at night, as a protection against harm. Guardian spirits are not always friendly, however. In some African belief-systems they are more ambiguous figures, either capricious or positively evil, requiring constantly to be placated by gifts and ceremonies.

It is possible that at least some of the European beliefs about FAIRIES derive from older and more primitive beliefs in guardian spirits of this kind.

GURDJIEFF, G I

The greatest of 20th-century European mystics, George Ivanovich Gurdjieff was born in Russia of Greek and Armenian parentage some time in the late 1870s. As a young man he set off on a quest for a 'real and universal knowledge', possibly travelling as far as Mecca and Tibet. By the time of the First World War he had a group of followers and was teaching his system of mystical thought in Moscow and St Petersburg. Central to this is the idea that ordinarily people are spiritually asleep, and that they must awaken themselves both to consciousness and to conscience before they can begin their true evolution as human beings.

Part of the process of awakening was what Gurdjieff called 'conscious labours and intentional suffering' and both of these were brought into play when he and his followers fled from the Russian Revolution and made an arduous journey to Western Europe. In 1922 at the castle of Prieure, near Fontainebleau, he founded his Institute for the Harmonious Development of Man.

In 1924 Gurdjieff made his first visit to the USA, where he attracted many new followers, and began work on his magnum opus, *All and Everything*, which was to occupy the rest of his life and be the basis of his teaching henceforth. In it he develops in detail the idea that mankind has a unique place in the cosmic scheme of things but that they cannot fulfil it until they acquire and develop their uniquely human attributes.

Left: *Gurdjieff believed that people were asleep, and only when fully awakened would they understand the difference between good and evil and their place in the universal scheme.*

In the 1930s Gurdjieff withdrew from public life and seems to have limited his teaching to a small inner circle of followers. He lived in obscurity in France during the Second World War but began to teach and to attract new followers from 1946 onwards, while the leading 'Seekers' established groups to spread his teaching in the USA and in various European countries. In the year of his death, 1949, he announced that he was finally ready to publish *All and Everything*. That work encapsulates his teaching, but the remarkable personality of the man, and his teaching methods, are captured in the reminiscences of his disciples and particularly in the work of his closest follower, P D Ouspensky, whose *In Search of the Miraculous* describes his early years with Gurdjieff.

HADES

The ancient Greeks and Romans had various beliefs about the afterlife, but the commonest idea seems to have been that most of the dead go to a sad, dark place that is the dominion of Hades, the god of death. Hades was seen sometimes as a land lying far to the west, sometimes as an underground place with several entrances, of which the most famous became the cave by the lake of Avernus near Naples, described by Virgil in his *Aeneid*. The Styx was the river of this underworld and Charon the boatman who ferried the dead across it.

The Greeks and Romans also occasionally refer to the idea of punishment after death, in the underground prison of Tartarus that lay below Hades, or in the burning river of Phlegethon.

See also HELL

HAND OF GLORY

One of the most gruesome of charms was the so-called Hand of Glory, literally a hand cut from the corpse of a hanged felon and ritually dried and prepared. It could be used in two ways: either it was set to hold a specially made candle, or the fingers themselves were set to burn. In either case it had the power to prevent any sleeping person in the vicinity from waking, or to render any waking person incapable of speech or movement until all the flames had died out.

Although witches were sometimes accused of using the Hand of Glory, it was of more obvious use to thieves and there are many accounts, from Britain and Ireland and from various European countries, of such use. Once the hand was lit it was believed that it could not be blown out or quenched by any liquid, except milk. In one version of the story a maidservant finds a thief in the house, a Hand of Glory burning in the kitchen, and the rest of the household in a sleep from which she cannot wake them. She tries to blow out the flames and then to extinguish them with water, then with beer. Finally she pours milk over them, the household is roused from sleep and the thief captured.

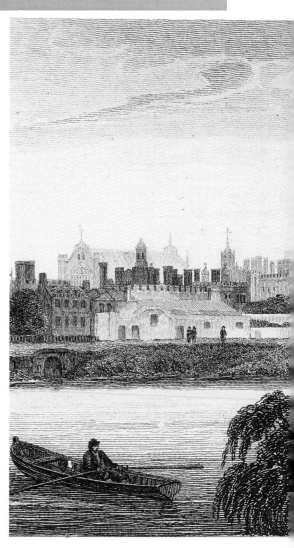

See also NECROMANCY

HAUNTED HOUSES

Ghosts may appear in various forms or manifestations: from simply an odour, a change in temperature, a noise, or an emotional atmosphere — to a fully formed human figure. Theoretically they may appear anywhere, at any time, but a substantial proportion are fixed in one setting: a house in which they lived in the past, or which was the scene of their death, or a moment of tremendous traumatic impact in their lives.

There have been many reports of haunted houses throughout history. Some ghosts appear regularly at known times, or to mark certain occasions. The ghost known as 'Dickie', whose skull is hidden in the walls of a farm in Derbyshire, is in this category. No one knows whether Dickie was in life a man or woman, but legend has it that death was violent. Dickie makes its presence felt by making noises, specifically when a death in the family is imminent, or in the

case of an emergency. Dickie also hates strangers and manifestations increase when anyone comes to stay. When extra labour is drafted in during haymaking Dickie's displeasure, shown by constant rapping and inexplicable noises, keeps everyone awake.

Some ghosts haunt modern houses, but this is considered to be a freak; usually it is found that a previous house existed on the site, and as far as the ghost is concerned, the modern house simply does not exist. Some very vivid manifestations, for instance, seem to float below or above the current floor level, and further investigations reveal that the original house on the site was correspondingly sunken or raised.

Older, larger houses may have more than one ghost, marking different moments in their histories. The royal palaces in Britain are credited with several ghosts each. The most spectacular is the ghost of Catherine Howard, the fifth wife of Henry VIII, who haunts the gallery at Hampton Court. Her voice can be heard shrieking in the gallery, and sometimes she is seen running along it very fast, and disappearing into the chapel.

No theory fully explains the phenomena of ghosts or why they should haunt houses. The most common theory is that they are visitations from the grave of those people who, for some reason or other, are strongly bound to these buildings. The usual explanation is that some unimaginable horror has to be relived time and time again — though some ghosts are said to return because they were so happy in those houses during their lifetimes. An example of this is one of the ghosts that haunts Longleat in Wiltshire. The old gentleman potters happily around the Red Library, wearing long, dark Elizabethan garments. He is said to be Sir John Thynne, the builder of the house that was his greatest achievement.

Other theories to explain haunted houses suggest that they are the result of telepathy between the living and the dead, which would explain why only certain people seem to see the ghosts, and why sensitive instruments, such as cameras and tape machines, do not always pick up what people have experienced. Sceptics insist that those who say they have experienced a haunting are suffering from hallucinations, or that the visions are a product of a fevered imagination — they wait for concrete proof that these manifestations exist.

Left: *Hampton Court, eternal home of many ghosts.* Above: *The most famous is Catherine Howard, who is regularly seen and heard.*

Above: The horrors of Hell fascinated artists who believed it was a region with real, physical existence. (Hell by Dieriq Bouts, c. 1410–75)

HELL

The horrors of Hell, the place of eternal torment, were Christianity's deterrent to sin, powerful enough to terrorize at least occasionally the most hardened sinner. In countless paintings and sculptures on medieval churches, in sermons and in the writings of churchmen, Hell is depicted as an underground place where lakes of burning pitch and a great variety of other tortures afflict the damned. Depictions of the punishments ordained there, of which Dante's *Inferno* and the paintings of Bosch are only two of the most famous, are often so lurid that they seem to have been drawn with a certain ghoulish relish, and from the 18th century on they began to diminish in ferocity, partly because they seemed to call into question the essential goodness of God. Hell was ruled by the Devil and his demons, but what he did there was presumably tolerated if not ordained by God and it began to seem to more enlightened minds that there was something unChristian about rejoicing in the suffering of adulterers, usurpers and unbelievers as well as of major criminals.

The idea of a place of punishment after death began to emerge in Judaism in the last centuries before Christ, sometimes being called Gehenna after an actual place where the rubbish of Jerusalem was burned. Similar ideas appear in Islam and in the popular religious beliefs of India, China and Japan, although they are foreign to the higher doctrines of Buddhism and Hinduism. The ancient Egyptians believed in a judgement after death, but the *BOOK OF THE DEAD* has little to say about punishments awarded to those found wanting.

See also DEVILS AND DEMONS, HADES

HOME, D D

Daniel Dunglas Home (born in 1833 near Edinburgh) was a medium with such energetic powers that the sheer range, number and violence of paranormal phenomena which raged about him whenever he was in trance was enough to ensure that fraud, as an explanation, had to be ruled out.

At the age of nine Home was taken by his aunt to live in America, and by the age of 17 his powers as a medium were already so developed that he turned professional.

In 1855, when he was 22, he returned to England and his reputation was soon established.

Wherever he gave a seance — often in places he had never before visited, so 'rigging' of the room would have been impossible — extraordinary evidence of apparent paranormal activity occurred.

His first major seance in England, the year of his return, took place in a strange house in front of 12 people, most of whom he had never met. Home preferred smaller gatherings for, he explained, large groups tended to inhibit spirit activity, 'but we cannot now do better than try'.

Almost immediately things began to happen. The quiet room, lit by candles, became a veritable hive of spirit activity. Raps were heard on the table, walls and floor. A handbell began ringing and a concertina started playing on its own. A disembodied spirit hand made its way round the table, then laid itself gently on the forehead of one of the gentlemen who leapt, screaming, from the table.

From then on Home was in much demand, and his sitters were rarely disappointed. Elizabeth Barrett Browning was delighted by the white spirit hand that placed a garland of flowers on her head, and was amazed by another hand that rose above the table, elongated itself and floated out of the window. In the opinion of her husband, Robert Browning, Home was an imposter, and Charles Dickens called him a ruffian and a scoundrel; but no one ever came up with proof of fraud. The best his detractors could do was suggest that the sitters were hynotized, or subject to mass hallucination.

Some of the happenings at Home's seances were so incredible that one scientist, William Crookes, convinced of Home's powers, wrote to a colleague about the happenings and implored him not to tell anyone else — because he did not want to be shut up in a lunatic asylum or turned out of the society of men of science.

Crookes saw tables levitated, and a fellow sitter rise in the air and be flung across the room. An accordion sailed around their heads playing sweet music, and when the sitters spontaneously broke into a round of 'For he's a jolly good fellow!' for Home, a spirit voice from above reproved then, saying, 'You should rather give praise to God!'

On other occasions sitters saw Home himself fly in and out of windows; tongues of flame lick round his head; and would watch as he handled red hot coals straight from the fireplace 'as if they had been oranges'.

In his later days Home never charged fees for his services, though he was always happy to accept presents such as jewellery from his admirers.

See also MEDIUMS

Below: *D D Home was an extraordinary physical medium who was seen by respectable witnesses to float in the air, in and out of windows.*

HOMOEOPATHY

The motto of homoeopathy *Similia Similibus Curantur*, or Like Cures Like, has a more vulgar rendering in the expression 'the hair of the dog that bit you', but the principle remains the same — a small dose of the same thing that ails you can actually effect a cure.

The man who formulated the ideas behind homoeopathy was the German Samuel Christian Hahnemann, who qualified as a doctor in 1779 but, never happy with the crude approach to medicine of his day, looked for a way to stimulate the body's own natural defences against disease.

It is believed that he produced his theory after remarking the reaction of his own body when he took a piece of Peruvian bark, from which quinine, used to treat victims of malaria, is extracted. Because he was not suffering from malaria the bark actually produced a fever in him; he reasoned, therefore, that it was active only in patients who had a greater fever than that which it provoked itself.

By developing this revolutionary idea, and by being a firm advocate of treating the whole person and not simply a disease, Hahnemann made enormous progress — indeed, when he died he was a millionaire.

He refined his technique by using himself and his friends as guinea pigs, and eventually determined that a large dose of medicine is counter-productive; the paradox of homoeopathy is that minute doses of, for example, Arnica, are far more effective than a larger dose would be. When the patient is given three microscopic pills he or she may be disconcerted, but homoeopaths insist that substances which might be fatal in very large doses are very efficacious if administered thus.

Hahnemann was a great promoter of his idea and products and the vogue for this new medicine spread to Britain in the early 19th century. A Dr Quin was physician to the aristocracy, and he introduced homoeopathy to the highest circles, from Prince Leopold, the Queen's uncle, to figures from the literary world, notably Dickens and Thackeray. A hospital was set up in Golden Square in the heart of London, and a bill was even passed through Parliament allowing medically qualified practitioners to set up as homoeopathic doctors, an act which set the seal on its acceptance by the British Establishment.

Even today this type of medicine retains its royal connection, for in 1969 Queen Elizabeth II appointed a homoeopath, Dr Margery Blackie, to be her personal physician. But its appeal is more widespread than that. Although it is nowhere near so widely practised as 'straight' or allopathic medicine, there are signs it may be experiencing a renewal of interest. With the current drive for healthier ways of living and natural foods, there is an obvious attraction in a type of medicine which involves drugs carrying absolutely no risk of side-effects or addiction through long-term use. The only obstacle to its resurgence is that all its practitioners must qualify in allopathic medicine first, and so are less inclined to spend longer period of training before beginning their careers.

Although still thought of as slightly 'cranky', those who have experienced the benefits, which tiny doses derived from bizarre substances such as snake venom and bee stings provide, almost invariably try to convert others to this gentle medicine.

Above: *Samuel Hahneman was the founder of homoeopathy.*
Right: *An engraving of the London Homoeopathic Hospital, which was founded in 1849 by Frederick Quin.*

HOROSCOPE

A horoscope is a circular astrological map, representing the known solar system, with Earth placed at the centre and the positions of the Sun, Moon and the planets charted around it. Horoscopes are complex to devise, as each one must show the precise planetary positions in relation to an exact moment in time and a detailed geographical location on Earth — often based on someone's birth. After casting an individual's horoscope, the astrologer uses it to make deductions about the person's character and future life.

See also ASTROLOGY

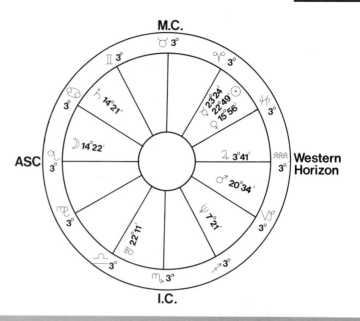

Above: *For a horoscope to be cast the planets are plotted on a birth chart and their significance divined.*

Left: *Blacksmiths working with 'magic' iron moulded by fire were thought to possess supernatural powers.*

HORSESHOE

The popular superstition that associates the iron horseshoe with good luck derives from an older and much more powerful belief that it was a charm with the ability to ward off evil, particularly evil from witches, demons and malevolent fairies.

Iron as a workable metal was discovered relatively late, much later than gold and copper, and both it and the men who had the skill to smelt and work it were regarded by their contemporaries with great awe; hence the belief that FAIRIES are terrified of cold iron. The horse too was sometimes regarded as a sacred animal. These associations, possibly combined with the horseshoe's resemblance to the crescent moon, may explain the power that it was believed to have. Until well into the present century it was very commonly hammered to the doors of houses to protect them from witches or to stable doors to prevent the horses being ridden by fairies or evil spirits. Sailors quite often fastened horseshoes to the masts of their ships (and not just common sailors — Nelson had one on the mast of the *Victory*).

However, the belief in the magical efficacy of horseshoes and of iron in general sometimes went even further. There are records of people curing their ills by drinking water in which a heated horseshoe has been dipped, and in at least one case a man is reported to have fed his horses on a soup made from horseshoes and other iron objects in the belief that they had been bewitched!

Above: *Mesmer called it 'mesmerism' and believed it was animal magnetism; later his discovery was renamed hypnosis and is still practised.*

HYPNOSIS

Hypnosis is the method of inducing trance in a subject, and using the altered mind state to effect certain mental or physical changes. Practitioners offer you the chance to give up smoking or stop compulsive eating by being hypnotized. And in many cases one session is enough — people really do give up smoking after hypnosis. Clearly, there is something powerful going on. What is far more striking is that some things are done under hypnosis which are normally impossible: someone in a deep trance can lie rigid, supported only by two chairs and bear the weight of a hefty man standing on the stomach. Or again, if a hypnotist claims to touch the subject with a red-hot bar, that person may develop a blister, even if the bar were actually a harmless metal rod.

It was once thought that such phenomena came about because the subject had abandoned his or her own will to that of the hypnotist, but the fact is that it is another manifestation of the tremendous powers of auto-suggestion. We know that the mind can affect the body — there are many examples of this, ranging from fire-walking to 'phantom' pregnancies — and under hypnosis the 'unconscious' mind is able to exert itself.

Charcot, at the end of the 19th century, remarked on the way that hypnosis could cure hysterical patients. Freud, who was once his student, picked up this idea, marvelling at the awesome potency of the 'unconscious' mind, and made the assumption that since it was evidently stronger than the 'conscious' mind, it was really the hidden master of our selves and our behaviour.

Charcot and Freud restored hypnosis to a position of respectability, after its eclipse during the greater part of the 19th century. Its roots lay in mesmerism and animal MAGNETISM, which put forward the idea that a vital fluid existed in the human organism and in magnets; the magnetist attempted to cure a sick person by channelling that vital fluid through his body.

It was in 1780, during his attempt to heal Victor Race, a shepherd, that the Marquis de Puységur, a follower of Mesmer, discovered a curious thing. He had tied the peasant to a lime tree, and had been passing a magnet over the man's head and body when he remarked that Race had apparently fallen asleep. He was startled, and ordered his subject to wake up and untie himself, but Race did so with his eyes still shut. Puységur realized he had put the man into a trance, or sleep (the word comes from the Greek hypnos — sleep) but he was uncertain as to how it had happened.

The phenomenon can be accounted for by pointing out that the brain is divided into two, and that when the 'conscious' side, the left cerebral hemisphere, is asleep, the other side, the right, takes over and is responsible.

Colin Wilson finds this of great significance and concludes that there is the left-brain, intellectual side, of us, which we think of as ourselves, and the right-brain, intuitive side, which is, as it were, another person. We are all victims of the syndrome known as 'the divided self'. If it is true that we can tap the forces of this other side to the brain, as seems to be the case in hypnosis, we should be able to develop abilities as yet barely recognized.

See also MAGNETISM

I CHING

The *I Ching*, also known as the *Book of Changes*, has been called a written oracle and is based on a belief that human existence forms a seamless web with its earthly surroundings and the cosmos. This ancient Chinese philosophy sees the universe as made up of two equal and complementary forces — yin and yang. Yang is the active mode of being — all positive and light-giving energies are represented by yang, while yin is darkness and passivity, embodying the negative principle.

In order to consult the oracle, the questioner tosses three coins six times. (Originally a bundle of yarrow stalks was used.) A note is made each time the coins fall and the pattern they make is transcribed as a broken or unbroken horizontal line. This is repeated until six lines, a hexagram, have been built up, and the appropriate hexagram is then consulted.

In keeping with the spirit of the *I Ching*, a hexagram has been chosen at random to illustrate the type of judgement the questioner might find. Number 15 Ch'ien/Modesty reads as follows: The Judgement 'Modesty creates success. The superior man carries things through,' and the Image reads: 'Within the earth a mountain: The image of modesty ... '. Following on from this there are passages on each of the six lines of the hexagram.

As can be seen, the interpretation of these hexagrams is delicate, because of the cloudy and cryptic nature of the ancient writings. Nevertheless, since it was first translated into English in 1882, it has gained a growing band of followers. Notable among these is Carl Jung, who thought it 'a great and singular book'. From his study of the *I Ching* Jung isolated a principle which he called 'synchronicity', a principle which has had great impact on Western ways of thought, and which is diametrically opposed to what the West has always valued — the idea of causality, or the search to classify and isolate laws which govern the human experience of self and the surrounding world. New discoveries in science have led us to realize that nothing in nature is cut and dried, that the element of randomness in the universe is present everywhere, and that, therefore, the ancient Chinese attitude, evolved over thousands of years, of taking whatever happens at any given moment as being absolutely of that moment and unrepeatable, is of startling modernity and relevance to modern scientific knowledge.

Are we, then, to think that the ancient Chinese sages had worked out an alternative philosophy to the causality of the West? It would seem highly improbable. What is almost certain is that the Chinese felt that 'spiritual agencies' were working through the book, and whoever consulted the book was being guided to the appropriate answer.

No case can be made out for this which would satisfy the rationalist, but we are urged to consult the book in a spirit of open-minded enquiry. The human race has advanced countless times by following methods that work without knowing why they work, and what begins as superstition may lead on to self-knowledge, which is, surely, the key to this body of rather oblique epigrams.

Once we who have been trained to search for logic and consequence learn to accept another mode of thought, then we may turn to the book more receptively. As Jung said, 'The less one thinks about the theory of the *I Ching*, the more soundly one sleeps.'

Below: *The Chinese traditionally used yarrow sticks to cast the hexagrams which are obliquely interpreted by the* I Ching *and used for divining the future. Nowadays coins are thrown.*

IMITATIVE MAGIC

Imitative magic stems from the universal belief that it is possible to achieve something by imitating the desired result. The cave paintings of prehistoric Europe which show hunters successfully killing game probably reflect thinking of that kind. But perhaps the most familiar example of imitative magic is the belief, found throughout the ancient and the modern world, that it is possible to kill or injure another person by making an image of that person, in the form of a picture or a doll, and inflicting injuries on it, perhaps by sticking it with needles or burning it. Images of that kind frequently incorporate material such as nail-parings or body hair from the intended victim to add to their power.

In the 14th century England a man named John of Nottingham was accused of making images like this in order to cause the deaths of King Edward II and some of his nobles, and a courtier named Richard de Sowe is said to have died as a result of John's activities.

There are many examples from this century of wax or clay dolls being used in connexion with WITCHCRAFT. As in the case of the CURSE it is possible that concentrated malevolence directed through the stabbing or burning of the images may have a mysterious power actually to cause harm, especially if the intended victims are aware that activities of this kind are being directed against them.

However, images are not always used to cause harm; they may sometimes be made in order to cause the person depicted to fall in love with the maker of the image. One textbook of magic recommends making two images, one of the lover and one of the person loved, and placing them in a vase. The vase is then buried in the hearth, a fire is lit, and a piece of ice placed in the fire. When the ice melts, the heart of the loved one will also melt.

Imitative magic may take many other forms. There is more than a hint of it in the Christian ceremony of holy communion, which re-enacts or imitates the Last Supper and therefore magically revives the mystery of Christ's death and resurrection and by extension the gift of his body and his blood.

Above: *This bottle contained a cloth heart stuck with pins — imitative magic to wreak harm on the target.*

INCANTATION

Incantation, derived from the Latin word meaning 'to sing', is the speaking of words in a ceremonial or rhythmical manner.

MAGIC may involve ritual, or special materials, or visual images, but the power of the spoken or written word is of supreme importance in most magical practices. 'In magic,' said the great French magician Eliphas Levi, 'to have said is to have done.' People have probably always been aware of the power of language, its ability to give names to things and thereby somehow to control them, its power to persuade or intimidate, to seduce or to charm, whether in political oratory, in war-chants, in poetry, in prayer or in the speech of lovers.

In magic, however, the power becomes more specific. The secret words of power must be discovered by the adept, for they are not the common words of everyday life; they must be spoken in the correct way, in the correct order, and even then they may be ineffective unless the speaker of them has been properly initiated, has reached the appropriate rank in that particular mysterious art or science.

There is an ancient and universal human belief that everything and everyone has a secret 'real' name, and that to discover and speak that name is to gain power over the thing or person concerned. That is why incantations designed to summon up spirits, for example, will frequently begin by listing the names and titles of the spirit concerned. The great folklorist Katharine Briggs in her book *The Anatomy of Puck* gives an example of an incantation, this one designed to compel the Judge of Hell to punish one of his demons:

O thou most puissant prince Rhadamanthus, which dost punish in thy prison of perpetual perplexity the disobedient devils of hell, and also the grisly ghosts of men dying in dreadful despair, I conjure, bind and charge thee by Lucifer, Belsabub, Sathanas, Jauconill and by their power, and by the homage thou owest unto them, and also I charge thee by the triple crown of Cerberus his head, by Stix and Phlegiton, by your fellow and private devil Baranter, that you do torment and punish this disobedient N.

(naming him) until you make him come corporally to my sight and obey my will and commandments in whatsoever I shall charge or command him to do. Fiat, fiat, fiat. Amen.

That address has most of the typical characteristics of incantation: not only the words themselves and the lists of names but also the alliterations, the repetition at the end, the strong rhythmic quality, designed to give the words an almost physical force.

The texts of incantations are to be found in ancient texts like THE BOOK OF THE DEAD and in the works of students of magic, but it is worth saying again that merely reciting them is hardly likely to be effective. The speaker of incantations must be ritually trained and prepared, and perhaps the most potent factor of all is the commanding personality of the magician.

See also MANTRA, RITUAL MAGIC

INCUBUS AND SUCCUBUS

In Christian demonology there were believed to be lecherous devils whose special business was the seduction of human beings, the Incubus in the case of women, the Succubus in the case of men. To do their work they could adopt human form, sometimes even taking on the appearance of their victim's wife or husband or lover. The Devil himself was believed to be able to take on the appearance of either a man or a woman in order to tempt mortals. The demonologists further believed that devils could impregnate humans, the incubus using human sperm which it had gathered earlier while in the guise of a succubus.

Not only witches and necromancers but also ordinary people were frequently accused in the Late Middle Ages of the sin of sleeping with devils and severely punished for it, but the belief was also quite often used as a convenient excuse for an unwanted pregnancy. Quite a few medieval nuns claimed that they had been raped by incubi and there was a famous 17th-century case in which a noble woman who became pregnant though her husband had been absent for four years claimed that she had been visited by her husband in a dream and impregnated by him. The judges speculated whether she might have been the

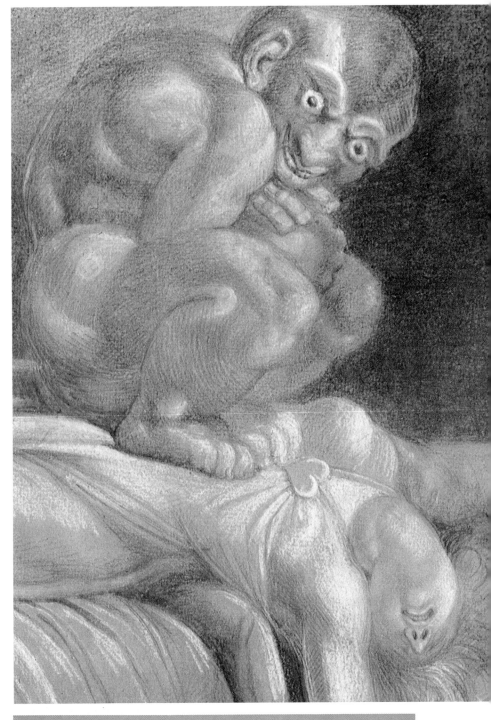

victim of an incubus, but the woman's own veracity was not publicly questioned, so strong was the belief in the demon lover.

The strength and prevalence of the belief probably stem from severe sexual repression in medieval Christian Europe, but the belief itself antedates Christianity. It appears for example in ancient Hebrew myth in the form of Lilith, the sexually voracious female demon referred to in Isaiah as 'the night hag'.

Above: *An incubus was said to feed on the sexuality of women, and could impregnate them. 'Mysterious' pregnancies were explained in this way.*

KARMA

The ancient Hindu concept of karma neatly sidesteps the dilemma concerning fate and free will, for one's destiny results directly from one's actions. Evil-doing in a previous life means that one is reborn a less fortunate creature, while righteous actions ensure reincarnation as a higher form of life. This belief acts as a constant incentive to lead a good life.

See also FATE

KIRLIAN PHOTOGRAPHY

It was not until 1970, with the publication of the book *Psychic Discoveries Behind the Iron Curtain* that the West became aware of a discovery which Semyon Kirlian had made in 1939. During a visit to a hospital in Krasnodar, USSR, he had seen a patient receiving treatment from a high-frequency generator and noticed that as the electrodes approached the skin there was a tiny flash. Inspired by this, Kirlian, together with his wife Valentina, attempted to

Below: *The aura of living things can now be captured on film using Kirlian photography, and can be analysed for problems.*

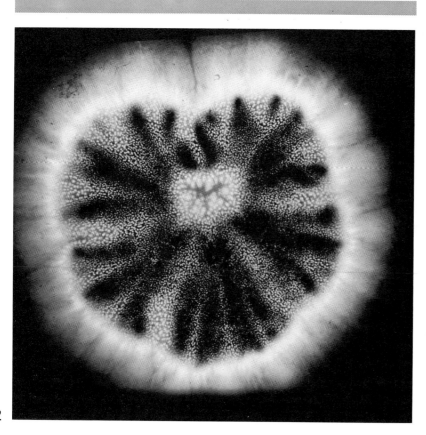

'photograph' human skin without the use of a camera. He rigged up two metal plates, on one of which was the light-sensitive film and then ran a high-voltage current between them; passing his hand between the plates, Kirlian managed to produce its image and the hand was surrounded by a glowing aura.

Experimenting with different objects, the couple discovered that inanimate objects give off auras or discharges of regular colour and form, while organic bodies produce different auras under different conditions. A newly cut flower stem seemed to be giving off sparks, while a man's hand photographed before and after he had drunk a glass of vodka showed that there was greater intensity of light after the alcohol. A section cut through a fresh cabbage appears vibrant, whereas once it has been cooked its aura seems flatter and deader.

What explanation is there for this? What is the nature of this aura? Some researchers claim that the Kirlians have succeeded in capturing on film the life-field, or L-field, discovered by Harold Saxton Burr in the 1930s. His belief was that all living creatures had a natural electrical field which fluctuated with sunspot activity, and this was measurable by electrical apparatus.

If the Kirlians are correct in believing that they can indeed record L-fields, then the implications for medical diagnosis are enormous, as are those for investigating many aspects of 'mind over matter'. Kirlian photographs show a striking difference between the fingertips of a girl before and after praying, and the medium Matthew Manning can control the extent of the discharges from his fingers.

More sceptical investigators claim that the flow of a high-frequency current is not constant, and therefore the 'auras' might simply be blurs caused by fluctuations. But if the patterns were brought about only by electrical ebbs and flows, they would show a uniformity that they clearly do not. If this were the case, the man's hand would give off identical discharges before and after drinking.

The balance of evidence seems to indicate that Kirlian photography is a phenomenon caused by the interaction of an electrical field set up in the laboratory and an innate electrical field within the organic entity. Further advances in the interpretation of this technique might mean we shall go to have our auras checked as a guide to our physical and perhaps spiritual health.

LAMA

Lamas are the fully ordained monks of Tibetan Buddhism but also the abbots of the great monasteries that ruled over the secular as well as the spiritual life of that country until the invasion by Communist China in 1950, which destroyed so much of Tibet's traditional way of life.

In the Tibetan form of Buddhism it is believed that certain saintly men, who have achieved supreme enlightenment after several incarnations, nonetheless choose to be reborn into this world in order to help and direct suffering humanity. A lama who has returned in this way is known as a *Bodhisattva*, a manifestation of the Buddha, and his earthly incarnation as a *tulku*. Almost all the heads of Tibetan monasteries were believed to be incarnations of this kind.

The leading church of Tibetan Buddhism was that of the Gelugpa sect, which ruled the country from Lhasa from the 17th century. The supreme figures of that sect are the Dalai Lama and the Panchen Lama. The former is claimed to be the most recent of a long series of reincarnations and as a manifestation of the national god of Tibet; the latter is a reincarnated manifestation of another Bodhisattva, the father of that god.

Since lamas were celibate, reincarnation offered the only method of succession to the great offices of Lamaist Buddhism. When the Dalai Lama or any other great tulku died it was believed that he was reincarnated in a child born at that time. Sometimes before his death he would indicate the part of the country where his successor was likely to be found; sometimes that information would be revealed to one of his followers in a dream; sometimes a child — often the child of very poor and simple parents — would declare that he was the latest incarnation of a particular lama. Once a claimant was found his claim would be tested, the chief test being his ability to recognize objects associated with his predecessor, since reincarnated lamas had the ability to remember their previous existences.

Once his claim was validated in this way the boy would succeed immediately to his office, whether as Dalai Lama or as abbot. Being still a child, however, he would receive instruction from senior monks until he reached his majority, at the age of 16 or 18.

From then on his authority would be absolutely unchallenged, and he would continue to rule till his death.

Reincarnation is of course a central element in Buddhist belief and it occurs at all levels of society, although not always with the power to remember details from previous existences. However, it is with the great abbots, the Dalai Lama, the Panchen Lama and the monks who ruled as regents during the minority of the Dalai Lama, that reincarnation took on political as well as spiritual importance. The majority of Tibetans today, after more then 30 years of Communist Chinese rule, probably still regard the Dalai Lama as their rightful ruler.

Below: *Lamas, the holy men of Tibet, are believed to be reincarnations of the Buddha.*

LEO

Leo the Lion, the fifth sign of the Zodiac, is a Fire sign, ruling those born between 23 July and 22 August.

Brave, bold, dignified, generous and noble, Leos seem born to lead. They have a certain 'presence' which commands attention. They love to delegate, as they feel trivial tasks are beneath them. Leos like to be treated with great respect, for even if they have not achieved great status, they feel that they are worthy of it — something which should be evident to others. They are proud, optimistic, faithful, kind and very affectionate people. Full of energy, persistence and ambition, they have the supreme confidence needed to reach their goals. A cat may look at a king, so the saying goes; Leos are bold, fearless, seldom overawed by important people or elegant surroundings.

The badges of success are important to Leos, who prize titles, trophies, honours, expensive jewelry, medals and uniforms highly. They play by traditional rules, aiming for conventional respectability rather than an inventive or revolutionary approach to life. They respect superiors, but can be rather snobbish, mean and patronising to anyone they regard as weak or inferior.

Leos just can't help wanting to be the boss in any situation, whether or not they're the best qualified person for the job. Sometimes they can be vain, pompous, boastful and ruthless. They may even steal the credit for a success from a subordinate, though they probably convince themselves that they are the ones who really deserve the credit. They may rationalize a triumph as the whole department's success, for instance, with the Lion's share of the glory belonging to Leo, the head of the department.

Napoleon, Mussolini and Fidel Castro as well as Coco Chanel show how strong Leos can prove in any position of power. They make good military officers, civil servants, diplomats and officials. They also succeed in banking, stockbroking or anything to do with money and gold. Leos may become head teachers, university principals, lawyers or actors.

Warm-hearted, straightforward Leos dislike secrecy and intrigue. Politics attract them, as natural leaders, yet they lack the perception and cunning they need to read between the lines. Leos can be gullible, believing that everyone else is as open and truthful as they are. They are easily taken in by unscrupulous adversaries, particularly as flattery does not arouse their suspicions — they enjoy it too much. Leos aren't used to losing, so when they are tricked, it comes as a terrible shock.

Rather domineering as friends or lovers, Leos are compatible with those born under ARIES and SAGITTARIUS. Leos try to be the boss at home, delegating the housework insensitively. Yet they are generous, open, warm, faithful companions.

Physically Leos often have large heads, big noses and huge eyes. They often have fair hair, and can be either tall and strong or of average height and slim build, depending on the sun's position.

Leos may have weak hearts, being prone to palpitations and fainting. Bad circulation, anaemia and back problems are also possible.

See also ASTROLOGY

Above: *Mrs Leonard was a great medium who received visions as a child and whose amazing powers were vigorously displayed for 50 years.*

MRS LEONARD

Gladys Leonard, who was born in 1882, started having visions when very young. But it was not until she experienced a premonition of her mother's death that she became properly involved in SPIRITUALISM.

Her first trance happened by accident, and friends had to tell her that her 'spirit control', a young girl called Feda, had introduced herself.

Mrs Leonard's work as a professional medium is better documented than most because she allowed the Society for Psychical Research to investigate her thoroughly. Once they even engaged a detective to discover whether she had had any other means of seeing inside a house that she had described with photographic accuracy.

Although no one seriously suspected Mrs Leonard of fraud, psychical researchers worked on the theory that the messages she received were a form of telepathy with her sitters.

To test this idea Mrs Leonard sometimes worked with 'proxy' sitters — people who were simply acquainted with the absent target — and some of her results were truly unbelievable. She told two proxies what their friend — thousands of miles away in Turkey — was up to, and inadvertently revealed this friend's well-kept secret about her adoptive father. On other occasions she predicted future events. Once she told a sitter about a letter he was to receive in the next fortnight. Only minor details were wrong: she slightly misspelt the town of the sender and said he would say that his son had been killed in a car crash. When the letter came as foretold, it turned out that the young man had died — but it had been in a *plane* crash.

See also MEDIUMS

LEVI, ELIPHAS

The noted French occultist and historian of magic was born in Paris in 1810, the son of a shoemaker, and died there in 1875. As a young man he studied for the priesthood but was never ordained. In early middle age he discovered an interest in magic to which he devoted the remainder of his life, reading deeply in the words of the ancient and medieval occultists and probably received instruction from a Polish expert, Hoene-Wronski.

In 1854 Eliphas Levi visited London, bringing with him a considerable reputation as a magical adept. He was taken up by, among others, the successful novelist Sir Edward Bulwer Lytton, author of *The Last Days of Pompei*, but also an acknowledged authority on magic and the occult. Although Levi regarded RITUAL MAGIC as a dangerous practice, he did attempt to invoke spirits by magical means and claimed on one occasion to have conjured up the spirit of the famous magician of ancient times, Apollonius of Tyana. On a later visit to London he and Lytton are said to have conducted a ceremony of invocation on the roof of a building in Oxford Street.

From the 1850s to the end of his life Levi earned a living by writing and teaching pupils. He was especially interested in the CABALA and later in the TAROT, which he believed to derive from cabalistic ideas. On one occasion he declared that if he were denied all books but one he would choose a Tarot pack, since he believed that the 22 major trumps represented a complete and universal system of esoteric knowledge.

Though more a student, historian and teacher than a practitioner of magic, Levi had a great influence both in his own country and on British magicians such as Aleister CROWLEY. His major works include *Transcendental Magic* and *The History of Magic*.

Below: *Levi invoking the spirit of Apollonius of Tyana in a private ceremony in a temple he constructed especially for the purpose. (By Gianetto Coppola)*

Above: *The line connecting Salisbury and Stonehenge.*
Above right: *The chalk man of Wilmington holds staffs used to plot ley lines.*

LEY LINES

These mysterious networks, linking prehistoric sites with holy places, seem to have been laid down for a purpose. Were they used by ancient peoples to predict lunar eclipses, or were they made to channel terrestrial magnetism?

Just before midsummer in 1921 Alfred Watkins, a 66-year-old flour merchant, paused on a hilltop and gazed down at the county of Herefordshire spread out beneath him. It was a landscape he had travelled since he was a boy, but on this particular day the familiar and well-loved sight was suddenly transformed, for in a flash he saw a web of perfectly straight lines connecting ancient sites with holy places, which in turn were linked to outstanding geological features. Standing stones, churches, wells and crosses, mounds, mountain peaks and notches in ranges of hills moved not an inch, but their systematic relation to one another had, of a sudden, become luminously clear to him.

Watkins hastened to test out his vision by reference to a one-inch Ordnance Survey map, and he found 'the align-

ment across miles of country of a great number of objects, or sites of objects of prehistoric antiquity'. Although these objects differed in age very considerably, the existence of straight trackways in prehistoric times seemed to him beyond question.

Pursuing his investigations, and noting, perhaps wistfully, that 'the method in the future is an aeroplane flight along the ley', he discovered that certain names occurred with unusual frequency along the alignment: Red, White, Black, Merry, Cold or Cole, Dod and Ley, and from this last he took the name for these old straight tracks.

The idea of ley lines did not find favour with many of Watkins's contemporaries, and even today there are many who find the case for them inconclusive. One argument levelled against the theory is that too many objects are admitted by ley hunters; no fewer than 17 sites or structures are thought to be significant.

Others, however, have hailed Watkins's discovery, notably the writer John Michell, whose book *The New View over Atlantis* pays tribute to him, and greatly expands upon the significance of these ancient tracks.

A concrete example of a ley line and

perhaps the most striking of all is pointed out by Michell — that of the 'St Michael Line', so called because, with a high degree of accuracy, from St Michael's Mount at the tip of Cornwall to St Michael's Church, Clifton Hampden, can be drawn a line linking eight churches or chapels dedicated to St Michael or the other dragon-slaying saints, George and Margaret. The line also passes through the Hurlers stone circles and the Cheese-wring stone on the south edge of Bodmin Moor, and through St Michael's Tor, Glastonbury, and the Avebury Rings.

These last two are among the most significant of all the ancient sites in Britain, and the inference we may draw is that the siting of the man-made Avebury Rings was largely determined by measurement against the line of hilltops across the West Country.

When Watkins made his discovery he believed he had found a set of traders' tracks, but as time passed he became increasingly convinced that the complex network could not have been laid down for this purpose alone, nor yet as lines and angles pointing to astronomical configurations or heavenly phenomena, such as eclipses.

Certainly, some do perform that function, and others seem to act as geographical markers, linking, for example, two headlands with each other, but there is evidence of the existence of these lines in many parts of the world, and the straight roads of South America, to cite one striking example, were built in the face of enormous hardships. Where any engineer would have designed a path around an obstacle, those ancient road builders made a way through, by tunnelling through mountains, fording rivers, throwing bridges across chasms and laying stone paths over swampy ground. No society would have gone to such pains without good reason.

Michell's Theory
Michell postulates the idea that ley lines were laid along paths or channels along which the earth's magnetism flows, and suggests that it was absolutely vital to prehistoric man that these channels should be followed.

It has long been established that phases of the sun and moon affect the earth's magnetic field, and we know that the function of many of the prehistoric stone observatories of Britain and elsewhere was the 'accurate prediction of lunar eclipses'. Professor Fred Hoyle has confirmed that the Aubrey holes around Stonehenge form a perfect eclipse predictor, and the imperative is to find for what purpose a civilization would produce such accurate and sophisticated instruments.

John Michell also puts forward the theory that the magnetic centres lie in straight lines across the land in a way that indicates they are man-made; that is to say, the great constructions may have channelled the flow of magnetism, rather than just marked it, for the currents of terrestrial magnetism in their natural state flow and curve as do currents of air.

If it is correct that early humans constructed those leys in order to channel terrestrial magnetism, then the logical sequence would be to assume that this force was tapped for some purpose long since forgotten. Michell likens the process to a sort of terrestrial acupuncture; the earth was kept fertile and productive by means of benevolent intervention by human beings — the crooked made straight and the rough places plain. Most important stones and earthworks were set into the ground at the appropriate spots to act as conductors through which solar or atmospheric energy might pass into the earth, thereby creating a bridge between earth and sky. Eclipses disrupted that flow and therefore measures had to be taken against them. This was why the prediction of eclipses was of such burning necessity.

Whether or not this last theory is correct, there does appear to be a strong connection between earth's magnetism and sacred sites situated along ley lines. Research into animals' homing instincts (consider that all the eels in the world originate in the Sargasso Sea and must disperse from there to unseen 'homes') may well shed light upon the forms and functions of these magnetic currents.

In the meantime, the sceptic may care to take up Alfred Watkins's invitation to test the theory both by map and — literally — in the field. Equipped with an Ordnance Survey map of one mile to one inch, the ley hunter should search to connect ancient mounds, moats or islands in ponds, churches of ancient foundation and the like by means of a straight line. The hunter should be satisfied with no less than four points, and should follow on to an adjacent piece of country where there is the beginning of a promising line. In Watkin's words, 'The great multiplicity in a small area will surprise and perplex you, but you will have to accept it as a fact.'

Above: *Bradgate ley, Leicestershire, showing the alignment of standing stone, Anstey church and old John Hill notch.*

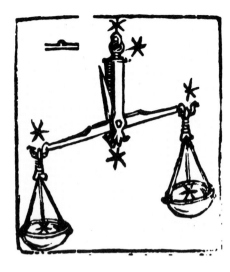

Above: *Margaret Thatcher, a Libran politician, weighing consequences before acting.*

LIBRA

Libra, the Scales, the seventh sign of the Zodiac is an Air sign, ruling those born between 23 September and 23 October.

Anything for a quiet life could be the Libran motto, for they like to preserve peace and harmony at all costs. They are polite, honourable, friendly, easy-going and get on well with almost everyone. They have a strong sense of fair play, are loyal, trustworthy, truthful and sympathetic. The sign is ruled by Venus, which gives Librans a strong appreciation of beauty and an enjoyment of the arts as well as a great capacity for love. Librans are charmers, who fall in love easily. Yet Saturn, the sternest of planets has a strong influence, giving the sign some much needed strength.

The problem with some Librans is that they bend over backwards to please everyone and end up pleasing no one. They can be over-timid, lacking in initiative, conventional and hesitant or even lazy. They can be moody, swinging from despondency to aggression. In company their flirtatiousness often gets them into trouble. Sometimes vain and weak, they should beware of changing their views to suit the occasion, which makes them look insincere. Despite these drawbacks, Libra is many people's favourite sign.

Symbolized by the Scales, Librans make good lawyers, judges and businessmen, for they are good at weighing up facts. Tactfulness and a willingness to seek a compromise make them good diplomats. The influence of Venus guides many Librans towards the arts, where they may become novelists, composers, artists, actors, dancers or poets. They are naturally talkative and enjoy speaking in public.

Despite a lack of ambition, some Librans become administrators, civil servants and even politicians, like Margaret Thatcher. The original 'iron lady' is far tougher and less willing to compromise than most Librans, but she likes to hear the views of many advisers before making decisions. She is also typically conservative in her appearance and ideas.

Those born under AQUARIUS and GEMINI are compatible with Librans, who fall in love regularly. They are easy to live with, because they hate rows and will often give in over small domestic matters. Their tendency to put things off could drive some partners round the bend, however. Ideally they need partners with enough initiative, ambition and energy for two. Librans should beware of making their partners jealous; sometimes their appreciation of an attractive newcomer is all too obvious.

Physically Librans are often well-proportioned, moderately tall and extremely graceful. They may have blue eyes, light brown or blonde hair and pale skin.

They can be rather delicate, with Libra ruling the kidneys, loins, skin, back, blood cells and urinary tract. They should watch out for kidney diseases, lumbago, skin rashes such as eczema, urinary problems and diabetes.

See also ASTROLOGY

LITTLE PEOPLE

The 'Little People' is only one of many names given to the FAIRIES, but it is particularly used of the small Manx fairies and of the piskies of Cornwall in the West Country of England. The latter are described as wizened-looking but generally neatly dressed in green suits and scarlet caps. They have a society of their own and when among themselves seem to behave with a certain gravity and dignity, but their dealings with human beings are generally mischievous. They delight in leading travellers astray and have been known to attack human beings when their own doings are disturbed.

The Cornish piskies are related to the pixies or pigsies of Somerset and Devon, who have the same tendency to mischief and who also dress in green.

The West Country fairies are sometimes said to be the souls of unbaptized children, sometimes the souls of heathens born before Christ and therefore unfitted to either heaven or hell. Whatever their origins, there is a surprising number of very matter-of-fact reports of encounters with them from as late as the 19th century.

People who believed in fairies often preferred not to name them directly in case of summoning them inadvertently. Vague or complimentary terms were therefore used instead — hence the term 'Little People'.

See also FAIRIES

LOVE MAGIC

The most popular love magic has always been the love potion, charm or aphrodisiac. Slip a love potion into someone's food or drink and it is supposed to send them into a frenzy of desire. Many are made from fruits or roots or creatures resembling male or female sex organs. Other love potions are hot and spicy, and as such should be able to engender the heat of passion.

The other form of love magic is the far more powerful individual charm, where lovers are bewitched. Here the would-be lover may have to obtain a lock of hair, nail parings or blood from their intended, for if these things are exchanged, love will ensue. Otherwise, some personal belongings may be charmed by a witch or wizard to induce love.

Such love magic could explain many ill-matched lovers. In Shakespeare's tale of supernatural illusion and trickery, *A Midsummer Night's Dream*, Oberon mocks Titania, using a love potion. He sprinkles the juice of a flower, shot through by Cupid's arrow, onto her sleeping eyelids, saying:
'What thou seest when thou dost wake,
Do it for thy true-love take;
Love and languish for his sake.
Be it ounce, or cat, or bear,
Pard, or boar with bristled hair,
In thy eye that shall appear
When thou wak'st, it is thy dear.
Wake when some vile thing is near.'

Hence Titania, Queen of the fairies, falls in love with Bottom, a simple man with the head of an ass.

A third form of love magic works *against* love and passion. Anaphrodisiacs, such as the poppy, or lizards soused in urine, or a lotion made from mouse droppings, suppress desire. Going one step further, there is also the art of rendering a man impotent. This can only be done by a skilled witch, using a cord-knotting ritual.

So powerful is the human need to be loved, that people have eaten and drunk the most revolting love potions and

Below left: *An enchantress prepares a love philtre.* (Morgan le Fay *by Sandys*)
Below right: *A love-spoon for measuring ingredients.*

aphrodisiacs. Again the lizard, thought to be penis-shaped, has also been revered as a reviver of flagging interest, as have the sexual organs of the stag and the horn of a rhino. The 'Spanish fly' or *Cantharides* is world-famous as a strong aphrodisiac. It is made not from flies, but from a dried blister-beetle. Unfortunately, its reputation for provoking lust is better known than the side-effects, which include vomiting.

One of the oldest known aphrodisiacs is the mandrake, a tuber with roots shaped like human limbs, which is said to scream when pulled from the ground. Ginseng, the liquorice-like root grown in the Orient, is another potent aid to sexual love. And when dissolved in goats' milk, another plant, *Satyricon*, gives a man the power to make love 70 times in succession. St John's Wort, a magical midsummer plant with the power to exorcise demons, cures infertility in women. All a woman has to do, it is said, is walk naked in her garden, pick this flower, and she'll be a mother before next Midsummer's Day.

Another aphrodisiac is the periwinkle, but it must be taken powdered with earthworms and eaten with meat. Artichokes, asparagus, leeks, turnips, parsnips, lettuce, cabbage and marigolds have all been ascribed with the power to promote desire in the past. The Romans prepared for their orgies with feasts of oysters, cuttlefish, octopus, red mullet and the electric ray, followed by pepper and myrrh.

Not all aphrodisiacs worked, however, and some drugs used by the magicians of Thessaly in Southern Europe had the side-effect of sending the patient mad. Other potions were sold in liquid form and contained some unpleasant surprises. Onions, ginger or cinnamon were common ingredients, together with narcotic perfumes, animal testicles, human brains, hearts, livers, urine and skin. Witches brewed especially nasty love potions, containing toads' venom, thieves' flesh, asses' lungs, ox bile and bits of bodies they'd dug up from churchyards. Love potions have all but disappeared in the western world, but 'sex shops' these days sell the modern equivalent, in the form of aphrodisiac pills and other sex aids.

Below: *The aphrodisiac mandrake root resembles the human body*. Below right: *In* A Midsummer Night's Dream *the use of powerful love potions wrought havoc.* (Fairies *by* Fuseli)

LUCK

'You've got the luck of the devil,' people say enviously as friends collect windfalls, land exciting new jobs or never seem to get found out in an indiscretion. Why are some people lucky and others accident-prone? Is our fate written in the stars for all to see?

Cruel, carefree Carmen, gypsy heroine of Bizet's classic opera seems to personify 'luck without effort'. She plays with men's affections, casting them aside when she's bored. Irrepressible and irresponsible, she's the free spirit who risks all and takes everything as a reward for her daring.

But even her luck runs out in the end — as she and Don José fall out of love and she consults the Tarot cards. Death! It's all written in the cards — and all comes true in dramatically tragic fashion.

Does this mean there is nothing we can do about our fate? Since the beginning of time, in all cultures, people have tried to bring themselves just a little bit of extra luck, in all sorts of ways.

They've worn St Christopher medallions when going to sea, prayed to saints and gods in hundreds of languages, crossed fingers for luck, avoided walking under ladders and held onto collars or buttons as ambulances drove past, letting go only on a certain sign, reassured that the danger is over. They have carried talismans, magic rings and other charms blessed by soothsayers, and men have gone to war bravely, clutching luck-bringing photos, locks of hair, rings and gloves from their sweethearts. People swear by their lucky sixpences, rabbit's feet, lucky hats, favourite colours and numbers — almost everyone has something which they secretly believe has brought them good — or bad — luck.

Indeed, superstitions are still alive and well: if a black cat crosses your path it brings good fortune, but you should always tread carefully on Friday 13th; and few brides ignore the traditional advice to wear, 'Something old, something new, something borrowed, something blue'.

Psychologists have tried to explain why some people are lucky and others seem dogged by misfortune — also shedding light on such sayings as 'on a winning streak' and 'trouble comes in threes'. They say that our personalities influence our luck — if we react with confidence to events in our life, we are

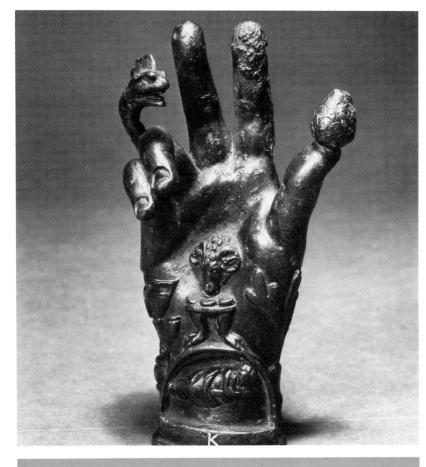

likely to come out on top but if we go around in a preoccupied, worried state of mind, we are quite likely to have an accident, or make an error of judgment. Naturally, the more success we have, the more confident we feel and the more good fortune seems to come our way. The reverse is also true, adding weight to the superstition that trouble comes in threes.

Even though our luck or fate seems to lie partly in our own hands, there are many ways people can try to predict fortunes. Reading tea leaves, ink blots, crystal balls, Tarot cards and the lines on our palms, for example. We pay great attention to the strangest of our dreams, and toss coins to help make difficult decisions. Those with the second sight may use occult chanting designed to conjure up images of the future. There is no doubt that some fortune tellers have had uncanny insights into the future, notably NOSTRADAMUS, who predicted so much that has come true. This suggests that, though we can influence our own fate, achieving much or little in our lives according to our efforts, some of the future is already written. Our luck is just waiting to be revealed.

Above: *People have always tried to influence luck; this hand was embellished with luck-bringing charms.*

A Table shewing the names of the Angels governing the 7 days of the week with their Sigils, Planets, Signs. &

Sunday	Monday	Tuesday	Wednesday	Thursday	Friday	Saturday
Michael	Gabriel	Camael	Raphael	Sachiel	Ana'el	Caffiel
☉ ♌	☽ ♋	♈ ♂ ♏	♊ ☿ ♍	♐ ♃ ♓	♉ ♀ ♎	♑ ♄ ♒
name of the 4.ʰ Heaven	name of the 1.ˢ Heaven	name of the 5.ʰ Heaven	name of the 2.ᵈ Heaven	name of the 6.ʰ Heaven	name of the 3.ᵈ Heaven	No. Angels ruling above the 6.ʰ Heaven
Machen.	Shamain.	Machon.	Raquie.	Zebul.	Sagun.	

Right: *The Magus, a book with a store of magic lore. These pages contain a table showing the weekdays and their governing angels.*

MAGIC

The ambitious magician seeks out secret forces in order to gain unlimited power, and will use any weapons to achieve this — including sex, drugs and cruelty.

'Magic,' wrote Eliphas Levi, the historian of the subject, 'is the traditional science of the secrets of Nature which has been transmitted to us from the magic. By means of this science the adept becomes invested with a species of relative omnipotence and can operate superhumanly — that is, after a manner which transcends the normal possibility of men'.

Magical beliefs of many kinds permeate human culture, as this book shows, but we are concerned here with the art or science which seeks to discover secret forces unknown to or ignored by rational and materialistic science and to use them to acquire unlimited power, the ultimate goal of the magical adept.

Magic in this sense is a European phenomenon, probably with origins in the last centuries before the Christian era when the religious and philosophical ideas of Greece and Rome began to meet those of Egypt and the orient in centres like Alexandria.

The Study of Magic

The student of magic is in pursuit of power. To acquire it he or she may begin by studying the traditional texts of the art or science of magic, which in itself might be a lifetime's work, but study alone will not take the student beyond the fringes of the subject. Further instruction must be given by a more advanced adept. Probably the learner will join a magical order and work up through the various stages of initiation in a hierarchy of grades, the number of which will have been determined by some mystical correspondence (seven for the traditional planets, ten for the sefiroth of the CABALA). The secrets revealed at each stage must not only be memorized but deeply contemplated so that they can be absorbed into the student's being, to develop the force of will, the power of compelling imagination which are also essential weapons in the magician's armoury in the quest to control the forces of the universe.

Ultimately the magician will seek the power to invoke Spirits of Intelligences from outside in order to win control of them and of the supernatural powers they can bring. The names given to these Intelligences vary from magician to magician and from order to order but the essential idea is the same. As the British magician J W Brodie-Innes remarked, whether these spiritual forces 'really exist is comparatively unimportant; the point is that the universe behaves as though they do.'

Black and White Magic

Conventionally we make a distinction between black (evil) and white (good) magic. But the scale of the magician's ambition reaches out to a cosmic reality which transcends good and evil. As in the legend of Faust, the promise of knowledge and power denied to ordinary mortals tempts the magician away from decency and morality.

To reinforce the power of will and to try to break through the bonds of conventional thought the magician will use any weapons that come to hand, and since sex, drugs and cruelty are powerful instruments they are not infrequently included in magical rituals.

Moreover the law of correspondences which is the basis of magical theory simply will not allow the magician to discriminate between what is good and what is evil; good and evil, kindness and cruelty, creation and destruction are part of the cosmic whole that the practitioner believes is incorporated in that person's own being and which has to be explored and controlled.

What we know about the great magicians of history does not necessarily suggest that they are all thoroughly evil, but none of them is strikingly good in the conventional sense and most convey a distinctly sinister aura. From a Christian point of view all of them are guilty at least of the sin of blasphemy for they have sought powers reserved for God.

Are the magicians merely charlatans? Some of them probably were, and many of them were probably charlatans in part, for they must soon have recognized how the mumbo-jumbo and paraphernalia of the magic arts could impress outsiders and win money and honours and sexual favours. The Elizabethan magician JOHN DEE for example, whatever his real gifts were, was offered a vast salary by the Czar of Russia for his services, and the 18th-century Italian Cagliostro made himself enormously attractive to fashionable women.

But many of the magicians of history are also described as having remarkably powerful personalities and the reports by many witnesses of apparently supernatural acts and phenomena represent a body of evidence too massive to be casually dismissed. Current scientific thinking makes some of the basic ideas of magic less totally nonsensical than they would have seemed a hundred years ago.

Below: *Invoking a spirit is dangerous; the magician must be the stronger or the spirit will control him.*

83

MAGIC HEALING

Primitive, and not-so-primitive people have attributed their misfortunes not to natural but to supernatural causes. Since one of the commonest kinds of misfortune is disease, people have looked for both causes and cures in the realm of magic and the supernatural. Magic healing therefore touches on virtually every aspect of magical beliefs and practices.

In tribal Africa, for example, disease is very commonly attributed to the malevolent activity of a witch, and the sufferer will resort to the services of a witch-doctor either to provide a powerful counter-magic or preferably to discover the witch and destroy him or her. In other cultures, for example in medieval Europe, possession by demons will be seen as the cause, and the recommended cure may be exorcism.

Whatever the cause, SPELLS and INCANTATIONS may be another cure, or the white magician or witch-doctor may resort to the use of 'medicines', the latter often combining pure magical belief with quite natural herbal efficacy. The practice of magic healing has over many centuries produced most of the valuable pharmacopeia of herbal medicine and homoeopathy. The discovery of genuinely useful herbs, however, has its origins in IMITATIVE MAGIC, based on the theory that resemblances in nature are invariably significant, not merely accidental: a yellow flower may offer a cure for jaundice, a plant that resembles the liver may provide a cure for diseases of that organ, and so on. A vast and complex medical system was based on ideas of that kind.

The idea that underlay the 'official' medicine of the middle ages was probably less useful than herbal medicine. It was the classical theory of the ELEMENTS, leading to the idea of the four basic Humours of the human body. All diseases could be attributed to an imbalance of the humours and the cure consisted in restoring the balance. The practice of bleeding, which persisted until quite recently, derived in part from this theory, but some of the treatments based on it were extremely bizarre.

Even more bizarre, however, was the notion that magic numbers had healing power (see NUMEROLOGY). In one recorded case a medieval Arab mathematician worked out a set of magic numbers as a cure for impotence, wrote them down, ate one set himself and fed the other set to his mistress!

Another important idea behind magic healing was the notion that people or things that are powerful in themselves are likely also to have healing powers. As late as the 18th century, for example, it was believed that kings had the power to cure particular diseases by touching those who suffered from them (scrofula was known in England as the King's Evil). The relics of saints and martyrs were also thought to have the power to cure or to ward off disease, and of course holy shrines such as Lourdes are still thought to offer cures to those who visit them.

One of the least reputable modes of magic healing was the use of pieces of dead human bodies. *Mumia*, or mummy, fragments of mummified corpses, was such a fashionable cure in the period of the Renaissance that it was faked in large quantities, and the use of pieces of recently buried corpses as medicine was so prevalent that tomb-robbing for this purpose was a major problem as late as the last century.

See also ELEMENTS AND ELEMENTALS, IMITATIVE MAGIC, INCANTATION, NECROMANCY, NUMEROLOGY, SPELLS, WITCHCRAFT

MAGIC SQUARES

Magic squares were once thought to be powerful talismans and to contain, special, magical properties. They are made up of numbers arranged in a square grid, in such a way that when added up vertically, horizontally and along the two long diagonals of the square the same total is achieved. Each number, from 1 to the highest must appear once, and no more. It is this achievement that lends them their magical properties. They were originally used as religious symbols or protective charms but in modern times, their original meanings lost, they are considered simply as curiosities, except by some Western mathematicians who continue to study them as problems in the theory of number.

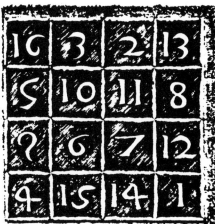

Above: *The mandrake was considered magic; as its scream on uprooting sent men mad, dogs were used to gather it.*

Left: *Magic number squares were thought to make powerful talismans, or even to have curative powers.*

See also NUMEROLOGY

MAGNETISM

When MESMER, the 18th century scientist who gave his name to the word 'mesmerize', spoke about 'animal magnetism' he did not, of course, mean the term to apply only to dogs, cats and so on, but to human beings also, and subsequent experiments seem to indicate that it should even be applied to plants and trees. It is a term Mesmer used to convey his idea that there is a hitherto unnamed fluid present in all matter, particularly in the nervous systems of animals, and in magnets. He conceived this idea by noticing that the movements of the planets and other heavenly bodies affected the course of an illness and that a sick person could be visibly assisted by someone in good health laying his or her hands on the body, or by passing a magnet over it.

None of those who went on to expand his ideas questioned Mesmer's initial assertion that a magnetic fluid existed, because the evidence of their senses told them there must be something of the kind to account for the way that the limbs of their patients would be attracted or repelled by the mesmerist, in just the way that a negatively or positively charged magnet behaves. The mesmerist did not even have to touch his subject — he could channel the fluid simply by willing it, and what is more, he could direct it to different parts of the body, and, if he wished, could put certain patients into a somnambulic trance, in which state they would respond obediently to his suggestions or commands.

Other 'proofs' were brought forward by proponents of the theory. Mesmerized subjects claimed they could see luminous AURAS around magnets, magnetists and magnetized people and things. This claim led Baron von Reichenbach to develop his concept that all matter has a quasi-magnetic fluid, which is either positively or negatively charged, and which is cold or warm accordingly, a force which may be generated by all kinds of chemical reaction or by friction, heat, light or electricity. He called this the 'Odyle' or 'Od Force'.

The whole subject continued to exercise the scientific minds of the early 19th century, but the tide began to turn against the supporters of animal magnetism as it was demonstrated that many of the phenomena remarked in the patients of magnetists could be ascribed to sheer suggestibility.

Nevertheless, the debate is not closed, because subsequent experiments seem to indicate that the human body may, after all, give off some kind of quasi-magnetic force. Human beings who held their hands close to wounded animals, without having actually touched them, seemed to accelerate the healing process, and plants treated in a similar fashion were observed to grow faster than is normal.

The problem with the theory of animal magnetism is that its most ardent followers deserted it in the middle of the last century in favour of SPIRITUALISM and it is now a cause with very few supporters to keep it alive.

Below: Mesmerists believed that they could harness 'animal magnetism' and make it work as a healing agent.

MANDALA

In Hindu and Buddhist ritual and mysticism the mandala is a mystical diagram, invariably circular in form. (In Sanskrit the word 'mandala' means circle.) It may be inscribed on metal or stone, painted or drawn in coloured sand or held in the mind and traced mentally in the air. Used ritually it somewhat resembles the magic circle of European RITUAL MAGIC, but rather than protecting the adept, it offers a focus or target for the spirit being invoked.

Within their essentially circular form mandalas carry symbolic designs of great complexity, sometimes numerological (see NUMEROLOGY). Whether they are used for ritual or for meditation they are thought to be embodiments of great mystical power, so long as they are drawn and used in the proper spirit.

The circle itself is universally regarded as a symbol of great significance and power, reflected not only in the stone circles of western Europe but in the ritual objects of almost every culture. The mandala as a symbol seems to set up reverberations in the collective unconscious of human kind that as yet we have scarcely begun to understand. For that reason it was intensively studied by the great Swiss psychologist Jung.

MANTRA

A mantra is a sequence of words or sounds which is thought to have a mystical or magical effect if repeated in the correct manner. As such it is related to the SPELL and the INCANTATION, since all three rely on the magical power of sound. In magic terms they are seen as keys that enable those who know how to use them to gain access to the secret powers of the universe; some of them are thought to be so powerful as to be positively dangerous if used incorrectly or with the wrong intentions.

Some mantras are described as 'seed' mantras, since they are thought to contain in a single syllable the concentrated essence of many thousands of words of occult wisdom.

Mantras are nowadays commonly used as tools for meditation. The apparently meaningless sound when repeated may help to empty the mind to the spiritual and physical benefits of an altered state of consciousness, which may also be brought about by the reverberations of the repeated sound within the cranium. The sound 'Om', itself a seed mantra, is the most familiar but also the most mysterious, since it is thought to contain within itself the secret of universal knowledge and power.

Above: *The mandala (circle) is a powerful symbol rich with significance in many cultures. Used in magic it becomes an engine of power; in Tantrism it is used as a meditation aid; divided by an S it is the Yang-Yin symbol of Chinese mysticism.*

MEDICINE-MEN AND WITCH-DOCTORS

Below: *Medicine men and witchdoctors carry out healing with significant rituals handed down from their predecessors.*

Medicine-man is the Western term applied to those specialists in African tribal societies who combine the function of doctor and priest. The functions are combined because no clear distinction is made in such societies between what we would regard as practical medicine and what we would regard as magic — or

between the material world and the spiritual. Most, if not all, ills are seen as having their causes in the workings of supernatural evil, which it is the business of the medicine-man to fight.

Like any practitioner of WHITE MAGIC the medicine-man has access to a vast inherited experience of the uses of plant-derived drugs, with which he can undoubtedly work effective cures for at least minor ailments. He will very often also use a large paraphernalia of weird magical materials, charms and spells, but these may simply reinforce the credibility of his real powers as a faith healer.

The medicine-man's standing in the community depends on his being seen to have success in the procuring of remedies for psychic and physical ailments, and there are plentiful reports of such successes, inexplicable though they may be to Western minds.

Because so many ills are attributed to WITCHCRAFT it is the business of the medicine-man's counterpart, the witch-doctor, to 'smell out' witches and destroy them. The witch-doctor is not himself a witch but another kind of magic specialist, who is likely also be be skilled in the arts of divination. It is the witch-doctor, too, who conducts the tribal rain-making ceremonies, directing the praying, dancing and singing that are designed to placate the god responsible for giving it or withholding rain, working himself into a state of ecstatic TRANCE in order to invoke the god. This may be dangerous work, since failure may result in the witch-doctor himself being accused of witchcraft, but it is an inescapable duty for those who are recognized as having the special gift of smelling out evil powers and gaining access to the gods.

Both medicine-man and witch-doctor are Western terms, and the use of Western terminology involves the imposition of alien concepts in such a way that can distort the situation as it is actually perceived by those who experience it at first hand. The medicine-man and the witch-doctor are probably best understood as important figures in a landscape in which the spiritual permeates the material and the supernatural overwhelms the natural; in which certain gifted men can from time to time restore the close understanding between man and the gods that existed before the Fall, for the notion that man and god once walked together in an earthly Paradise pervades African as much as it does Judaeo-Christian religious belief.

MEDITATION

Meditation was once thought, at least in the West, to be the province of the exceptional person, the mystic, but the great upsurge of interest in eastern religions and ways of thought has brought the concept, if not the practice, into the common vocabulary of the lay person. Very few who speak of it, however, have any but the haziest idea of what it entails, those who do know something of it tend to be familiar with only the method of meditation peculiar to their own particular creed or school of thought.

Some things are common to all systems of meditation — most people require a private, quiet place in which to meditate, and at least 20 minutes which will be undisturbed. Most Eastern systems recommend a sitting position, although many Christian mystics would meditate while kneeling. Whatever posture is adopted, the body should be completely relaxed, and then the object is to empty the mind of all worldly cares and all stray thoughts. An aid to achieving this is to find something symbolic on which one's concentration may be focused — this symbol will vary according to the creed or philosophy of the practitioner. When the mind is focused on this symbol, meditation has not yet been achieved but it may blossom from the stillness so created.

A common image of meditation is that of the Hindu yogi sitting contemplating his navel, but while there is no denying the benefits to be had from even the most elementary knowledge and practice of yoga, there is a world of difference between evening-class exercises and the hard-won achievement of samadhi, the eighth stage of yoga, by which stage the adept has reached union with the Absolute.

While yoga imposes great mental and physical demands, Taoism urges an immense non-striving on its followers. By doing nothing one can, paradoxically, achieve everything, it claims, but for the impatient human heart this is also very difficult. Zen Buddhism represents a middle way, tending more to the Taoist path, but giving some guidance to the acolyte. For example, a Zen master may give pupils a puzzle to think on, in the hope that it might surprise them into a satori, or sudden illumination or understanding. One such is: What

is the sound of one hand clapping?

Among the theistic religions the techniques differ. Sufis, the mystics of Islam, build up to a vision of the Face of Allah by a total concentration on Him, constantly repeating His name. Certain Jews, following cabalistic tradition, employ a meditative device arranged roughly like a tree, having 10 centres, or sefiroth. Many Christians seem to have found their own system of meditation, but some have set them down on paper for others to imitate, the *Spiritual Exercises* of St Ignatius of Loyola being a good example of these.

Whichever system of meditation is used, all schools insist that there are dangers inherent in exploring the uncharted reaches of the spirit, which is what the Christian mystic St John of the Cross referred to when he wrote movingly of the 'Dark Night of the Soul'.

Few of us seem likely to reach such depths or go through them to attain the complete ecstasy which meditation can lead to; we can, however, look towards the peace and regeneration which it promises to those who practise it.

Above: *There is no correct way to meditate, but the object is usually constant: to achieve peace by a fusion with a higher force or through contemplation.*

MEDIUMS

Important information on mediums and how they work came from a well-known psychical researcher who was drowned in the *Titanic* disaster. But these findings were not released by him until after his death.

A medium is a person (usually a woman) who can apparently make contact with the dead. Many mediums operate in a TRANCE, or semi-trance, during which they are 'controlled' by spirit guides.

There are two main types of medium: physical and mental. Physical mediums are able to produce verifiable physical phenomena: such as furniture moving, bangs and raps, and outpourings of ECTOPLASM, which may form into recognizable human shapes. Mental mediums produce no such phenomena, but filter messages from the dead; they are further subdivided into 'intuitive' and 'direct' mediums. Intuitive mediums pick up messages in the form of ideas, which they repeat or write down 'automatically'; direct mediums are taken over by the spirit while in trance, and the spirit speaks directly through the medium.

During a sitting a medium will usually repose quietly at first with eyes closed. The beginning of a trance is usually marked by a change in the medium's breathing, which becomes heavy and rapid. After this she seems to fall asleep. Within minutes she is apparently awake again — but if she is a direct, mental medium, her own personality will seem to have disappeared, to be replaced by the spirit who purports to be in control. Most mediums have one or more 'spirit guides' who mediate between the medium and spirits who wish to communicate. Many spirit guides claim to be red indians, or ancient Egyptians, or from some other ancient civilization, though sometimes they are 'innocent' children.

W T Stead's Posthumous Communications
In the 19th and early 20th centuries there was much serious, widespread interest in SPIRITUALISM, and many scientists and scholars turned their attention to psychic investigations during their lifetimes. Some of these seem to have attempted to communicate from beyond the grave, to help living researchers, and extend human knowledge

Above: *Psychical researchers, such as Sir W F Barrett, maintained open minds as far as the paranormal was concerned.*

about eternal survival of the spirit.

W T Stead was one such well-respected researcher who had the misfortune to go down with the *Titanic*. Two years later the French medium Madame Hyver began to receive messages from him, which she took down as 'automatic' writing. These were published by The Greater World Association under the title *Communication With the Next World*, and if they are truly teachings from Stead, they tell us a lot about mediums and the problems that spirits have when trying to communicate.

The book concerns mainly mental mediums, both intuitive and direct. Madame Hyver was an intuitive medium, and it was clearly this type of medium to which the spirit of Stead felt most drawn.

Stead described the different auras of mediums. Some 'Intuitive' mediums had very powerful and radiant auras, which the spirits could not penetrate, but through which they could communicate by vibration. Vibrations of ideas and emotions, he asserted, are stronger than those of facts, such as a name or a date, so the messages may be profound and elevated, but not precise. Other, 'direct' mediums have auras that are more easily penetrated and therefore more precise manifestations may be produced. The kind of spirit attracted to each medium depended, he said, on the medium's own spiritual advancement: 'A spirit of elevated character cannot approach a very material medium without suffering as if from asphyxiation, sometimes nearly to the extent of becoming unconscious; but with the same medium a coarse spirit would be quite at

ing, I have often tried to take possession of a direct medium by penetrating within his aura. The first contact revived in me the impressions of my death by drowning — the feeling of suffocation.'

Stead was particularly interesting when he described the way spirits viewed the physical world. In works of art, for instance, 'I see only the ideas the artist had in producing them. Thus I see not colours but a harmonious rhythm.' People appeared only as minds and spirits: 'Magnetic waves, thoughts and feelings vibrate from them. They are beautiful or ugly, brilliant or dull, or of intermediate degree, according to the state of their soul.'

Physical Manifestations

Physical mediums produce manifestations that do not correspond to the laws of science as we know them today. Tables rise in the air; musical instruments fly around the room, being played by an unseen musician; wispy ectoplasm forms into solid-looking people, or disembodied hands that move on their own and touch the sitters.

Many learned, sound and sensible men in the 19th century reported seeing these manifestations with their own eyes, and the evidence of some of them cannot be doubted. Those who suspected fraud could not but be convinced by testimonies such as this one, from the respectable Sir William Barrett in 1913, 'I saw the table rise about 18 inches and made all the sitters hold up their hands which were clearly visible whilst the table remained suspended. Then I was allowed to go within the circle and try to force the table down, which was impossible. I sat on the table and could not force it down. The table then of its own accord turned upside down and I was allowed to try and lift it but it was impossible, the top seemed riveted to the floor.'

Psychical researchers have found that these phenomena are often accompanied by a distinct drop in temperature.

Can Paranormal Happenings Be Explained?

Many explanations are offered as to what is the real cause of these paranormal happenings by those who do not believe in the continuation of the spirit, or its ability to communicate with us from beyond the grave. Straight fraud is sometimes cited — and some mediums have been discovered to be falsifying phenomena. But most of them perform quite genuinely.

Left: *A physical medium can cause extraordinary phenomena. Instruments sailing through the air, played by invisible hands, are common occurrences.*

ease. On the other hand, with a medium of more refined type, the coarse spirit would feel as would a peasant in a drawing room: he would not know how to act.'

Explaining to Madame Hyver how he was communicating with her, he said, 'I do not transmit words. I think, and the vibrations of my thoughts are transmitted by the intermediary of our spirit bodies. Your spirit body then gives consciousness of my thoughts to your brain and you translate these thoughts into corresponding written expressions.

'I would be able to convey very complicated and subtle thoughts to you so long as you had in your mind words adequate for the expression of these ideas; but I could not convey through you an algebraic formula or a scientific or historical term which you did not know. If, for example, you knew the name Nebuchadnezzar, I could make you write: "The pride of a Nebuchadnezzar." If you did not know the name, you would write "The pride of a great potentate," or something equivalent. The idea would be the same.'

Stead also compared a medium to a musician. A well-educated and talented medium would interpret sensitively the messages she received, whereas some mediums were unable to give adequate expression to the ideas, so they sounded banal and uninspired.

Some spirits, Stead said, like the experience of taking over a direct medium, though others, such as himself, preferred dealing with an intuitive medium for, 'memories of earth are very clearly and even painfully revived when he first tries to communicate through a direct medium. For the purpose of manifest-

Telepathy with sitters is one explanation of a mental medium's ability to give information of which he or she is not consciously aware; or that the medium has subconsciously drawn clues from the look and personality of the sitter, or from the way the sitter responds to questions. Unconscious memory — of things the medium has read, seen or heard, and subsequently forgotten — is another explanation. There is also the possibility that the medium has clairvoyant abilities, and has been able to 'read' a document not yet discovered.

However it is in evidence such as cross-correspondences (see AUTOMATIC ART/WRITING/MUSIC) that the only explanation seems to be communication from the dead. Fragments of writings communicated separately to different mediums, which made no apparent sense, have been joined to make a coherent whole, containing knowledge, allusions, foreign-language quotes and in-jokes that seem to be transmitted by one guiding intelligence.

Fraud on this scale by undeniably respectable people has been completely ruled out.

But one strange fact is true: nowadays there are far fewer physical mediums operating than in the golden age of the mid 19th to early 20th centuries. Partly this can be explained by the fact that many mediums who used to be classified as physical mediums, no longer attribute the forces that create the phenomena to spirits outside themselves. In the past Uri GELLER might have been thought to be a physical medium, whereas nowadays his psychic powers are recognized to be under his own control. Another theory suggests that the many women who possessed the powers of physical mediumship grew up in a time when repressed sexual feelings gave rise to deep guilt and anxiety which might have created the necessary energies. Spiritualists disagree, and say that the spirits have turned their powers to healing instead, rather than wasting them on producing useless phenomena.

Below: The power of the medium is most likely to be revealed at a seance with the right atmosphere and sympathetic participants.

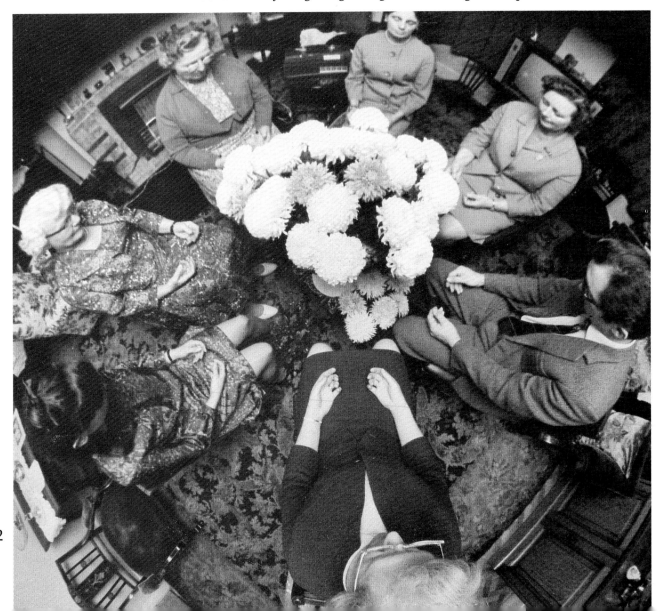

MERLIN

The figure from the Arthurian legends who above all takes them out of the realm of history and into the realm of myth and magic is surely that of the magician and seer Merlin. In both French and English versions of the tales it is Merlin who arranges Arthur's birth, helps him obtain the sword Excalibur, instructs him as a boy, gives him magical help in war and foretells the future.

On the whole he is a benevolent figure, although in some versions he plays a more sinister role. He is sometimes said to have been conceived by a human mother and a demonic father, in an attempt by the Devil to create a Satanic child, but the attempt went wrong and Merlin retained demonic powers but chose on the whole to serve good rather than evil. In later life he fell helplessly in love with the enchantress Nimue, who eventually tired of him and cast a spell on him, confining him to imprisonment in a cave for all eternity.

Like Arthur, Merlin was regarded in the middle ages as an historical figure and his prophecies, as recorded, for example, by the 12th-century historian Geoffrey of Monmouth, were frequently studied and quoted.

One of the candidates for an historical Merlin is the ancient British bard and seer called Myrddin, who actually lived a little later than the historical Arthur. Myrddin was certainly used by Geoffrey of Monmouth as the basis for the Merlin, shifting his birth by a hundred years.

However, several of the tales surrounding Merlin suggest much earlier, even prehistoric origins. He is associated for example with the building of Stonehenge, two thousand or more years before the lifetime of Arthur. Since some of the massive stones of that mysterious monument were certainly transported to Wiltshire from west Wales it is not surprising that they are associated with magic. Although Stonehenge is pre-Celtic, the character of Merlin also suggests that of the Celtic druids, who were also seers, teachers and repositories of ancient laws and ancient wisdom. It is more than likely that the stories which Geoffrey and other medieval writers drew together to write their tales contain folk memories of that Celtic priesthood, which must have enjoyed a revival of its powers in the period between the departure of the Romans and the final triumph of the Saxons. While Arthur represents military power in the last struggle of Celtic Britain, Merlin represents the power of magic and of the spirit.

Above: *One of the myths surrounding Merlin suggests that he used his magical powers to move the great stones of Stonehenge.*

Above: *For a time Mesmer's healing sessions were very popular; he was a showman, dressed in magician's garb, playing mysterious music.*

MESMER, F A

Franz (or Friedrich) Anton Mesmer (1734–1815) was a trained doctor, who developed revolutionary theories about the treatment of illness by harnessing magnetic forces. His work was discredited in his lifetime, partly because of the extremely eccentric way in which he carried it out, and many believe that his theories put him on the wrong track. But his treatment, which came to be known as 'Mesmerism', was the forerunner of HYPNOSIS, and was developed to good effect by other practitioners after his death.

Mesmer was educated in medicine at the university of Vienna, where he presented a thesis on his theory of the magnetic influence of the stars on human beings. His theory led him to try to treat sickness in people by the use of magnets, which he did with great success.

However Mesmer soon decided that it was not the action of the magnets that was having a beneficial effect, but something he called 'animal magnetism'. In other words, the magnetic force came directly from the person treating the patient. He believed himself to be particularly adept at controlling this force, and harnessing it so that he could influence others.

In 1778 Mesmer moved his practice to Paris, and gathered around him a school of pupils, and many sick people hoping to be cured. His healing ceremonies were distinctly odd. Dressed as a magician, Mesmer conducted his surgeries to the accompaniment of soft music and low lighting. His curative tool was a large wooden tub filled with water and iron filings supporting many bottles of magnetized water and iron rods. He had charged the rods with his own 'animal magnetism' by stroking them, and he effected his many cures by laying the rods on the site of the problem.

In 1784 a committee of the French Academy of Sciences, made up of the eminent scientists of the day, studied Mesmer and his clinic. Their findings acknowledged that Mesmer, indeed, seemed to have presided over many cures, but concluded firmly that the so-called animal magnetism had nothing to do with them. After this public denunciation, Mesmer left Paris, and lived the rest of his life in seclusion.

But his many pupils continued to believe in the validity of his work, and continued to experiment in their own ways.

One of them, the Marquis de Puységur, discovered that by using his 'animal magnetism' he could put his patients into a trance-like state, during which he could treat them. Often he would find that they would speak to him, diagnosing their own problem, and sometimes suggesting treatment. When they woke, most of them were unaware of what had passed.

This twist in the application of the treatment began to be more widely investigated. 'Mesmerism' came to be synonymous with the trance-like state, and followers increasingly stopped using the magnetized iron rods in their treatments. As understanding about the process grew, the theory of magnetism was dropped altogether. The seductive atmosphere, the tone of voice, even the belief in magnetism, all contributed to put the subject into a suggestible state in which the subconscious could be addressed directly. Subsequently the process was renamed 'hypnotism'.

See also HYPNOSIS

MIDSUMMER EVE

To pagan people the main turning points of the year, the spring and autumn equinoxes and the summer and winter solstices, were of literally vital importance. In the hot days of midsummer they were all too aware that the sun had now reached its peak and must start its decline towards the bitter dark and cold of winter. They were also anxiously awaiting the harvest, knowing that success or failure of the crops would mean life or death.

In a world ruled by the supernatural action simply had to be taken to placate whatever forces could sustain the dying sun and bring good crops. The habits of associative thinking that underlie all magical beliefs led to the custom of lighting midsummer bonfires, which at one time could be seen blazing all over Europe at this time of year. Men and women would dance around them and the more vigorous would leap over them to enhance the fertility of the crops (a custom which survives in some bonfire ceremonies today).

The Christian festival of the Nativity of John the Baptist, three days later than the solstice, is a survival of these ancient pagan customs, though the practice of lighting bonfires has largely died out.

Midsummer Eve was also a dangerous time in other respects. Witches and evil spirits were thought to be particularly active and many of the midsummer ceremonies were designed to drive them away. But it was also a time when young women could cast spells to see images of their future husbands, and many of the plants that blossom at midsummer were thought to have special magical powers, among them St John's Wort, which could drive out demons, and Midsummer Eve fern seed, which was though to convey the power of invisibility.

Below: *Oberon exploited the romantic atmosphere of Midsummer Eve in Shakespeare's 'A Midsummer Night's Dream', by engineering love mix-ups.*

MIND-OVER-MATTER

The Indian fakir has practised mind-over-matter in the Indian rope trick for centuries, and since early Christian times saints have exhibited stigmata and other mind-over-matter phenomena — but today mind-over-matter is being used efficaciously in medicine by doctors who administer 'placebo' drugs.

'Mind-over-matter' is the non-scientific term for the ability to control the environment, using psychic ability alone (PSYCHOKINESIS); and it also refers to the ability to affect your own bodily responses, using mental power.

Both these kinds of mind-over-matter can be performed consciously by those who have studied to enable themselves to do so, or can happen spontaneously, without conscious effort.

An example of a conscious effort of will is shown by Maikeli Masi, a Fijian boy, who walked barefoot over white hot coals at a recorded temperature of 400°F (200°C). In Fiji this story was only considered remarkable because Maikeli was 11 years old at the time, and therefore the youngest person to have attempted the feat — any number of older people had done exactly the same before him. But when D D Home (the 19th-century medium) handled red hot coals straight from the fireplace 'as if they had been oranges', he believed he was being controlled by spirits, and that divine intervention stopped him from experiencing pain or physical damage. Nowadays it can be seen that both these cases show the mind's incredible power over the body when harnessed.

Mind-Over-Matter in Medicine
This power, consciously used or not, has begun to be explored by doctors. Previously only hypnotists tried to tap the ability of the mind to affect the body — and under hypnosis subjects have raised blisters on their skin in the belief that they were touching something red-hot, or else suffered no ill-effects when really in contact with something burning hot. Now conventional medicine has started to tap this power. 'Placebo' drugs — sugar pills with no active ingredients — are sometimes prescribed to patients who seem to obtain relief from them. Doctors have shifted from believing that this was because hypochondriacal patients simply needed to feel they were doing something or being looked after to feel better, to discovering that real changes can take place in the body after taking these pills. Simply believing that completely useless pills are having some effect can stimulate the body to produce its own natural painkilling or tranquilizing hormones.

In the same way, doctors have discovered that patients can bring down their own blood-pressure just by using force of will. Once wired up to a machine that shows them what high and low blood-pressure look like, the patients can use this visual aid alone to lower blood-pressure to a more acceptable level.

Mind-Over-Matter in Religion
The religious produce a fair number of semi-miraculous mind-over-matter stories. The various saints who genuinely exhibited stigmata — bleeding wounds in the same places as Christ's — are outstanding examples. The fact that the stigmata vary from person to person in positioning or shape seems to prove a psychological rather than divine cause. The church shares this scepticism. The stigmata of Father Pio Forgione, first received in 1915, were declared not to be supernatural by the Holy Office.

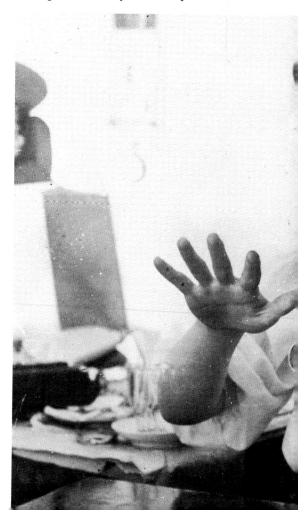

Nobody hinted that they had been fraudulently produced by the pious Father, but he was known for his psychic abilities, including telepathy or 'reading of hearts'. It was decided that his stigmata were merely another manifestation of this power, which also affected his body temperature, so that it occasionally ran so high that it broke a clinical thermometer. Other methods of measurement showed that it reached 112°F (45°C).

Stories of psychokinesis can be found in religious records, too. The Curé of Ars told how the host moved from his fingers and flew onto the tongue of a communicant — a clear case of psychokinesis, particularly bearing in mind that the Curé had been the centre of poltergeist activity for years.

Reports of psychokinetic mind-over-matter have been recorded in all cultures over the centuries — from the fakir's Indian rope trick, a coil of rope slowly unravelling itself upwards out of a basket, to the ultra-modern experiments in the laboratories of the parapsychologists.

Spiritualism and Mind-Over-Matter

Psychokinetic phenomena are often spontaneously produced. The editor of an investigative magazine into the para-

normal tells how his entrenched scepticism took a knock during the course of its run. His deputy editor frequently clashed with him because of what she called his 'closed mind' — she herself was more prepared to give the reports they published the benefit of the doubt. One day, they were arguing fiercely when he was suddenly hit on the head.

'I looked round in surprise and saw that I had been struck by a chunk of plaster that had somehow leapt out of the wall behind me and travelled a distance of 18 inches or so to land on my head. Now there was no natural explanation for this at all. I was completely dumbstruck — and so was my deputy editor. She felt guilty because it seemed that she was the unwitting agent for this happening.'

The greatest body of information about psychokinetic mind-over-matter is to be found in Spiritualist records. Seances with mediums produce remarkable phenomena, attested to by respectable independent witnesses. These curious happenings were usually attributed to spirit activity — but if that is ruled out as a possibility, then mind-over-matter remains the only explanation.

A good example of this is the case of the medium Anna Rasmussen, who was studied in her native Denmark by Dr Christian Winther. In a series of sittings Anna was able to affect pendulums encased in glass. More extraordinarily, she was able to make one of a pair move independently from the other, changing direction, slowing down and then accelerating again.

Nowadays people try to produce similar effects in laboratories in the name of parapsychology. Subjects in full control of their powers, such as Uri Geller and Matthew Manning, are able to bend metal without touching it. Other people, quite unaware that they possess powers, or what faculty they are exercising, have also produced strange effects. Specifically, experiments with dice show that they can be 'willed' to fall a certain way if the person throwing them has the ability. It is hoped that finally these experiments will not just prove that the mind can control matter, but that they will come up with the answer to the great question, 'How is it done and can anyone do it?'

See also MEDIUMS, PARAPSY-CHOLOGY, PSYCHOKINESIS, SPONTANEOUS PSI EXPERIENCES

Above: *Walking on white-hot coals without feeling pain is a mind-over-matter trick that anyone can learn.*

Left: *Stanislava Tomozyk was photographed levitating these scissors using the power of her mind alone.*

MIRACLES

Are miracles performed only by religious power, and can they totally cure serious diseases such as cancer? And why were some of the saints so reluctant to reveal their miraculous powers?

We often use the world lightly, declaring, 'If City win the Cup it'll be a miracle', or speaking of 'a new miracle drug' but we are hard put to define it when it is applied more seriously. A miracle, is indisputably, a marvel, something which defies the natural order, the normal physical laws. But what brings about this marvel?

The history of miracles is largely a history of religion. When we look back at the stories of the ancient Greeks, we find tales of marvels being wrought by divine beings and not by mortal men. Asclepius, the god of healing, worked his cures while the sick man slept at one of his temples. At Epidaurus, a man called Euhippus went to sleep with a spear tip lodged in his jaw and when he awoke he found that his dream of the god removing it had been true — the spear head was gone!

Biblical Miracles

While there are many examples to be found in the history of ancient Greece, the oldest and most detailed body of writing to record miracles is the Bible. The Jewish tradition of one God, a tradition which is carried through to the New Testament, gives us numerous instances of miracles brought about by God with the purpose of showing his determination to care for his Chosen People and to promote their spiritual progress. None of the Old Testament miracles are performed with a worldly goal in view — when the Red Sea opened to let the Israelites pass through, it was so that they might be strengthened in their belief and free to worship the One True God — not that they might triumph over the Egyptians.

This theme of the miracle always being performed for spiritual ends is repeated and strengthened in the New Testament. Jesus often showed a reluctance to work a miracle which could be interpreted as mere wonder-working. A striking example is the story (Mark 2.1–12) of the sick man whose friends let him down to Jesus through a roof. When he saw their faith he said, 'Son, thy sins

be forgiven thee.' But the scribes muttered that this was blasphemy, and Jesus asked them if they thought it was easier to forgive sins than to heal the sick. 'But that ye may know that the Son of Man hath power on earth to forgive sins, (he saith to the man sick of the palsy,) I say unto thee, Arise and take up thy bed and go thy way into thine house.' The miracle was a visible sign of Jesus's divine powers and was intended to help lead mankind to salvation.

Other Religious Attitudes to Miracles

Passing from the Judaeo-Christian world, we can touch upon the status of miracles among other religions. In theory Islam allows that Allah works miracles, but little emphasis is put upon them. There are, by way of illustration, saints, but there is no lengthy and exigent canonization procedure such as there is in Christianity.

Moving further away, in religious tradition and geographically, we come to the great religions of the East. The whole world-view of the Asian religions is very different, and a way of thinking which already admits a fluid relationship between cause and effect is ill disposed to the concept of a miracle.

Confucianism and Taoism both conceive of gods as unable to move outside the evolved system — there is nothing beyond what there is. Buddhism reaches its apogee in Tibet under the guidance of the LAMAS or priests, who speak of a great Beyond, made up of an infinite mind-energy which underlies all of nature. The marvels which lamas reputedly perform are brought about by their mastery of a mind-power technique, and the lama, by using his own mental energy, can make his thought take substance. The Tibetan word for a solid thought-form is *tulpa*, and a *tulku* is a person who has been created in this way. (Each Dalai Lama is said to be a tulku.)

If this were all, we would still have an instance of magic, rather than a miracle, but it appears that there are cases of tulpas being governed by the Mind Beyond, which transcends nature in the way that God is thought to transcend nature to work a miracle. A comparative study of Lamaistic Buddhism and Christianity would reveal some essential similarities, even though the basic premises seem so very disparate.

All the marvels which have been reported from Tibet — yogis who levitate, who can endure amazing extremes of

temperature, who can go into suspended animation and perform other bodily feats — can be found in India, although the Hindu yogi will protest that there is nothing miraculous about them — they are the products of will, a species of magic, for what lies Beyond is impersonal and could not intervene in human destiny.

Even if we examine the Vishnu cult, the belief that the Supreme Being came to earth in the guise of Krishna and performed miracles, it seems not to matter much within Hinduism. What is stressed by both Hindus and by enlightened Christians is that a miracle is a spiritual sign and not to be viewed in isolation. St Teresa of Avila, for instance, in common with many saints, tried to conceal miraculous events in her life for fear that they would disturb her mission.

We have seen that nowhere is emphasis laid upon miracles as strongly as in the Judaic tradition and in Christianity, and it will be useful to concentrate our investigation within this field. There are two broad classes of miracles. The first is that which affects only an individual, although visible signs may be observed by outsiders. Typical of this class are cases of people suffering the stigmata (wounds which reproduce those of the crucified Christ), levitating, giving off an inexplicable sweet smell, surviv-

ing months or even years without sustenance, and appearing physically at the same time in two different places (bilocation). The other type of miracle occurs to more than one person or may affect inanimate objects, and is less intensely personal. In this class we may place manifestations of holy figures, cases where prayers directly or indirectly to God are answered, and instances where inanimate objects are made to defy the natural laws, such as is the case of the Turin Shroud.

Modern Miracles

Current scientific knowledge in no way equips us to explain such a remarkable phenomenon as the reported visions of the Virgin Mary to a group of young people in Medjugorje, in Yugoslavia. Since 1981 there have been over 2000 of these visions and even sceptics have seen inexplicable lights in the vicinity. A battery of tests have failed to account for the simultaneous ecstasy of the youngsters. If we believe that this is a modern-day miracle we must see its purpose as being to stimulate religious ardour among Christians and promote peace throughout the nations. Other well-known cases of Marian appearances are those of Lourdes and Fatima, and a concomitant of such visions is the phenomenon of miraculous healing.

Above: *Are miracles exclusively religious, such as Jesus healing a blind man, or are they meant to shatter our ideas of reality? (By Agosfinidi Duccib)*

There is no question that some of the so-called 'miraculous' cures at Lourdes, Fatima and elsewhere are produced by auto-suggestion in people who are of a clinically 'hysterical' nature. There is equally no question that many cures cannot be explained away in this fashion. The facts of one recent case are well authenticated: John Fagan, a Glasgow dock worker, had a cancer confirmed at Glasgow Royal Infirmary in 1967. Mr Fagan was in the terminal stages of his illness when a priest suggested that Mrs Fagan should pray to Blessed John Ogilvie for her husband's recovery. Following a prayer session around his bedside, the dying man made a full recovery. A panel of doctors examined him, and he submitted to a series of tests in an Edinburgh hospital in 1971, tests which showed he was entirely free of cancer and found 'no satisfactory explanation' for his recovery. Largely as a result of this cure Pope Paul VI canonized the saint in 1976.

If these can be seen as miracles designed to recall to the mass of people the transcendent power of God, 'private' miracles are outward signs of an interior spiritual progress and those experiencing them often try to conceal or suppress them. We know that St Teresa of Avila tried to prevent herself from levitating after receiving communion by desperately clutching a grille. Similarly, Padre Pio, an Italian friar, was very reluctant to reveal his stigmata for fear that a personality cult might grow up around him. One might say that such humility is a pointer to saintliness.

The Roman Catholic Church, when examining the case of a candidate for canonization, investigates alleged 'miracles' rigorously, but even when it accepts them it insists that they were worked by God, although saints and people on earth can focus them. Eastern religions tend to admit the existence of what appear to be miracles but locate them within a total reality in which context they are not remarkable.

The ufologist Jacques Vallée believes that there is a 'control system' somewhere in the universe which stimulates us into reassessing our perceptions of reality, and it is this that miracles may do — they occur and we are suddenly and forcibly reminded that people are not in control of their own fate, that our earthbound visions cannot feed an innate desire to look beyond the stars. To the believer, the miracle makes the logic and the science of human beings dissolve in the face of evidence of a greater truth.

Below: Morgan le Fay's power to raise phantom castles from water led to mirages on water being named Fata Morgana, after her.

MORGAN LE FAY

In Arthurian legend Morgan Le Fay is Arthur's half-sister and the ruler of the enchanted island of Avalon, where Arthur goes to have his wounds healed after his last battle. She is supposed to have studied under MERLIN but her name in French means Morgan the Fairy and there are constant hints of her non-human or semi-human origins. In all probability Morgan was originally a Celtic deity, possibly the goddess the Irish call Morrigan. When the Celts were Christianized she became a fairy or half-fairy, half-human. She retained the powers of an enchantress, including the power to change herself into a bird. In the later versions of the Arthurian tales, under medieval Catholic influence, she becomes a more wicked and sinister figure. When the Arthurian legend reached Italy she became Fata Morgana and gave her name to a mirage seen in the Straits of Mesina.

See also MERLIN

NECROMANCY

Necromancy is sometimes thought of as being synonymous with BLACK MAGIC but its meaning is actually more specific than that for it comes from two Greek words that mean 'dead' and 'divination'. Divination from the dead can be performed in two ways, either by summoning their ghosts, one of the most skilful and dangerous arts of the magician, or by working from corpses.

It was believed that the dead did not normally return as ghosts but that for 12 months following death their spirits might linger near the grave. During that period the skilled magician could, by means of the appropriate ritual and INCANTATION, compel the dead to come to him and impart some of the knowledge that the dead were supposed to have. His motive for wishing to converse with the dead might be his endless quest for wisdom, but all too often

necromancy was used for baser ends, such as the search for hidden money.

The ritual used in this kind of necromancy was not only designed to invoke the spirit of the dead but also to protect the magician from the immense dangers involved. Invariably some kind of magic circle would be drawn on the ground, inscribed with protective symbols and holy names. The slightest departure from correct ritual might involve not only the death of the necromancer but the possibility of damnation also.

The use of corpses or parts of corpses to make potions or as part of a ritual is one of the darkest aspects of BLACK MAGIC and WITCHCRAFT. The practice undoubtedly led to grave-robbing — the graves of unbaptized children and people who had suffered violent deaths being particularly favoured.

See also BLACK MAGIC

Below: *Necromancers believed the dead were all-knowing so secrets could be discovered by talking to them.*

NOSTRADAMUS

Nostradamus is the Latin name of Michel de Nostradame (1503–1566), who became the most widely known Renaissance prophet. His writings were extensively read in Europe during his own lifetime and, because they are seen to cover events up to the present day and beyond, the premonitions he made remain relevant and of widespread interest. This is reinforced by the fact that many of Nostradamus's predictions have already been seen to be fulfilled in an uncannily precise way.

Nostradamus was born at St Rémy in southern France. His family was Jewish but he was raised as a Catholic and, early in life, became a brilliant student in Hebrew, Latin, Greek, mathematics, astrology and medicine. It was medicine he went on to study at university in Montpellier and, after graduating without difficulty, he began travelling and applying his medical knowledge to curing victims of the plague which was endemic in southern France at the time. He became known as a generous and skilful practitioner, refusing to 'bleed' plague sufferers as was the convention in the 16th century.

After returning to Montpellier in 1529 and completing a doctorate, he subse-

quently travelled widely across France again and came into contact with the renowned philosopher Julius Scaliger in the town of Agen. Scaliger, who had himself studied under the famous Italian astrologer Luca Gaurico, was probably the influence which fuelled Nostradamus's growing interest in the subject of prophesy.

In 1547, after the plague had claimed many of his family, Nostradamus settled in Salon en Craux de Provence. He married a rich widow, who bore him six children, and remained there for the rest of his life. It was at Salon that Nostradamus began writing books, some on medicinal remedies and beauty recipes and others predicting the course of history.

In the early 1550s his first prophetic writings appeared in the form of annual *Almanacs* and *Prognostications* which were modest publications predicting local events and foretelling such things as climatic changes and agricultural trends. Imitators, using his name, swamped the market with similar texts and Nostradamus's reputation was badly undermined by their activities. Then, in 1555, he sent the first part of his major work to press — a book titled *Les Prophéties de M. Michel Nostradamus.* This text, which was added to when the full text appeared 13 years later, firmly established the author's international fame as a visionary.

Below: Over the centuries Nostradamus's cryptic prophecies clarified as they came true, one by one.

This extraordinary manuscript was written in an obscure, old-fashioned mixture of Greek, Latin, French, Romance languages and local dialect. It was divided into ten 'centaines', or centuries, each containing a hundred individual prophesies written in the form of rhyming quatrains. As well as being linguistically difficult for even Nostradamus's own contemporaries to understand, the predictions were presented in no apparent order — a deliberate ploy, for the author wanted to prevent the uninitiated from understanding his book and to avoid accusations of witchcraft by the Inquisition. This accounts for the many attempts to decipher and interpret the meaning of *Prophéties* over the years and perhaps why the work has remained so tantalizingly elusive and fascinating for centuries.

But, amongst the more esoteric of Nostradamus's premonitions — which he would 'see' by staring into a bowl of water on a tripod when in a trance-like state — were a number of tangible accounts of events which definitely occurred after they were predicted. In his own lifetime he predicted the death of Henry II in a duel. When travelling in Italy as a young man, Nostradamus met a monk named Felice Peretti along the way. Both the monk and bystanders were amazed when Nostradamus fell on his knees before the man and said, 'I kneel before His Holiness'. Peretti, in due course, became Pope Sextus V. Nostradamus, when visited once by Catherine de Medici from the court in Paris, focused on a boy with the royal party and pronounced that he would, one day, be crowned King of France. In fact the boy was Henry of Navarre who went on to become Henry IV.

Nostradamus, who claimed that the earth revolved around the sun 100 years before Galileo, also predicted the French Revolution and the accession of an emperor named 'Napoloron'; he named Pasteur and described a person called 'Hister' (Hitler) who would one day turn Europe into a battlefield. Nostradamus made specific references to General Franco and the Spanish Civil War. He predicted King Edward VIII's abdication and two unparalleled scourges which interpreters see as referring to the bombing of Nagasaki and Hiroshima.

Nostradamus prophesied an apocalyptic terror just before the end of the 20th century, followed by a great famine. He also foretold the time and place of his own death in Salon in 1566.

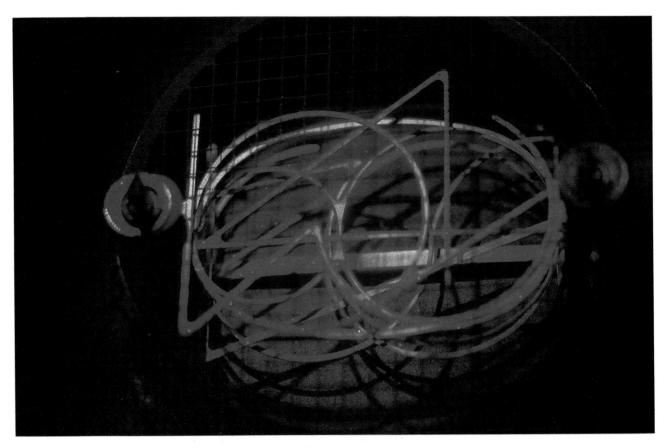

NUMEROLOGY

By adding together the representative numbers of your full name you can find out your personality type, and by adding the vowel values together you discover what sort of person you are at heart.

Numerology was bequeathed to the West by the Pythagorean philosophers who believed that everything was a number, numbers representing order in an otherwise chaotic universe. It is this principle of numbers being clues to the true structure of the universe, combined with the belief that the very essence of every person or object is contained within its name, that has resulted in modern numerology.

The Pythagoreans saw the existence of opposites, too, as a crucial characteristic of the universe. Among these pairs of opposites were good and evil, odd and even, male and female. Good and male were thus associated with odd numbers while evil and female were represented by even numbers. The basic meanings attributed to numbers by modern numerologists still correspond neatly with this table of opposites – 1 being active and positive, 2 passive and receptive, 3 lucky and spiritual, 4 unlucky and earthly, 5 multi-faceted and adventurous, 6 plain and domestic, 7 signifies retiring from the world while 8 represents involvement in the world (in this case 9 is left over at the end).

Before reaching the modern world in its present form numerology continued through the Middle Ages when it was still used to explain the mysteries of the universe, and was also applied to reach an understanding of the Bible. In the latter case 1 was the number of God, 2 that of his opposite the Devil, 3 obviously was the number of the Trinity, 4 of the earth, 5 of the senses and the flesh, 6 the number of creation (the world having been created in six days with God resting on the seventh), 8 represented fullness and balance, 9 cosmic significance — and 10 was the number of completeness. Any number beyond 10 can be reduced to another, smaller number by adding together its component digits e.g., 342 = 3 + 4 + 2 = 9.

Know Yourself Through Numerology
Modern numerology is a combination and refinement of all earlier instances of the science, and concentrates on specific numbers such as your 'Personal Number' and your 'Birth Number'. Adding together the representative

Above and below: *Each number has its character and significance, and you can find its personal relevance by determining your own number.*

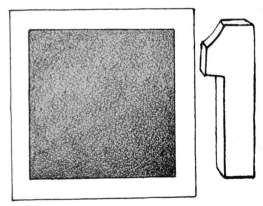

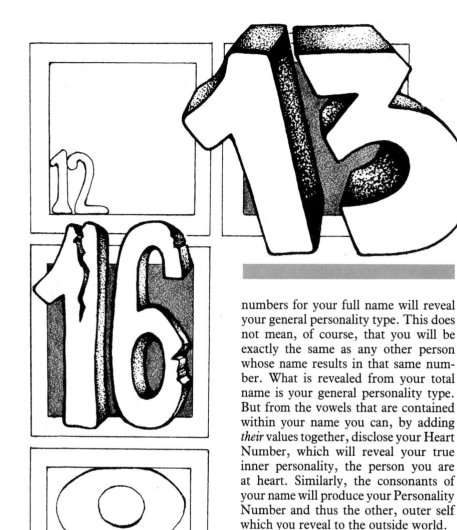

Far right: *The table shows the numbers relating to each letter. Use it to discover your name number.*

numbers for your full name will reveal your general personality type. This does not mean, of course, that you will be exactly the same as any other person whose name results in that same number. What is revealed from your total name is your general personality type. But from the vowels that are contained within your name you can, by adding *their* values together, disclose your Heart Number, which will reveal your true inner personality, the person you are at heart. Similarly, the consonants of your name will produce your Personality Number and thus the other, outer self which you reveal to the outside world.

As well as determining your general, inner and outer personalities from your full name, you can also assess the way in which you are seen by others according to the way in which they address you. By considering any nicknames, short forms or other variants of your name in the ways described you will see how you present yourself to others. If you change your name you can, numerologists suggest, alter your personality. A married woman's maiden name should, therefore, reveal her character before her marriage while her married name will indicate the way in which she has changed since her marriage.

Another important number is your Birth Number, which can be discovered by adding the month, day and year of your birth together. This number will reveal the mould in which you were cast at birth and the destiny you are meant to follow. Numerologists believe that if your Birth Number does not accord with, or harmonize with your Name Number you are likely to be prone to considerable inner conflict.

All manner of other aspects of your life can be assessed and considered through numerology — taste, for example, in music, furnishings, where you choose to live, and diet. People with names adding up to 1, 3 or 9, for instance, will opt for loud, martial music while 6 people will opt for more romantic music. The numbers generated by different foodstuffs will tell you whether they are suitable for or beneficial to you personally.

Time, of course, is measured numerically and the significance of dates to the numerologist is considerable. The numbers of the present century add up to 1 which suggests a period of innovation, new theories and discoveries, while the advent of the year 2000 is not looked forward to with much enthusiasm, its number being 2, which indicates that it will bring with it the influence of evil, although it is not all gloom since the year 2001 will bring with it the more fortunate influences of a 3 year. A combination of the number of the year and our own Birth Number will reveal to us our Personal time cycle and allow us to determine a course of action at any given time. This number can be reached by adding to the present year the day and month of our own birth.

As well as being used to discover your true character, numerology can be applied to help smooth your journey through life. For example, if your Name Number is 5 you should always try to attend to important matters on days that result in the same number. You should, if possible, live in a house whose number is 5 (or whose name adds up to 5) in a street whose name adds up to 5 — the continuity of numbers will make your life more harmonious and successful. The Heart Numbers of the cities of the world reveal their inner characteristics quite accurately. New York, for example, is a city whose vowels add up to 3 — a number representing brilliance, vivacity and glamour, while those of London amount to 5 — multi-faceted and sensual. And Paris is a 2, the number of both women and the Devil — very suitable for a city famed for its women and its wickedness.

1	2	3	4	5	6	7	8
A	B	C	D	E	U	O	F
I	K	G	M	H	V	Z	P
Q	R	L	T	N	W		
J		S			X		
Y							

OBJECT-READING

Object-reading is a term used to describe what psychometrists (people with extra-sensory perception) do when they hold an article and are able to give information related to its owner. Similar effects can be created without actually touching the object, but simply by concentrating on it — even if it is miles away or has ceased to exist. The information perceived in this way may describe events that have happened in the past — though they sometimes predict the future.

So precise can some of this information be, that it is not uncommon for the police to use the expertise of someone talented in object-reading to help solve a crime when they have reached a dead end.

As part of some psychometric experiments, one young object-reader was given the cap of a man who had murdered his baby. He became agitated and handed it back, saying that he did not receive any impressions from it. Two days later he described a dream of a man murdering a baby, which exactly coincided with the truth. He recognized that he had originally repressed the images he was receiving because they disturbed him, but when his 'censorship' was weakened during sleep the images emerged.

Some psychometrists operate in trance or semi-trance; others seem to be operating normally, though they might have a rather 'distracted' air. When concentrating on an object they experience visual, hallucinatory images, or what feels like the surfacing of a half-forgotten memory.

The object-reader is able to describe the impressions he sees, but not to analyse them. It has often been found that scenes or unseen objects described are somewhat distorted. This is partly because the visions he receives may 'condense' time: fragments from past, present and future amalgamating into a single picture, or else 'portmanteau' rooms may be described: a chest of drawers from one part of the house, next to a chair from another.

In 1946 the 'chair experiment' was developed as a way of testing object-readers' abilities to gather information about future events. The object-reader examines a chair in a public hall and is given a random date in the future to concentrate on. He then gives his impressions of the person who will occupy the chair at that time. Of course, it is seen to that the object-reader has no opportunity to arrange for someone he knows to take the seat. Talented psychometrists are often able to give startlingly precise information about this person.

A well-documented example of unwitting object-reading happened when Dr Soal, an amateur psychic researcher consulted a medium about a friend he thought had been killed. He gave the medium a photograph of his friend, and the medium transmitted 'messages' from beyond the grave, also describing the house the friend had lived in before he died. Dr Soal, as was his practice, took extensive notes of the seance, and had them witnessed.

Three years later Dr Soal found out that his friend was still alive. He visited him and saw that his house was as the medium had described. But Dr Soal's friend had moved into the house a year *after* the seance had taken place.

See also MEDIUMS

Below: *The medium is able to see events and people simply by concentrating on a related object.*

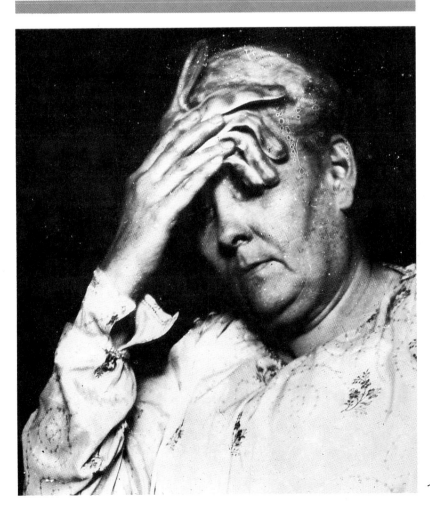

Above: *The oracle at Delphi was enormously influential. The sibyl would deliver her enigmatic messages while in a mediumistic trance.*

ORACLES

The gods know the future, but they either cannot or will not reveal it to humankind in a simple, direct fashion. Ways can be devised, however, of addressing questions to the gods in such a form that they receive answers. This ancient human belief has led to a variety of forms of divination, of which one of the best-known is the oracle. In the oracular practices of ancient Greece a temple was built at a place associated with a particular god — Apollo being the most popular for the purpose — and tended by priests or priestesses dedicated to the cult. Questions would be put to the god by individuals or by the representatives of communities or states and the reply would come through the voice of a man or woman in a state of mediumistic TRANCE or POSSESSION. The replies were frequently enigmatic, ambiguous or simply baffling to the ordinary inquirer and had to be interpreted by the priesthood, which demanded substantial payment for the service provided.

By far the most famous oracle of the ancient world was the one at Delphi, where the medium was known as the sibyl. Because states as well as private individuals took their problems to Delphi the priesthood there enjoyed considerable political influence.

An important rival to Delphi was the oracle dedicated to Zeus at Dodona in a remote mountainous region of western Greece. At Dodona the inquirers scratched their questions on thin pieces of lead, which were then rolled up so that they could not be read by human eyes. Hundreds of these lead strips survive and the questions inscribed on them provide us with a fascinating picture of the preoccupations of men and women in the ancient world.

When the centre of ancient Greek power and wealth moved from mainland Greece itself to Asia Minor new oracles sprang up there, especially along the western coast of what is now Turkey. Chief of these were Didyma and Claros, both dedicated to Apollo. It was perhaps because of their political influence that the Romans destroyed some of the Greek oracles, but the pagan Romans themselves consulted them and oracles survived in the classical world until Christianity put an end to them.

Although the oracle is associated with the ancient classical world, essentially similar beliefs and practices are found in many other cultures: among African witch-doctors, Asiatic shamans and voodoo priests, even in the Western cult of SPIRITUALISM, wherever men or women go into a TRANCE state in order to be possessed by Gods or spirits.

See also DIVINATION, SPIRITUALISM, POSSESSION, TRANCE

OUIJA BOARDS

The ouija board is a device for communicating with the dead. The board itself is an oblong, with the letters of the alphabet in a crescent shape along one side. Messages are spelt out by the people present placing an index finger on a smaller board with a pointer, mounted on tiny wheels — this then moves to the various letters. The fingers are intended to be a focus of spirit power; the small board moves with no conscious effort on the part of the participants.

'Ouija' derives from the French and German words for yes — presumably as the answer to the question often posed at seances, 'Is anybody there?'

It is generally acknowledged that a ouija board should only be used by serious researchers, preferably with a medium present, because the fact that forces (whatever they might be) are conjured up has been shown to be true. Mediums say that there are mischievous or evil spirits always clustered ready to manifest themselves where possible. The function of a spirit guide, for instance, is to 'vet' all spirits who wish to communicate through a medium, so that he or she is protected.

However, many people improvise a ouija board as a game. Letters are cut out of paper and arranged on an ordinary table, and a glass is used instead of a pointer board to spell out the message. Where there is no protection from 'evil forces' (which might simply be misdirected psychic energy from one or more of the 'players') extremely frightening things can occur. Sinister messages can be spelt out, purporting to come from the devil. As if to prove that no one person is purposely pushing the glass, tales have been told of all removing their fingers except one, and the glass continuing to whizz round in manic fashion — or of the glass jumping up in the air or hurling itself off the table and smashing.

A similar device to the ouija board is the planchette. In this case the pointer has a pencil attached to it, so that when it is moved a message may be written, and therefore preserved.

The big question is whether the communicators are indeed the spirits of dead people, or the unconscious minds of the participants. Sometimes messages have been given — prophetic in form or about facts that the people around the table could not know — that seem to prove they came from beyond the grave. Other sessions produce messages that could just as easily be explained by the other theory — sometimes offering knowledge that a participant has forgotten, but which had remained buried in the subject's subconscious.

Another proven theory is that the messages are, at times, telepathic. On one occasion six Dutch spiritualists received communication from a dead Englishman. None of them had more than a rudimentary grasp of English, but when the spirit spelt out a poem, they took it down word for word. It so happened that it was discovered that a schoolboy who lived over the road, and who intensely longed to join the seances had *that evening* been learning the very

same poem for his English homework.

Whether the ouija board proves survival after death or the power of the subconscious and telepathic connection, it is a useful tool of study.

See also MEDIUMS

Above: *The ouija board allows spirit messages to be received without a medium going into trance.* Below: *Occultists believe we possess a spiritual body which is radiant but formless.*

OUT-OF-BODY EXPERIENCES

Near-death, overwork and even extraordinary happiness have caused out-of-body experiences, when people have found themselves floating near the ceiling while observing dispassionately their own body below.

An out-of-body experience is usually involuntary. From one moment to the next, with no warning, you are suddenly aware of being quite separate from your own physical body, which you can see as if watching a stranger.

This kind of experience is somewhat different from using the ASTRAL BODY to travel. In astral travel you consciously will yourself out of your body, and your second self can be seen as clearly as your real body. An out-of-

body experience is a private experience, undetected by anyone else, and normally takes you by surprise.

Clinically Dead

The most famous and well-documented cases involve people who are close to death, or who have indeed clinically 'died'. There is a curious uniformity about the stories that these people (who have never met each other) tell about their near-death, out-of-body experiences.

Usually they feel they have 'come to', during an operation or similar. The difference is that they find themselves above the scene, hovering near the ceiling and looking down with a sense of detachment. Once conscious again, they are able to describe precisely what went on, and to retell the conversations between the doctors and nurses. Often they are witness to desperate attempts to revive their physical bodies — and even when these attempts meet with failure they rarely care. The stories usually go on to describe what happens when they draw away from the scene and attempt to enter the 'after life'. The stories always end, of course, with them returning to their bodies — usually unwillingly.

This happy detachment is often used to add weight to the theory that the spirit survives after death, and in an elated, happy state.

Other Stressful Situations

But these positive feelings, and the detached regard of the physical body are common to all out-of-body experiences. Most, like the near-death experiences, happen at a time of stress.

One writer describes how he worked through each night for a week to complete an impossible working schedule. 'I kept myself awake with amphetamines, bought over the counter in the days before they were known to be harmful. Suddenly I found myself floating on the ceiling, looking down at myself hunched over the typewriter. I saw myself continuing to type, and I remember thinking how tired I looked. It was just a passing thought — I felt completely uninvolved with that man down there. I also remember feeling alert and alive — better than I had felt for weeks. Unfortunately the experience didn't last long. I was soon back in my heavy, tired, overstressed physical body.'

Even very happy experiences, of course, can be stressful. One woman remembers soaring out of her body when

'I had just become engaged and I cannot remember any other time of feeling such pure happiness'.

But some people do have out-of-body experiences when in quite normal frames of mind, or simply when in a very relaxed state between sleeping and waking.

Parasomatic and Asomatic Experiences

There are two distinct kinds of out-of-body experiences — 'parasomatic', which means apparently inhabiting a

get in touch with them, they had over 400 replies, after their appeal had had minimum coverage.

The curious thing that all the cases had in common was that the subject often watched his or her waking self continuing as usual. Like the writer who continued writing, a dentist saw himself extracting a tooth, while others watched themselves driving cars or motorbikes, or performing on stage. Rather than being aware of the two bodies simultaneously, they were only conscious of experiencing the out-of-body state, yet their performance in their physical bodies seemed unaffected.

Few people were nervous or afraid in the out-of-body state. Most felt entirely natural and at home, or even better than normal. Perceptions were usually brighter and more vivid than normal and the feeling of well-being was extremely common.

As one man said, 'The escaped me felt absolutely wonderful, very light and full of the most wonderful vitality, in fact more well than I have ever felt before or since.'

Some subjects find that their senses are heightened: 'I wondered, as I saw my physical body in the bed "Is my hearing acute without ears?" and I approached a patient who was asleep and listened to her breathing. I could hear it extremely clearly. I thought, "My sight is acutely clear too".'

Sometimes while in this state people are able to travel, often to great distances — and see and hear things they could not otherwise know. One woman wrote about finding a friend of hers sleeping in a strange bedroom, and was able to describe the room exactly. Her friend, who had stayed at the house of a relative because of a crisis was amazed and mystified at the detailed description.

It is hard to find explanations for these experiences. Little research has been done into the brain waves of those who can leave their bodies at will while they are 'travelling', but it is research such as this that will help us to understand the phenomenon.

For most people, these out-of-body experiences are quite involuntary and happen only once in a lifetime. But the memories they carry of the happenings are so clear and pleasurable, that many long for them to happen again, or to be able to reproduce the experiences at will, and may experiment with astral travel.

See also ASTRAL BODY

body identical to your own, down to the very same clothes, and 'asomatic', in which you see, hear and experience without a body. One person who experienced this second state described it as feeling as if he were a pin-point of presence. Others say it is like looking at yourself 'from nothing', but this is in no way an unpleasant experience.

Out-of-body experiences seem to be fairly common. When the Institute for Psychophysical Research appealed for people who had had this experience to

Left: *The astral body can spontaneously leave the physical body during sleep or trauma — and leaves forever after death.*

PALMISTRY

The Life Line expresses vitality, the Head Line intellect, The Heart Line emotional nature. The lines on the left hand show what we were born with, and on the right hand, how we have developed — but what if we are left-handed?

All the police forces in the world recognize the truly astonishing fact that every single one of the world's millions of people has a unique set of fingerprints (and toeprints, if it comes to that). This is also true of the human hand — no two are alike, and the recognition of this has claimed people's attention since the earliest times.

We know that Aristotle, in his *De Coeli et mundi causa* recognized the significance of this. He wrote: 'The lines are not written into the human hands without reason, they come from heavenly influences and man's own individuality.'

History shows us the subject was highly regarded in ancient times in India, Tibet, China, Persia and in Egypt, but it reached its highest point of development in Greece. There are, today, some palmists active in the West, many of them gypsies, but the art is most commonly practised in the Orient, notably among the Indians and Chinese.

Palmistry — or chiromancy, as it is also called — was often closely associated with astrology in its earliest days and this may have accounted for the hostility displayed towards it by the Church, but when the Templars returned from the Crusades, they brought back with them a belief in hand reading, and by the time of the Renaissance there was tremendous interest in it all over Europe.

There are three areas in which palmists interest themselves: medical palmistry, palmistry outlining the character, and the prediction of the future from studying the past and present manifest in the hands. There may be some antagonism between the practitioners of the separate disciplines; there is, however, a general agreement on the names given to the principal lines and mounts of the hand, even if interpretations differ. In addition, there is a general consensus that both hands merit study, for the left hand represents what we are born with, while the right hand shows how we have developed our gifts or weaknesses —

there seems to be some doubt as to whether someone naturally left-handed should have the readings reversed.

Some palms display a fine criss-cross of lines, with stars and crosses at various points, while others are relatively smooth with only a few lines defined. The fact that most people, regardless of being left- or right-handed, have more lines in their left than in their right hands shows that sheer movement of the hands does not account for the lines on the palm. Yet even among sparsely lined hands certain lines are almost invariably found. They are the Life Line, the Head Line and the Heart Line. Other lines to be looked for include the Line of Fate or Destiny, the Girdle of Venus, and the Travel Lines.

The most commonly misunderstood line is the Life Line. Its length does not reveal how long the owner is likely to live but rather it expresses a person's vitality — a long, vigorous line may occur in someone whose life ends abruptly, while short or broken life lines may sometimes be found in people of great longevity.

The Head Line indicates intellectual abilities, and according to its degree of sloping the owner tends to be practical and direct or idealistic and subtle — a wavering line indicates wavering thoughts, and cuts and islands on the

Below: The mounts mean different things: Venus is sensuality; Jupiter ambition; Saturn scepticism; Apollo art and imagination; Mercury finance; Mars aggression; Moon clairvoyance.

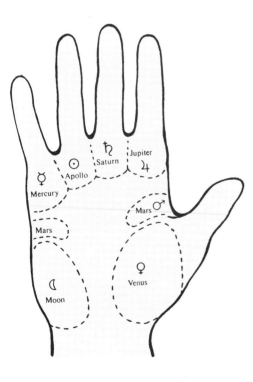

or more sensitive types of people.

Apart from the lines on the palm, chiromancers take many other factors into consideration in their readings — the very shape, appearance, texture and temperature of the hand all mean something to the experienced palmist. There are palmists who can learn a great deal by studying only the fingernails, or by observing the fingers and thumbs, their relative length and shape. There is, in folklore at least, such a thing as a 'murderer's thumb', one which is, typically, large and bent outward and backward. And every hand is also divided into regions or mounts. The names of these, such as the Mount of Venus and the Mount of Apollo, bear witness to the old links with astrology, and a strong development of any one mount will show an innate drive towards the characteristics peculiar to it, so that a fleshy Mount of Saturn reveals a sceptical, down-to-earth nature.

Medical Palmistry

This form of palmistry can claim a distinguished history, but is still regarded today with suspicion among most practitioners of orthodox medicine. Nonetheless it does not seem so far-fetched that the malfunction of one part of the body should show itself in the hand — anyone with a knowledge of acupuncture will know that the site of trouble is not necessarily that which the acupuncturist will treat directly.

One example of how medical palmistry operates is that when there is a cross-bar cutting the Life Line and terminating in a split, island or break in the Heart Line below the Finger of Apollo, then heart disease is indicated. Palpitations are shown by a row of dots along the Heart Line, and the Mount of Apollo will bear many fine, vertical lines.

There are so many charlatans posing as palmists that the art/science of palmistry has, of late, had a bad name in the West, yet the conviction persists that our hands can tell a story to those able to interpret them.

Whether we are consulting a medical palmist, or going to learn more about ourselves and our natures, or, most common among half-believers, hoping to learn what the future has in store, we are asserting a certain faith that the hand is the person in little. In that belief we are joined by Aristotle, Plato, Virgil, Julius Ceasar, the Emperor Augustus, Galen, Paracelsus — even Savonarola — so we are in excellent company.

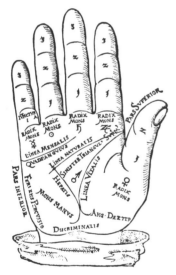

line suggest an incapacity for sustained concentration.

The Heart Line tells of a person's emotional nature and it is important to assess it in relation to the Head Line, for the correlation between the two is most revealing.

The Line of Fate or destiny runs vertically up the hand and is the most irregular of the lines. It is not always to be found in every hand, for it seems to imply a degree of self-awareness and is best marked in reflective, introverted

Left: Palmistry is an old science, stretching back at least as far as 500 BC. Below: The lines are examined for direction, depth, length and interference from crosshatching.

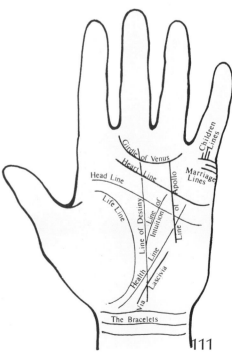

PARAPSYCHOLOGY

Spirits appearing to loved ones at the time of their death, messages from the dead, metal-bending and poltergeists are just some of the paranormal phenomena which are investigated by the Society for Psychical Research. But it is recognized that in research experiments Spiritualists make the best subjects.

Parapsychology is the new, scientific term for what has been known since Victorian times as 'psychical research'. Indeed, the most august body set up to deal specifically with alleged paranormal manifestations is still called the Society for Psychical Research (SPR), although many of its younger and highly qualified members call themselves 'parapsychologists'. At least two of them are engaged in research, funded by ordinary British universities, into the nature of paranormal metal-bending and telepathy. And today there is even a Chair of Parapsychology, created by the Arthur Koestler Foundation, held by Professor Robert Morris at the University of Edinburgh.

The supporters of this strange science include biologists, such as Dr Rupert Sheldrake (called by one respected scientific publication 'The New Darwin'); psychologists such as Dr Carl Sargent of Cambridge University; mathematicians such as David Bohm, physicist Professor John Hasted of London University; the astronomer Professor Archie Roy of Glasgow University and a host of non-academic notables from Steven Spielberg to Prince Charles.

As a young science it seems to have a lot of well-connected friends, but it has a great many more enemies — some, it seems, thriving within the ranks of the SPR itself. The basic problem is that, in order to establish your research next door to your 'straight' colleagues, first you must catch your ghost, poltergeist or whatever — and then put it through its paces to order, just as you might prove that a flame needs oxygen to burn, time and time again.

Establishing constants in parapsychology is a major headache. Some friends of the subject maintain that researchers ought to stop trying to put parapsychology on the same level as 'rat psychology', simply because of the nature of the beast. A rat can be trained to show off your pet rat theories (if suit-ably rewarded); a poltergeist is, by its very definition, mischievous and will do its best to wreck your experiments, as well as your laboratory (but only when there is no one present to see it). So should good old-fashioned psychical research even try to become a science? Should it go to its present lengths to try to mollify the scientific establishment when it seems likely that sceptics will remain sceptics and believers believers?

The SPR was founded on 5 January 1882 by a group of Cambridge scholars, many of whom had belonged to the Cambridge University Ghost Club. Its first and major aims were to conduct experiments into thought transference, or telepathy. Interest in such matters ran high at the time due to the craze for Spiritualism that had swept the USA and Europe from the mid-19th century.

The SPR's greatest corporate work of those early days was to produce a survey, the results of which were published as *Phantasms of the Living* (1886). Many of the cases investigated in its pages concerned 'crisis apparitions' — seeing or hearing hallucinations of persons at the moment of crises in their lives — especially at the moment of death. *Phantasms of the Living* had revealed that of 300 cases of visions of recognized human beings 80 related to people who had died at that time.

Although the SPR had rapidly fallen foul of the Spiritualist movement — any suggestion that telepathy between living beings might account for the alleged doings of 'spirits' being an anathema to them — within a few years the founders were themselves to add to the literature of survival of death.

F W H Myers died in 1901; soon after this several well-connected mediums received fragments of automatic writing (produced by a pen held by an entranced medium) purporting to be messages from the discarnate Myers. In themselves the messages seemed to be mere ramblings, but each concluded with the name of another medium whose automatic writing held the next clue to the puzzle — a highly literate, and apparently brilliantly conceived, jigsaw emerged, bearing the distinct characteristics of the living Myers.

Gradually, as the founder members of the SPR died, the number and complexity of the scripts grew. Mediums in Europe, the USA and India were drawn into the network. Often they had no idea what their individual messages meant; they were typically studded with classi-

Above: *F W H Myers, one of the founders of the Society for Psychical Research; he added to its records, through mediums, after his death.*

cal allusions and snatches of obscure poetry. But together they make arguably the most persuasive case for a life after death. Of course these 'cross correspondences' have been ascribed to unconscious telepathy between the mediums — or to downright collusion. But more than 3000 scripts were produced by a changing cast over more than 30 years; few frauds, conscious or not, are so dedicated.

While the SPR's archives were growing from beyond the grave its living members threw themselves into an intensive programme of research into the nature of mediumship, pioneering the use of modern equipment such as infrared cameras to detect fraud in the seance room. Mediums frequently obliged by producing genuine physical phenomena one minute and crude frauds the next. This set the pattern for all psychical research and persists in its new incarnation as parapsychology.

Phenomena previously only connected with mediums — such as the levitation or other inexplicable behaviour of inanimate objects — became the subjects of an experimental free for all. Psychokinesis (PK), the results of mind over matter, suddenly owed nothing to the work of invisible spirits and everything to unconscious forces. In the USSR in the 1950s and 1960s Nina Kulagina caused scissors to hop and snap in the air as she concentrated on them. This was filmed, just for the record at the time, but then everyone knows about special effects . . .

The President of the SPR from 1945 to 1946, electrical engineer G N M Tyrrell, designed a machine for testing ESP (extrasensory perception) using a sequence of lights in boxes, and producing an automatic trace recording some very impressive results.

The Displacement Effect
In the USA J B Rhine began to develop his famous telepathy experiments using a system of describing specially designed (Xener) cards that were out of the subject's view. SPR members Dr S G Soal, Mrs K M Goldney and Basil Shackleton also conducted experiments into telepathy and came across the bizarre phenomenon known as the 'displacement effect'. That is the prediction of a card *before* it was selected — by random number tables — as target. Unfortunately years later the Soal-Goldney results were discovered to be dubious.

The present author took part in a telepathy experiment at Cambridge University, under the control of Dr Carl Sargent, in 1981, with remarkable results. Yet the experiment was deemed a failure, because it 'only' proved the displacement effect: swaddled in a form of subdued sensory deprivation known as the Ganzfeld, the subject describes anything and everything that comes into his or her mind for the duration of the experiment. Meanwhile in another room a randomly selected set of four different picture postcards is given to the 'sender'. Of course the sender takes only one and concentrates on 'sending' mental images of it to the subject, snug in the cocoon of dim red light and soft white noise. After half an hour the subject comes back to a normal state of consciousness and matches all postcards in a duplicate set to individual comments made during the 'stream of consciousness'. This can be astonishingly accurate: 'I see a purple fish . . . frolicking' is obviously matched with a postcard of a cartoon dolphin, bright purple. In this case I realized I had 'homed in' time and time again on one particular card. I had described it in detail, 'seen' it vividly in my mind. Yet it was not the target picture, the one that was being so feverishly 'sent' to my mind. The one I described faultlessly had remained in its envelope; nobody knew what it was, nobody saw it or sent it. It wasn't the target picture, so the experiment was recorded as a failure.

This apparent delinquent wandering of the unconscious has provided some of the most exciting parapsychological experiments of recent times — the 'remote viewing' tests of California's Stanford Research Institute (SRI). Russell Targ and Harold Puthoff of SRI began in the mid-1970s, using psychic Ingo Swann and retired police commissioner Pat Price as subjects. They were secretly set a possible nine target locations, which were noted down and locked in a safe shortly before the experiment began. One of them was chosen at random; Puthoff and another researcher set off for that location and wandered around it, talking about its peculiarities and generally soaking up the scene. With astonishing accuracy, Swann and Price described the locations.

The late Dr Kit Pedler took part in one of the remote viewing experiments for his British television series *Mind Over Matter*. Subject Hella Hammid spoke and drew her mental impressions, while Pedler and another researcher wandered around the target site. Yet

Above: *Harry Price, the famous ghost-hunter, one of the first to bring science to bear on the paranormal.*

Above: *Telepathy is a power that has been exhaustively investigated by parapsychologists, who are little closer to understanding how it works.*

Hammid described in detail — unmistakably — one of the *other* potential sites that had been on the list. Pedler said he thought the displacement effect just as exciting in its own way as getting a string of 'direct hits'. Targ and Puthoff maintained that remote viewing is 'probably a latent and widely distributed perceptual ability'. For discovering this remarkable human ability these two scientists have been remorselessly pilloried by 'straight' scientists and parapsychologists alike. Their experimental protocol has been repeatedly tightened. Their findings seem, in the light of the quality and quantity of the evidence accrued, to prove irrefutably that the phenomenon exists.

Spiritualists as Subjects

There is also the 'heads I win, tails you lose' factor of 'the experimenter effect'. This is demonstrated when one researcher, using precisely similar experimental protocol to another, gets perhaps only a 'just above chance' result, while the next — because of that person's enthusiasm and belief that anything might happen — gets wildly significant results, way above chance. Of course sceptics pounce on such results — to their minds a believer will go to any lengths to prove the point (including fraud), so what else can one expect? Whereas an objective researcher will get much more negative results, presumably because the phenomenon being investigated just doesn't exist. But one has only to take part in a metal-bending party thrown by tremendous enthusiasts, and

a mere novice can cause cutlery to twist into figures of eight. Julian Isaacs, the British-born investigator into paranormal metal bending — himself exuding a Geller-like charisma — firmly believes that only those who crash the 'boggle threshold' will get spectacular results. You get what you believe. He has also discovered that he personally gets the best results for any of his experiments (including those into *teleportation* of objects) if he uses Spiritualists for his subjects.

One of the most positive aspects concerning Spiritualists and parapsychology, is their complete disregard of criticism. In the 25 years since its inception in Rollo, Missouri, the Society for Research into Rapport and Telekinesis (SORRAT) has produced phenomena — on film and in front of many investigators — that border on the miraculous. Spiritualists all, the original group of about 20 discovered that simply by meeting regularly, sitting around in a lighthearted manner and believing something would happen — it did. Tables, toys, hats and books levitated; raps thundered up and down walls, furniture 'walked'. Then J B Rhine's PK specialist William Cox became involved and decided to try to 'trap' the phenomena. He constructed a 'minilab' — essentially an upturned aquarium with a sealed bottom, containing several objects for the PK agent — whatever or whoever it is — to play with. A home movie camera went into action if there was any movement of objects inside the minilab. Since 1977 when the first films were shown extensively to selected audiences (including the SPR), 'Cox's box' has become the source of vicious controversy. The films show such phenomena as packs of Xener cards sorting themselves into suits, pens writing by themselves, spontaneous combustion of objects and rubber rings linking and unlinking — then jumping through the glass wall of the minilab *between frames* of the film. As one eminent scientist said 'If it is a fraud then it's not very good. I've seen better special effects on a small budget. If it's not a fraud we've just witnessed the most significant film ever made.' The SORRAT minilab experiments continue.

Interestingly enough, all the phenomena investigated by parapsychologists have been recorded in Victorian seance parlours. The only thing that has changed is the climate of belief — spirits were responsible yesterday, the unconscious is today.

PATH SYMBOLISM

It is common for human life to be likened to a journey, a description of the quest for spiritual salvation. The Path, Road, or Way are frequently used symbols that everyone is familiar with. Phrases like 'the straight and narrow', 'the steep thorny way to heaven', 'to fall by the wayside' need no explanation. The path a person chooses to follow is as important as being aware of the danger of wrong turnings. The place where two paths meet has always been held to have great power and significance and to be a popular site for black magic rites.

The 22 paths of modern western occultism correspond to the 22 characters of the Hebrew alphabet and the 22 major trumps of the Tarot pack. Depicted as lines running from one safira to another on the cabalistic Tree of Life, each path belongs to one of the Tarot trumps whose symbolism is the key to its nature. For example the Day of Judgment is the path taken by those aspiring to a higher life, the path of the Sun is illuminated by true intelligence, and the Falling Tower warns of following false teachings. The path of the Fool is the way of the Holy Madman or man as God.

PENTAGRAM

The pentagram or five-pointed star is a symbol of supreme importance in MAGIC. The number 5 itself has considerable symbolic significance, representing among other things the five human senses and the human figure itself, the one upward-pointing arm representing the head and spirit and the four others the limbs. For that reason the pentagram must normally be drawn or held with a single upward point. The reversed pentagram is a symbol of evil; the magicians of the Order of the Golden Dawn, for example, used it only if it was absolutely necessary to converse with spirits of an evil nature.

In its upright form the pentagram is typically inscribed by magicians around the rim of a magic circle in order to keep evil spirits at bay, or it is worn on their robes or carried in the hand.

The magicians of the Golden Dawn had a 'Lesser Ritual of the Pentagram' involving an INCANTATION and the drawing of an imagined pentagram on the body with a steel dagger, and an extremely complicated 'Supreme Invoking Ritual of the Pentagram'. Similar rituals would certainly be found in all magical orders and among occultists.

See also MAGIC, BLACK MAGIC

PHALLIC SYMBOLISM

When Freud once addressed a group he prepared to smoke, saying, 'You will observe, gentlemen, that I am holding a phallic symbol, but you must not overlook the fact that it is also a cigar.' This is a salutary warning to those who see everything, both in the natural world and in people's works, such as architecture, in terms of sexual symbolism.

Below: *Sexual congress of the gods, and the phallus, were important elements in Tantric religion and art.*

Those who do so, feel that they are in touch with an ancient wisdom, attuned to nature, and point to the multifarious genital symbolism to be found in early societies and in religions. The Bible is replete with phallic symbolism, with allusions to both the male and female reproductive organs and the process of procreation. Puritanical editors have unfortunately frequently bowdlerized the text, but much escaped their attentions.

There is no doubt that ancient people prized symbols of the sexual organs, the fonts of fertility, for their powers to invoke the gods to send a similar fertility to the land. They also felt that coitus was a mysterious quasi-religious act, and this idea can be found running through many religions worldwide, principally in early times, although the belief is still very much alive in India. Hindus set up lingams and yonis in their temples, representations of the male and female organs, and Tantrism exalts the deities Shiva and Shakti, whose sexual congress keeps the cosmos in being.

Today, images of the phallus and vulva are, for the most part, debased, whereas once they were an integral part of society. On very old Christian churches there can still be seen carvings of a woman displaying her sexual organs, the sheila-na-gig; these are vestiges of an earlier recognition of the significance of human sexuality and fertility.

MRS PIPER

Mrs Piper (1857–1950) became a medium at the age of 27 when she went to consult a healer about her health. With no warning she went into a trance and produced her first example of automatic writing.

From then on this young American woman turned to mediumship full time and gave many hundreds of sittings. Like most famous mediums she was also intensively studied by psychical researchers who were agreed that her apparent communications from the dead were very remarkable. One young man, George Pellew (who had sat with Mrs Piper on one occasion, using a pseudonym), became her 'control' for a time — just weeks after he died. During the period that he communicated through her at sittings she saw numerous people. Without fail Pellew recognized those people he had known in his lifetime and mentioned things he could only have known as their friend.

But over the years many people from the 'other side' communicated through Mrs Piper — from the anonymous 'mighty dead' to Richard Hodgson, who had been a member of the British Society for Psychical Research, and, when alive, had taken charge of the investigations into Mrs Piper. What disturbed researchers was that whatever the earthly calling of the dead people who 'controlled' Mrs Piper, they showed inexplicable ignorance about matters that, when alive, they would have known about. More than that, they shared Mrs Piper's feminine fascination with clothes and hats. This led some researchers to believe that, quite unconsciously, Mrs Piper was 'creating' her spirit communicators, and that the knowledge they purported to impart was gathered telepathically from her sitters.

Other researchers strongly disagreed. Mrs Piper often gave out information that was quite unknown to the sitters, and only verified later. As was common in those times, psychical researchers also put detectives onto her for some length of time to check that she was not attempting to obtain information before her sittings. Not only that, Mrs Piper's spirit controls showed distinctive personalities. One, a Dr Phinuit, came across as a rather unsavoury character. When he was in charge, Mrs Piper often gave a poor performance — apparently trying to elicit information from the sitters and blustering when any wrong information was given out. But under the control of more steady characters (like George Pellew) the impression was vastly different. He only gave out information that he knew, and rarely made a mistake.

Usually Mrs Piper's controls spoke their messages to the sitters, often using characteristic gestures. But quite often Mrs Piper would communicate the messages through automatic writing — occasionally both at once.

In 1911 Mrs Piper found that she had lost the ability to go into trance. Some say this was because of the methods used by G Stanley Hall, a psychologist who studied her for the American Society for Psychical Research. However, she never lost the ability to transmit messages through her automatic writing.

See also MEDIUMS

Above: *Mrs Piper's personality changed according to who spoke through her.*

PISCES

Pisces, the Two Fishes, the 12th sign of the Zodiac, is a Water sign, ruling those born between 19 February and 20 March.

Pisceans are hopelessly romantic and love to wallow in emotion. They are imaginative, inspired, self-sacrificing, humane and warm-hearted. Peaceful people, they are extremely receptive to other people — sometimes to the point of telepathy. Pisceans may find that they are natural mediums and will be drawn to spiritualism. They are always willing to forgive because they find it easy to understand other people. They are very popular because they are good listeners, enjoy good company, adore gossip and have a happy disposition. They are also intelligent and sensible, with a love of animals.

Yet they can be held back by their dreamy natures. Sometimes they just can't make decisions, can't concentrate and, for all their obvious intelligence, seem dim when it comes to the practicalities of life. Sometimes they're very gullible. Because they are sensitive to the opinions and emotions of other people, their own moods can swing wildly from jubilation to despair, with little in between. They must beware of turning to alcohol or drugs, as they could easily become hooked. In a bad mood, they may be disorganized, hysterical, secretive, untruthful and guilt-ridden. Or they may go on a disastrous spending spree. Anxiety attacks sometimes make them feel unable to cope, occasionally leading to suicidal unhappiness. They need to learn assertiveness and a few practical skills to make the best of their hidden depths of creativity.

Pisceans love to travel, as did the mystics and astronomers of the past. They may become travel writers or sailors, seeking distant places and new ideas. Ruled by Neptune, Pisceans often find work connected with the sea or with liquids. They may be doctors, chemists, or pub managers. The arts also lure these imaginative people, whose creativity sets them apart. Rudolf Nureyev is one Piscean dancer who shows just how expressive a body can be. Literature, religion, philosophy, psychology and music or architecture are all attractive options for versatile Pisceans. Their humanitarian ideals may lead them to devote their lives to helping people, without thought for themselves. The same impulse may guide them towards working with prisoners.

Compatible signs CANCER and SCORPIO contain those who will take great delight in the wildly romantic, pleasure-loving Piscean nature. Those born under the sign of the Two Fishes need constant emotional reassurance and are also very physical. If they cannot find inner strength, they may seek it in a compatible partner on whom they can depend.

Physically Pisceans are often short, with a tendency to overweight, though they are well made. They may have round faces, large brown eyes, snub noses and brown hair.

Although sensuous, Pisceans tend not to look after themselves enough. Trouble spots are feet, liver, circulation and blood clotting mechanisms. They should beware of bunions, corns, gout, cirrhosis of the liver, heart disease, tumours, colds and influenza. Excessive alcohol is particularly dangerous to their weak liver.

See also ASTROLOGY

Below: *Rudolf Nureyev, the great dancer, personifies the Piscean qualities of imagination and the power of artistic interpretation.*

POLTERGEISTS

Accounts of poltergeists or 'noisy ghosts', the literal meaning of the word, can be traced back to the pre-Christian era, and this disturbing behaviour seems to have occurred throughout the centuries. There have been strange bangings, furniture and objects moved or hurled about, sometimes inexplicable smells, and, perhaps most disturbing to the people who are the object of all this turbulence, cases where people are thrown about or tossed in the air.

One of the best authenticated cases of poltergeist activity is that which happened in Enfield, on the outskirts of London. It all began on 31 August 1977 in an ordinary semi-detached council house occupied by a mother in her forties and her four children, then aged between seven and 13 years of age. Strange knockings were heard, furniture was moved and objects flew through the air. The mother was understandably concerned and contacted the council, the local vicar, even a medium and the police — all to no avail.

Finally neighbours rang the Society for Psychical Research and two investigators moved into the house and were eye-witnesses to several types of poltergeist activity.

Another man, a Daily Mirror photographer, Graham Morris, who had visited the house when the story was first reported, returned out of personal interest to try to photograph some of the uncanny events taking place. His best sequence shows bedclothes being whipped off one of the girls, a pillow thrown down, curtains twisted into a tight spiral although the window was shut, and a girl hurled into the air.

Many of the events, in fact, did seem to focus particularly on the young girl and the most bizarre took place on the day of her first period, or menarche, when she and some cushions were observed being whirled up in the air in broad daylight. She also spoke in a deep, rasping voice which was produced by a part of the larynx known as the false vocal chords, or *plica ventricularis*.

The family were eventually rehoused and it appears that the trouble stopped. But the questions did not stop — questions to which various solutions have been put forward. What is almost certain, because of the vast numbers of cases which testify to this, is that poltergeist activity centres on one particular person, very often a child or adolescent, more frequently a girl than a boy, although there are cases where a grown man is involved, such as the 17th-century 'Drummer of Tidworth' case.

Either these individuals are the chosen prey of poltergeists, or spirits of the dead, or else they are, in a sense, themselves the poltergeists — that is, they are the unwitting cause of the things which happen around them.

The latter argument seems to find favour with many modern researchers, who feel that in some way emotional tension, anxiety or suppressed sexual excitement generate the energies which exhibit themselves in the variety of ways we have examined. William Tiller, of America's Stanford University, feels that the human 'somatic system', or physical energy system, has at least one other adjunct, and that extremely powerful magnetic activity given off by disturbed people is picked up by the 'etheric body' and rejected.

If it is right to look to the individual concerned for the source of this disturbing activity, then we also may discover why it is that the phenomenon suddenly ceases. Some change in the emotional or mental state of that individual will mean she or he is no longer producing quantities of energy, and the rappings and levitations will naturally stop. Or is it that a malevolent spirit suddenly gets tired and decides to go 'home'?

Below: *The terrifying Drummer of Tedworth, Wiltshire, an early poltergeist outbreak recorded in 1662.*

See also HAUNTED HOUSES

POSSESSION

The belief that it is possible for the personality to be invaded or 'possessed' by a spirit or demon is found in all human cultures and at all periods of history. Perhaps the best-known example in Western society is the New Testament story in which Jesus drove out a legion of demons from the body of a madman, which then occupied the bodies of a herd of swine.

In a typical instance of demonic possession the victim will go into convulsions, writhing on the ground, frequently speaking or screaming in an unfamiliar voice and uttering obscenities. There are literally thousands of reports of phenomena of this kind, both from tribal societies and from medieval and modern Europe and America. In most, though by no means all, cases the victims are women, and the records of, for example, the SALEM WITCHES or of possession among nuns in French convents in the 16th and 17th centuries suggest that one of the causes of the phenomenon may well be sexual.

However, it is by no means only women who are possessed, possession is quite often induced voluntarily, and it is not always seen as demonic — the possessing spirit may be neutral, or a good spirit, or even a god. In tribal Africa, for example, it is not uncommon for a healer to induce a TRANCE state to become possessed by a spirit in order to remove evil spirits from others. The shamans of central Asia will similarly induce possession through intense ritual drumming in order to heal or to prophesy. In ancient Greece and Rome the priests and priestesses who tended the oracles were believed to be possessed by the gods and goddesses who resided in them and thus to speak with their knowledge of future events. Even in Christian mysticism there is a belief in the possibility of being possessed by God, especially by that aspect of God known as the Holy Ghost.

Possession is also central to mediumship, the medium being temporarily possessed by the spirit of the departed, who uses the medium to communicate with the living.

Apart from shamanism, probably no religion places more emphasis on possession than the voodoo of Haiti and similar religions of the Caribbean and Latin America. In such religions not the priests only but all the initiates will seek to dance their way into a trance state in which they are 'ridden' or possessed by the *loa*, the gods or spirits.

Possession is also an element in MAGIC, where drugs and sex are sometimes used in order to induce it. However, the magician will often try to induce the spirit to appear outside rather than *within* the magician's body.

See also TRANCE

Above: *Possession was supposed to be the result of the devil claiming a man's soul after keeping his part of a Faustian pact.*

PRECOGNITION

Precognition is the alleged ability to foresee future events. It manifests spontaneously in dreams, premonitions, trances as well as through well-known fortune-telling methods such as astrology, palmistry, omens and the summoning of spirits or ghosts. As a psi ability it has been the subject of much scientific investigation.

See also SPONTANEOUS PSI EXPERIENCE

PSI

Psi is the 23rd letter of the Greek alphabet. It is also the umbrella name given to all psychic abilities and phenomena.

Although attempts have been made to classify psi into sub-divisions, such as telepathy, psychokinesis, clairvoyance, etc, these classifications are in many ways arbitrary. While the five ordinary senses of sight, hearing, taste, smell and touch can be considered separately (even though they do inter-relate) because of the different organs of the body involved, the regions of the brain that govern the psi senses are still a mystery. We do not know whether telepathy and clairvoyance are different manifestations of the same sense, or wholly separate.

It is believed that all of us have psi abilities, but because of our lack of understanding of how they work, most people are unable to tap them. It is suggested that people such as Uri GELLER do not have exceptional abilities, but simply a well-developed method of harnessing powers that all of us possess. Credence is given to this by the fact that many people at some time or other have a SPONTANEOUS PSI EXPERIENCE — an 'intuitive' knowledge of something they could not rationally know, a premonitory dream or something similar. These experiences often occur at a time of stress, which suggests that normal inhibitory mechanisms in the brain are temporarily absent.

See also ASTRAL BODY, AUTOMATIC ART, ESP, MIND-OVER-MATTER, SPONTANEOUS PSI EXPERIENCES

Above: *Precognition in the form of clairvoyant flashes is more often concerned with disasters than triumph.*

PSYCHIC SURGERY

Psychic surgery is the performing of operations in a state of trance, through the intervention of spirit doctors.

To Dr Ary Lex — a distinguished surgeon specializing in internal medicine, lecturer at the Surgical Clinic of São Paolo University and author of a standard text book for Brazilian medical students — the scene he was witnessing could only be described as horrific. In a cramped, grubby kitchen a near-blind woman was having the cataracts cut out of her eyes by a man wielding a pair of unsterilized nail scissors. He used no disinfectant, no anaesthetic, and wiped the unorthodox instrument on his sports shirt when he had finished. The operation was over in a matter of seconds. There had been no blood and no sign of discomfort from the fully conscious patient. As Dr Lex was later able to testify, the woman regained her sight. She was cured.

The man responsible for this remarkable feat was José Arigo, the greatest psychic surgeon of all times. From the early 1950s to his death in a car crash in 1971 he was a Brazilian national hero and scarcely a day passed without a newspaper report proclaiming his latest miracle. Desperate people from all over the world flocked to his clinic and a conservative estimate stated that he'd treated half a million people for complaints of every type and seriousness over a five-year period.

José Arigo was made aware of his extraordinary talent quite unexpectedly while paying his respects to a dying woman. Although later he couldn't recall any detail of what had occurred, he suddenly rushed from the room to return immediately with a large knife. Frozen with disbelief and horror, friends and relatives watched transfixed while he ripped off the sheet and plunged the knife into the woman. A few savage twists and he withdrew the knife, inserted his hand, and pulled out a growth the size of a grapefruit. The local doctor was summoned hurriedly. After a careful examination he was able to reassure the terrified onlookers that there was no haemorrhaging and testified that the growth removed was a cancerous uterine tumour. From that moment the woman began a rapid return to health. Within hours the whole town was buzzing with what had happened. A lot of people were intrigued but disbelieving. A few days later Arigo was approached by a man with a huge goitre, asking for help. Using a blunt knife, Arigo made a cut in the skin, popped the goitre out, wiped the opening with a dirty piece of cotton and sent the man on his way. José's life as a psychic surgeon had begun.

Arigo alleged that a German doctor who had died in 1918, Adolphus Fritz, was working through him. During operations he would go into a light trance, speaking with a German accent and often prescribing obsolete medicines that chemists had to make up especially for him. Although he could have been a very rich man, Arigo never accepted payment from anyone for his services. He cured people for whom the medical profession held no hope and in all the years that he practised there was never a single allegation that his unconventional method of treatment caused anyone any harm. But what he was doing was against the law and twice he was jailed for the illegal practice of medicine. On both occasions the judges used every loophole to make his sentences as short as legally possible. Many people, doctors included, testified to the miraculous work he was doing. Arigo himself was never able to explain how he diagnosed or why he knew just where to make an incision. He gave full credit to Jesus and Dr Fritz. The one time he watched a film of himself performing an operation . . . he fainted.

Below: *A woman uses her psychokinetic powers to change the balance of a pair of scales without any mechanical aid.*

PSYCHOKINESIS

Psychokinesis (or PK) is the ability to make objects move or change, using the power of the mind alone.

Records of this kind of activity have been found throughout history, long before it was given this name: previously it was described as magic, witchcraft, or the intervention of gods or ghosts.

But now, as then, people who are able to harness their PK powers have little or no understanding of how they do it, or even if it is truly under their control. In the past, 'physical' MEDIUMS, whose seances were accompanied by the movement of objects — accordians sailing through the air playing tunes, the table rising or tilting — truly believed that this was caused by spirit activity, focused through their mediumistic presence. Nowadays, psychics produce similar phenomena, and are aware that they are causing the phenomena, though are unable to explain or teach their methods.

How many people have this unconscious mind control is not known, but research has thrown a new light on people who believe themselves to be 'lucky' in games of chance. One parapsychologist was intrigued by gamblers who, when they consider themselves to be 'hot', seem to guess the fall of the dice far more often than can be explained away by chance. Experiments were set up to test the resultant hypothesis that they were, in fact, affecting the fall of the dice to suit their call. Experiments showed that in many cases this was true.

Although the volunteers could not explain how they did it — some of them even being unaware that they had done anything at all — it was found that 'preference' or 'good feelings' were a contributory factor. Subjects performed best with dice of a weight and size they 'liked'. Throwing two dice was preferable to throwing one. Whenever a preference was stated the results were consistently better. This adds weight to the theory that psychic phenomena need a 'sympathetic' atmosphere, and that test conditions are not always conducive to successful results.

Other PK experiments have had astonishingly good results: specifically controlling the random generator which causes a series of lamps to light up.

But stories of PK activity are by no means confined to the laboratory. At times of acute stress, such as the moment of death, pictures have leapt from the wall and clocks have stopped. Many poltergeist phenomena are believed to be the result of unconscious PK. And psychokinetic metal-bending, as demonstrated by Uri Geller and Matthew Manning, has caused a copycat spate of similar cases, particularly amongst children who seemed to have tapped a 'knack' that perhaps we all share.

See also MIND-OVER-MATTER, PARAPSYCHOLOGY, POLTER-GEISTS

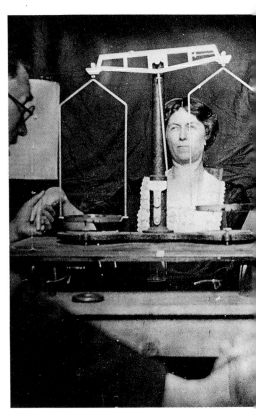

PSYCHOMETRY

Psychometry, or object reading, is the deducing of facts about people or events by the touching of objects connected with them. In the hands of psychically endowed individuals an object becomes the focus for extra-sensory perceptions and often leads to the location of a missing object or person.

See also OBJECT-READING

PYRAMIDS

The mystery of the pyramids, who built them and how, remains one of the great unanswered questions. These vast stone structures have a rectangular base and four triangular sides, which slope inwards, to meet at an apex. The most famous pyramids are to be found in Egypt, though there are also pyramids in Central America.

The explanation put forward by archaeologists, and accepted by most people, is that pyramids are extravagant tombs for the noble dead. That they were *used* as the burial place for pharoahs is undeniable, but whether they were built for the purpose is not quite so clear.

The Pyramid of Cheops, for example, comprising more than two million large blocks of stone, would have taken 600 years to build if the usual theory that men alone, using primitive wooden rollers, transported and constructed the pyramid. But it is not just the fact that the labour and time involved would have been so enormous that has caused people to question further the very existence of the pyramids. The technical expertise needed to level the ground and join the blocks of stone so precisely seem beyond anything we can connect with ancient Egyptian knowledge.

Much more unsettling is the discovering that a meridian running through the pyramid divides continents and oceans into two equal halves, and lies at the centre of gravity of the continents — something the ancient Egyptians could not have known on their own. A similarly extraordinary fact is that the area of the base of the pyramid divided by twice its height gives the value of pi.

In fact the shape and exact dimensions of a pyramid have been shown to have unusual powers in their own right. Researchers insist that unknown, possibly gravitation, forces are still at work in the pyramids. Scale models of pyramids have been shown to have inexplicable powers. Eric McLuhan, and his team of researchers, have carried out countless experiments using the scaled-down measurements of the Pyramid of Gizeh. They have placed eggs and meat inside these mini-pyramids for weeks at a time, and the food has not gone bad. Even stranger, when a razor blade is placed inside it mysteriously sharpens itself.

It is not surprising, then, that in Victorian times, when some of these facts about the pyramids came to light, many people took them to mean that the pyramids were constructed by God, and act as a concrete message to us from him. Thus Pyramidology became, for a time, a fashionable, 'scientific' religion.

Nowadays some people use the pyramids to aid the theory that 'God was an astronaut' — which says that highly developed beings from other planets visited earth thousands of years ago, and were thought by primitive people to be gods. The pyramids, among other things, were built under their guidance, either for their own unknown purposes at the time, or as a message to be unravelled at such a time when people became more sophisticated — as now.

Below: *This view of the Giza plateau shows the Pyramid of Mycerinus, with its subsidiary pyramids in front, Chephren behind and Cheops in the far distance.*

REGRESSION TO PAST LIVES

Under hypnosis a 20th-century Welsh housewife claimed that she had been put to death during the 12th-century Jewish pogrom in York; and a journalist said that she had been an 18th-century Curzon Street prostitute. Are these examples of cryptomnesia — or of regressed personalities?

Those who believe in reincarnation say that it is possible to re-experience past lives under the influence of hypnosis.

Hypnosis, despite continued opposition from parts of the medical establishment, is gaining in respectability as an alternative form of anaesthetic (limbs have been amputated painlessly while the patient was 'under') and in therapy, to eliminate anything from traumatic dumbness to drug addiction. Its use in this field is uncontested by anyone who has benefited from it. But whether it can really take a person back to other lives of long ago is still disputed.

In Britain in the 1970s two hypnotists made names for themselves as experts in regression: Joe Keeton and Arnall Bloxham. Both of them collected impressive libraries of tapes, recording hundreds of sessions in which their subjects spoke of lives as sailors under Nelson, as medieval French princesses, as persecuted Jews in old York and as starving servant girls in Victorian Liverpool. These were not vague romantic tales, but full of detail, even the sort of trivia that fills an average life (the servant girl's craving for 'taties and gravy, that's best of all'). The sailor gave a highly charged account of his last battle, interrupted by his terrible scream when his leg was blown off.

The Persecution of Rachel of York
It was the battery of names and dates given in these sessions that was to give ammunition to both believers and sceptics alike. Bloxham's best subject, a Welsh housewife, told one particular tale that rapidly took a hold on popular imagination, especially after it had featured in a British television programme fronted by the respectable academic Magnus Magnusson. Mrs Evans, under hypnosis, related the sad and often sickening tale of life as a high-ranking Jewess, Rachel, in York in the 1190s. There had been a flourishing Jewish community in

the ancient city up to that point, but growing anti-semitism was rapidly moving towards an all-out pogrom. Naturally Rachel was terrified; the day came when a mob, including armed soldiers, moved in on the Jews and chased those who were not massacred in their own homes towards York Castle. Rachel and her children took refuge in the crypt of a church near the castle and huddled together, hearing the mob closing in on them. Mrs Evans's telling of this appal-

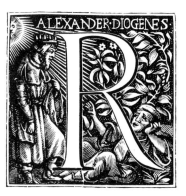

ling story was as vivid as any eye-witness account of atrocity can be. Inevitably the soldiers arrived and put the children to the sword. Then it was her turn. As the television cameras rolled viewers saw Mrs Evans scream and moan and writhe in a way suggestive of both rape and murder.

Very few historians — let alone ordinary Welsh housewives — know details of that dreadful night in York. Magnusson's team took the transcript of Bloxham's tape to local historians and medieval specialists at York University's history department. They had to look up the names and dates given — and discovered them to be entirely accurate. Even ap-

Above: A housewife remembered life as a persecuted Jewess in York, and details were historically accurate.

parently vague terms used by 'Rachel', such as a reference to the 'great gate', were seen to be, in fact, specific. In York one of the city gates is still known as 'Micklegate' — or 'great gate'. Only one puzzle remained; there was no crypt in St Mary's Church. One was discovered, however, during an excavation several weeks after Magnusson's programme had been made. He was so impressed by this that he added a few minutes to the programme to tell viewers the news.

The 18th-Century Prostitute

Once regressed under hypnosis, the memory of your experiences while 'under' remain with you afterwards. One journalist was amazed by her own experience when, writing an article on regression, she allowed herself to be hypnotized. This was her account, written some years later.

'Now where are you?' The hypnotist's gentle voice came quite clearly through the darkness and profound sense of physical comfort that is, for me, hypnosis. I could only respond to her questions without prevarication or taking time to say something for effect. Whatever else it was, my answer was no conscious fabrication.

'In Curzon Street. Where else would I be?' The voice was perky, bright and quite young. As I spoke I distinctly saw in my mind the wheels of a cart and swishing skirts, men with buckled shoes and a rough, dirty roadway entirely unlike today's Curzon Street in London's smart West End.

Whenever it was, it wasn't the 20th century, and whoever 'I' was was sitting on the ground, feeling cheerful. When asked what year it was this young lady sighed deeply with irritation but replied '1794'. Through patient question and answer, Mary, the hypnotist, elicited a few more details. Annie — for this was the character who was speaking through me — was a prostitute, newly arrived in London from Sussex ('because of some trouble with a Man o' God). She lived with the other girls in 'the house on the corner' (clearly she thought Mary could see it as she spoke), a brothel, where petty theft was also a way of life.

Mary persuaded Annie to take an overview of her life — and then a series of progressive images took over from the previous vivid scene.

The thieving had backfired when

Annie had robbed a client ('a grand gentleman') of his silver watch, and had been put in Newgate jail for an indeterminate term. But Annie was bailed out by one of her previous rich clients, Lord [sic] Robert Worsley, on condition that she live a respectable life in a small house he owned up north. It was a dull Georgian house in a tiny Yorkshire village. Describing years of incredible tedium the voice grew weary and lacklustre. Annie had been tamed. Gently, the hypnotist took me through Mary's death and into another life.

Years after that session of hypnotic regression I can still recall some of the images and accompanying emotions. But I have no definite views as to whether I had been describing a real life once lived by the person who is now me in another incarnation, or whether it was an instant creation of the subconscious mind, triggered off by the change in consciousness brought about by hypnosis. Compared to the more famous cases of hypnotic regression, my vague tale of the prostitute Annie seems insubstantial. After all, I only gave one full name — Lord Robert Worsley — and one date. I thought that perhaps, as a northerner, I had thought of the name Worsley because of the York-

each other, and him, during the time when Cathars were hunted down and burned at the stake. Many of them died on the same day. The evidence as given by Dr Guirdham is extremely persuasive; however, further investigation is almost impossible due to the cloak of secrecy the group maintains around themselves. Perhaps old habits die hard.

In India and Pakistan there are recorded cases of young children giving explicit accounts of lives as other people. Children as young as five tell of a life as a grown (and named) man, married and with children, even giving details of the last illness. In some cases it emerges that the named man died as the child was born, and lived only a few villages away. Taken to the scene, a little boy has been known to have rushed up to an elderly widow and exclaim tearfully, 'This is my wife!' Sceptics simply cannot explain it — the open-minded rarely have such difficulty.

In Australia a group of people were regressed hypnotically as an experiment. Many talked of previous lives back in Britain, of little villages, and details of their previous families. This was potentially 'good television'. They were flown to England so that, while the cameras rolled, they could visit the places mentioned.

For a start it was extraordinary that the places actually existed. In some cases the villages were so tiny that they were not even featured on maps of Britain commonly available in Australia. Once there, the subjects took the investigators confidently over the old ground. It really was as familiar to them as the territory back home. One commented on 'a new bridge', green with age. Indeed, old maps showed that in the time he claimed to have lived there was no such bridge. One lady found her old home still standing and led the cameras to an outhouse, now used as a barn. She told how the flooring was an unusual mosaic in her day, and volunteers got to work, scraping away centuries of dirt. There for everyone to see was the beautiful old floor — something the present occupants knew nothing about.

Some believers in reincarnation maintain that we should leave well alone; that we are simply not meant to know who we have been in previous lives — and that the point of being incarnated time and again is to cope anew with fresh problems.

Above and left: *A journalist remembered life as a prostitute, incarcerated in Newgate before an admirer bought her freedom.*

shire Worsleys (the family of the Duchess of Kent). It was only during a casual conversation with a local historian for the Isle of Wight that I found out that one of the island's 'better' familes were also Worsleys. He checked up for me and said that, indeed, there had been a Sir Robert — who had been disinherited for helping a woman of the streets!

Is There an Alternative Explanation?
Sceptics and self-appointed debunkers have tried very hard to find alternative explanations for 'past lives'. One fashionable theory is that of *cryptomnesia*, long-buried knowledge that can surface dramatically under hypnosis. In the case of Mrs Evans and her regressed personality of Rachel it was suggested that a romantic novel had given her every bit of the story; the deception, it was suggested, was unconscious on her part, but it was a rattling good tale told to please Mr Bloxham and the television crew.

Another *cause célèbre* of regression in the 1970s was that of Arthur Guirdham — a Bath-based doctor — and his belief that he was part of a group, reincarnated now, who had once been persecuted Cathars (a medieval French sect). He believed that many of his patients had revealed through their dreams and under hypnosis that they had known

See also REINCARNATION

REINCARNATION

The Hindu and Buddhist theory of reincarnation is that people are reborn in circumstances predetermined by their past lives, and that reincarnation will continue until the soul has achieved purity and perfection.

Physical death is the only certainty a human being can ever rely on and yet people still refuse to accept its inevitability. Their yearning for immortality expresses itself in art, architecture and science, and is beautifully represented in the myth of the phoenix, the legendary Arabian bird who sets fire to itself and rises anew from the ashes every 500 years. Some would say this yearning simply reflects our mortal terror at the annihilation of the ego, others that it is our instinctive perception of the birth–death–rebirth cycle governing the whole universe.

The Central Theory of Hinduism and Buddhism

Reincarnation — the incarnation or embodiment of a soul in a new body after leaving it in physical death — is a widespread belief rooted in the earliest days of our civilization. Accepted by many philosophies and cultures, the theory of reincarnation is central to the teachings of Hinduism and Buddhism. It says that the soul journeying towards purity and perfection is reborn in circumstances predetermined by behaviour in past life. This theory gives an explanation, albeit a harsh one, for the brain damaged baby, the crippled young man, the barren woman. Some receive punishment, some rewards. We are all merely adjusting the balance sheet of our previous lives according to the strict karmic rule of Cause and Effect. Placing the responsibility for our lives entirely in our own hands absolves God from accusations of injustice, cruelty, favouritism or what sometimes looks like spiteful caprice. We and only we weave the pattern of our own destiny.

Although some Hindu sects teach that serious misdeeds can result in a soul being reborn as a plant, insect or animal, it is generally believed that once a soul has evolved to human stage it doesn't regress to a lower life form. There is also the belief that Nirvana, final release from the cycle of reincarnation, can be obtained by the practice of spiritual disciplines that lead to extinction of all desires and individual existence. These disciplines include prayer, meditation, renunciation, asceticism, ritual and strong faith. These highly evolved beings, however, often choose to return to Earth to help others in their evolution towards perfection. Buddhism calls such beings Bodhisattvas and teaches that

Below: Children can be born retaining memories of other lives; child prodigies are said to bring knowledge and talent from earlier existences.

some will continue to reincarnate until all people are saved. For the Tibetans each successive Dalai Lama (their spiritual leader) is a reincarnation of the Bodhisattva Avalokitesvara. When a Dalai Lama dies his soul immediately occupies the body of a boy-child born at the precise moment of his death.

Case Histories

The theory of reincarnation has always fascinated people whatever their religious beliefs and there have been countless mysterious occurrences to keep that fascination alive. The Greek philosopher Empedocles, for example, who lived in the 5th century, recalled existences as a bird, a young girl and a youth. Annie Besant, the Theosophist, knew she'd had two other lives and Aleister Crowley believed himself to be a reincarnation of Eliphas Levi. Contemporary writer, A J Stewart, is so convinced that she is a reincarnation of James IV of Scotland that she has written a vivid description of her life as King in the book *Falcon*. But even more thought-provoking and fascinating, perhaps, are the extraordinary details of past lives given by ordinary people during a form of hypnosis called age-regression. Professor Hemendra Banerjee, director of the department of Parapsychology at Rajasthan University, India, spent many years researching the subject. He dealt with several cases where very young children refused to recognize

the family they were born into, insisting their real parents lived in another village which they were able to describe with astonishing accuracy and in considerable detail.

Another curious and common phenomenon related to reincarnation theory is *déjà vu* (French for 'already seen') in which a person has a sudden overwhelming conviction that they have already encountered, or known well, a person or place in some other existence. There was a case of an illiterate Italian peasant woman from Sicily who, at the age of 72, visited her daughter and factory worker son-in-law when they emigrated to Manchester. This woman had left her village only four times in her life and had never been further than the capital of Italy, Rome. And yet the moment she arrived at the basement flat everything became uncannily familiar. She didn't have to be told the location of a Catholic church with an ancient oak in the adjacent churchyard a good 15 minutes walk away, or the small park tucked behind the new shopping centre. She just knew. Two days after her arrival a vestige of memory took her halfway across the city to a Victorian terraced house in a narrow treeless street. All she could say when questioned by her worried and bewildered daughter was, 'I used to live there, I used to live there.'

And then there is the phenomenon of child prodigies. The famous 'Infant of Lubeck' born in Germany in 1721 was talking a few hours after his birth, knew all the major events of the Bible at the age of one, the whole of the Bible at two, and had mastered world history at three. Fluent in Latin and French, he was sent for by the King of Denmark who wanted to verify for himself the child's remarkable abilities. Another prodigy was Pascal. Aged 11, he worked out a new geometrical system, the following year he published a treatise on acoustics. There are mathematical prodigies who astound the world, solving intricate problems involving astronomical numbers at the speed of a computer and musical geniuses in the tradition of Mozart who was composing at the age of five. For reincarnationists these children have been re-embodied, conserving knowledge from their past lives. They have come back in order to develop their talents further for the benefit of the world.

See also REGRESSION TO PAST LIVES

Above: *Ritual is all-important in magic ceremonies such as this. Years of study are essential to provide the necessary knowledge.*

RITUAL MAGIC

At the highest level of MAGIC the adept believes that it is possible to invoke Spirits or Intelligences or Higher Powers and bring them under the magician's power in order to acquire knowledge and power from them and thus advance still further in the art. The adept may have spent a lifetime in preparation for the ceremonies involved, which are at the centre of what is known as ritual magic, as practised, for example, by Aleister CROWLEY.

The rituals for the summoning of spirits have been described in numerous textbooks of magic over many centuries

and the description that follows is a conflation of many different accounts. It should be remembered, however, that all the elements of the ritual, however fanciful they may seem, have a serious purpose with a perfectly comprehensible psychological basis: to take the magician out of a normal and into an abnormal state of mind and body and to strengthen and focus the power of will, which that magician may have spent years developing and which is the essential instrument of the art.

Before the ceremony begins the adept will spend a number of days in preparation, typically nine. During that time the magician will fast, ritually cleanse the body and be continent in order to build up a store of sexual energy. The adept may also pray to God and receive Holy Communion, not necessarily out of Christian piety but because it is believed that these are acts that give access to power quite irrespective of motives.

Magical 'weapons' will have been obtained and prepared by the magician: certainly a wand, a sword and a dagger and probably several others. Aleister Crowley required also a swastika, crown, crook, spear, scourge, lamp, girdle, apron, sandals, tripod, cup, cross and sickle. Whatever weapons are used they must be 'virgin', i.e. new and unused, and preferably made by the magician. Furthermore they must be specially prepared, often with very elaborate annointments and incantations and at particular times. The wand, for example, should be made of hazel wood, cut at sunrise with the magic knife, and measuring $19\frac{1}{2}$ inches long.

When the time for the ceremony comes the magician will put on robes, normally white, inscribed with appropriate magical symbols (see PENTAGRAM), and while dressing will repeat an INCANTATION. The time will have been chosen carefully in accordance with astrological principles and the place, whether outdoors or indoors will also have been chosen with great care with a view to the appropriate atmosphere and the avoidance of interruptions and distractions.

The magician's first act will almost certainly be the drawing of a magic circle, both to exclude forces from outside it and to concentrate his own power within it. The circle will be drawn with the magic knife and inscribed with symbols and names of power. Accounts vary as to whether the spirit summoned manifests itself inside the circle or in a triangle drawn outside it.

Various scented substances are burned, chosen for their appropriateness to the subject of the ritual, their smoke and perfume adding to the powerful atmosphere of the ritual. The central element of the ritual is the INCANTATION, the recital of words and names of power with which the magician commands the spirit to appear. In an incantation used in the ritual magic of the Order of the Golden Dawn the magician addresses an 'angel', calling out its names and attributes and then saying: 'I invoke Thee, the Terrible and Invisible God Who Dwellest in the void place of the Spirit' and continues in this fashion, in a state of higher and higher excitement, constantly increasing urgency and compelling power in the voice until the 'angel' or spirit appears.

Once the spirit makes an appearance and submits to the will of the magician it will be compelled to answer questions or obey commands. But for whatever purpose it has been summoned it must also, in a final ritual, be dismissed, for no human being can safely leave the protection of the magic circle until the spirit has returned from where it came — and some are reluctant to leave.

RUNES

Runes are the earliest form of Germanic writing, dating back at least to the 3rd century AD and found all over Europe from Russia in the east to England and Scandinavia in the west. Probably originating with the Goths in south-eastern Europe, they seem to be derived from the Greek and Roman alphabets but differ considerably from them.

The 24 letters of the runic alphabet were used mainly for the purpose of giving the spoken language a fixed form, but they probably also had magical associations from the very beginning, being used, for example, for the purpose of divination or as a talisman. A stone from Sweden probably dating to the 7th century AD, bears the runic inscription 'This is the secret meaning of the runes: I hid here power-runes, undisturbed by evil magic. In exile shall he die by means of magic art who destroys this monument.'

The runic alphabet came to England with the Anglo-Saxons and was increased by them to one of 28 and later 33 letters, which remained in use until the Norman conquest. In Sweden on the other hand the runes were still being used in remote districts until quite recent times.

At the beginning of the 20th century German nationalist occultists turned to the runes in their attempts to create or recreate a Germanic occult tradition in opposition to the main European tradition, with its Greco-Roman and oriental roots. These attempts were linked to theories of German or Aryan racial supremacy and as such have more than a superficial connexion with the mystical side of Nazism. The insignia of Himmler's SS was based on the runic form of that letter.

Top: *12th-century runic writings left by the Vikings in the Orkney Islands of Scotland.* Above: *11th-century runic stone from Uppsala in Sweden.*

Below: *The witches' sabbath was a time for lewd cavortings and meetings when ceremonies to conjure evil powers took place.*

SABBATH, WITCHES'

Sabbath, or Sabbat, is the name given to the ritual assembly of a group or coven of witches. Such assemblies commonly took place at night and in the open air, though sometimes also in houses, or even in churches.

Witches were thought to travel to them by magical means. The sabbath was presided over by the Devil and the ceremonies began with ritual worship, including the 'obscene kiss' on the Devil's buttocks, and indecent parodies of Christian ritual. When homage had been duly paid the witches would move

to the business part of the assembly, reporting their evil deeds since the last sabbath, introducing new recruits and sometimes conducting weddings or even baptizing their own children.

The business over, the witches would move on to feasting and to wild dancing which would take them to the point of ecstasy, leading to unrestrained sexual intercourse, both hetero- and homosexual, in the course of which the female witches would have intercourse with the Devil himself.

Such are the main features of the witches' sabbath as described in countless confessions during the period of the great witch hunts in Europe. Some, perhaps most, of these confessions were extracted under torture, but many accused witches confessed willingly, even boastfully, to having taken part in sabbaths of this kind. Typically, one beautiful young woman stated that 'she had more pleasure and happiness in going to the sabbath than to Mass, for the Devil made them believe him to be the true God, and that the joy which the witches had at the sabbath was but the prelude of much greater glory'.

The balance of the evidence seems to suggest that sabbaths did take place, that they were presided over by a man wearing an animal mask and probably also an artificial phallus (which would describe both the frequency of his acts of intercourse and the fact that they are often reported as painful).

Those who attended them were probably from the poorest classes of society in remote country districts, leading lives that were normally deprived, tedious, sexually repressed and without hope of betterment. Cheated, as they saw it, by the promises of Christianity, they sought and occasionally even found some perverse consolation in the frenzy of the sabbath and in the cult of God's antithesis, the Devil.

See also SATANISM, WITCHCRAFT

SACRED MAGIC OF ABRA-MELIN

The Book of the Sacred Magic of Abra-Melin the Mage, is the English title of a magical textbook known from an 18th-century French manuscript, but purporting to have been written in Hebrew in the 15th century.

Claiming to offer a method of achieving power over evil demons via conversation with the adept's guardian angel, it disdains the use of most of the paraphernalia of RITUAL MAGIC recommended by other grimoires or magic textbooks, and instead offers a prolonged and intense process of prayer and concentration. Nonetheless, it had a considerable influence on the British magicians of the Golden Dawn and in particular on MacGregor Mathers, who translated it into English, and on Aleister CROWLEY.

SAGITTARIUS

Sagittarius, the Archer, ninth sign of the Zodiac, is a Fire sign, ruling those born between 22 November and 21 December.

True to their symbol, the Archer on horseback, Sagittarians love most sports. Outdoor activities, especially riding, mountaineering, hunting, flying and of course archery or shooting bring out the best of their character and physique. Competitive but fair, they believe in true sportsmanship. They are idealistic, almost to the point of extremism, pursuing ambition wherever it leads. Above all, they enjoy life whatever the setbacks and they always remain optimistic that their next scheme will finally lead them to fame and fortune. They have no time for dull hard work, preferring to take risks which may prove to be short cuts to success. They never give up hope of winning the jackpot, and gambling often becomes their favourite pastime, a sport that some would be considerably better off without.

Sagittarians are extroverts, with lively, energetic, generous personalities, which make them very popular. They are independent, clever, love travelling and may be religious. They are honest, always speaking their mind. This sometimes means that they are tactless, however. They can also be big-headed, boastful and extravagant, exaggerating their successes beyond belief. Idealism can lead them outside the law, perhaps getting them mixed up in riots and revolution. Sagittarians know a little about a lot of things and love to show off their knowledge. They crave attention and admiration, sometimes trying too hard to impress.

Charitable Sagittarians like to help people, so they make good teachers, and take a great interest in their pupils. They find it very satisfying to see their students succeed and offer them every encouragement, inspiring them with their own enthusiasm. Their interest in religion often leads them to become clergymen. A more general interest in ideals may prompt a study of philosophy, where they could follow in the famous footsteps of Sagittarian philosopher Bertrand Russell. They may also become excellent public speakers, judges or civil servants, bankers or traders. Sagittarian business people are never content with a monotonous job, even if it happens to be well paid. They are always keen to progress to a more challenging position and enjoy recognition for their efforts in terms of promotion or some kind of honour. Where many of them feel most fulfilled, however, is in a job connected with the outdoors. They may be sports professionals or coaches, explorers or travellers. They are clever enough to succeed in their chosen career, provided they concentrate. They must not allow themselves to be distracted by too many risky ventures on the way.

Ambition can vary among Sagittarian personalities. While always strong, it can take the form of the natural wish of a young person to succeed in life, to the burning and ruthless desire to create a vast fortune. A quality which can only help them to succeed is the eternal Sagittarian optimism. Despite innumerable set-backs, they will not easily be deterred from pursuing their goals, and their customary attitude that better luck is around the next corner will always carry them through.

Sagittarians are compatible with those born under ARIES and LEO, two equally lively, energetic signs. Like LEO, Sagittarius has connections with royalty, but unlike the other two signs, Sagittarius is not quite so desperate to be the leader. They may find it difficult to express affection, especially the women, but they are generous, carefree and amusing companions.

Physically, Sagittarians are often tall and athletic, with light brown hair, grey or blue eyes, an aquiline nose and an oval face, with a high, intelligent forehead. Loins, thighs, hips, sciatic nerves and the femur are likely to trouble Sagittarians. They should beware of sports injuries, hip diseases, sciatica and rheumatism.

Above: *Bertrand Russell has the typical face of the Sagittarian: both a high forehead and aquiline nose.*

Above: *The anti-witch hysteria in Salem resulted in an extended trial and the tragic execution of many innocent people.*

SALEM WITCHES

One of the most famous witch hunts of all time occurred in the year 1692 in the small community of Salem Village (now called Danvers) near Salem, Massachusetts. Though a relatively minor affair by the standards of witch-hunting in Europe in the 17th century, it was particularly well recorded and is notorious as an outstanding example of the hysteria and blatant injustice underlying witchcraft persecutions.

The story began in the winter of 1691–2 when a group of young women from the village began to meet regularly in the company of a black female slave called Tituba. Whatever happened at these meetings, two of the younger girls began to show signs of hysterical illness, shrieking and moaning and falling into convulsions.

These symptoms soon began to spread among the other young women and, given the common beliefs of the age, there was an immediate assumption that they had been bewitched. At the end of February the girls began to make accusations, naming Tituba and two other women. Soon afterwards Tituba herself made a 'confession' in which she accused several more people of being witches.

The matter was taken seriously enough for the governor, Sir William Phips, to appoint a special commission of judges to sit in the town of Salem. The accusations henceforward flowed thick and fast. Anyone casting doubt on the proceedings was liable to be accused in his or her turn, although virtually the only 'evidence' produced was the fact that the young women fell into fits whenever the persons they had named were brought near them. The number of accusations grew to as many as 400, more than 200 people were imprisoned, including several of Salem's most worthy and respectable citizens, and at least 19 were executed before the accusations became so wild and implausible that a reaction set in and the governor brought the proceedings to an end.

Suddenly the hysteria was over, the magistrates of Salem Village made a public admission of error, and the death sentence was never again carried out for witchcraft in Colonial America.

Whatever might have been the case elsewhere it seems likely that those who were accused in the Salem witchcraft trials, with the possible exception of Tituba, were entirely innocent. Whether the girls themselves were suffering genuinely from some kind of hysterical illness, or were caught up in a fabrication originally designed as a cover for some unsavoury practices of their own, or were acting out of sheer malevolence will probably never be known for certain.

See also WITCHCRAFT

SATANISM

Satanism is the worship of the Devil as the rival to God or even as the One True God. Witches were commonly accused of worshipping the Devil and performing obscene and sacrilegious rites in his honour. Satanism proper, however, is a perverse intellectual cult, practised by a relatively small number of people, that probably has its origins in the early 19th century.

Intellectually and emotionally satanists are utterly opposed both to the God of Christianity and to the virtues and values that He represents. In particular they loathe such virtues as compassion, self-restraint, humility, purity, all of which, following Nietzsche, they see as the expression of the slave spirit in human beings. To such values they oppose their own: pride, hardness, ruthless self-interest and the extremes of self-expression, particularly in matters of sex, in which they deliberately seek out the most elaborate and even brutal and disgusting perversions.

To symbolize their opposition to the Christian God satanists will practise rituals which deliberately invert or desecrate those of Christianity. Aleister CROWLEY was being particularly inventive when he baptized a toad as Jesus Christ and ritually crucified it, but satanists will commonly use black candles and vestments in their rituals or conduct mass on the body of a naked young woman.

Montague Summers in his *History of Witchcraft and Demonology* quotes a description of a Satanic chapel discovered in the Palazzo Borghese in Rome in 1895, hung with curtains of scarlet and black silk and furnished with an altar, a huge tapestry woven with the figure of Lucifer and all the furnishings required for an elaborate liturgy, 'the chamber being lit by electricity . . . arrayed so as to glare from an enormous eye'.

Not only witches but also Christian heretics and the Knights Templar have in the past been accused of satanic practices, probably falsely, but there is no doubt at all that Satanist groups did and still do exist in many parts of the world.

See also BLACK MAGIC, RITUAL MAGIC, SABBATH, WITCHCRAFT

Above: *Satanist ceremonies include specific violations of Christian beliefs and rituals, such as the trampling of the crucifix.*

SCORPIO

Scorpio, the Scorpion, the eighth sign of the Zodiac is a Water sign, ruling those born between 23 October and 21 November.

Sympathetic, emotional Scorpios form deep and lasting friendships. When they fall in love they do so utterly, with heart and soul. They are ruled by the warlike planet Mars, which spurs them on to action. It gives them great courage and determination as well as impatience. They love work, which seems more of a pastime or a means of self-expression than a chore to them. They are extremely thorough in everything they do, going to great lengths to ensure that they do the best job they possibly can.

Yet too often excessive caution prevents Scorpios from enjoying life to the full. They may become jealous and suspicious of their friends and lovers, with no real cause. Then they can be vengeful, vindictive, treacherous, aggressive and cruel, flying into a rage that has to be seen to be believed. When Scorpios are in such a mood, stay away from them. Boastfulness and over-indulgence in sensual pleasures can also bring them misfortune.

Secrecy and magic surround Scorpios, giving them an alluring aura of mystery, danger and sexuality. Their naturally secretive natures and investigative minds could lead them to spying, like Kim Philby, or detective work, privately or in the police force. They are natural healers, often becoming doctors, surgeons, homeopaths, herbalists or spiritualists. They may also do well as teachers, scientists or sports professionals. The influence of Mars in the sign means that they often make good soldiers.

Scorpios are compatible with those born under CANCER and PISCES.

They are not selfish or materialistic, nor are Scorpios constantly on the defensive, but they can be a bit bossy. They usually have a healthy, positive outlook on life and have an enormous appetite for sex. In fact, they pursue all sensual pleasures energetically. As lovers they are emotional and sometimes jealous, for they give themselves completely to their partners and expect loyalty in return.

Physically Scorpios are often strong, sturdy and possibly a little heavy. They may be shorter than average, with strong legs. Often they have dark brown or black curly hair, with brown eyes and an olive complexion. They may have small pointed chins, with aquiline noses and large nostrils.

The genital organs are ruled by Scorpio, along with pubic and nasal bones, the bladder, colon, prostate gland and haemoglobin. This makes Scorpios prone to ulcers, hernias, nasal catarrh, syphilis, and problems with the womb.

See also ASTROLOGY

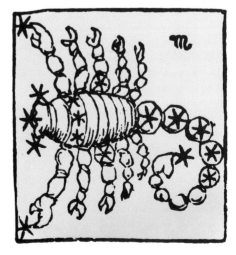

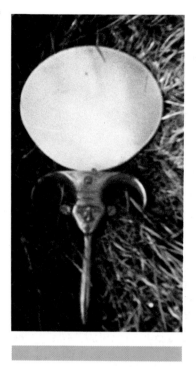

Right: *The Egyptian goddess Hathor is connected with scrying with a mirror.* Above: *George Alexander's modern version of the original mirror of Hathor.*

SCRYING

The word 'scrying' originally meant simply seeing, but it has come to refer to means of seeing the future, especially means that use transparent or reflecting materials: water or other liquids, mirrors and crystals.

Catoptromancy, or mirror-scrying, was used by a wide variety of ancient peoples, including the Aztecs of pre-Columbian America, and by such medieval adepts as Roger Bacon and NOSTRADAMUS. Crystallomancy, or crystal-gazing, is found in an equally wide range of cultures. By the 17th century in Europe it had become the most popular form of scrying among occultists and by the 19th it had become, as it remains today, a popular form of FORTUNE-TELLING.

The crystal used may be a simple sphere of glass, but serious crystal-gazers tend to use spheres made of crystalline rock such as quartz; in the past the greenish or reddish-coloured rock known as beryl was much favoured by scryers rich enough to afford it.

The explanation for the great popularity of the crystal as a means of divination probably lies in its essential simplicity — simplicity, that is, for those who have the psychic or clairvoyant power to see visions in it and to understand the meaning of what they see. Arguably, the crystal is only a simple instrument to assist those who already have the power to 'scry' events that are remote in time or space. Those who had an interest in keeping their divinatory skills exclusive tended to dislike this essential simplicity, and many authorities in the past suggested a variety of accompanying paraphernalia. The crystal should for example be mounted in a special silver frame inscribed with various names of power, or laid on a table meaningfully inscribed with magic words or symbols. Special perfumes should be burned in the room in which the crystal was used. The crystal must be handled ritually and in accordance with particular astrological rules.

More modern and perhaps more reliable authorities seem to agree that all that is required, apart from the necessary psychic powers, is the crystal itself. Looked at with those powers, it will first become foggy and then suddenly clear, to reveal the visions it offers to the clairvoyant's special sight. These may be cloudy shapes whose meanings have to be interpreted or quite clear and unambiguous scenes, as precise as photographic images. If the visions are cloudy, certain rules for interpretation have been established: white, green and blue indicate happy omens; black, red or yellow unhappy or evil ones. Movement upwards means 'yes' to any question that may have been asked.

The crystal offers perhaps the readiest means of discovering what psychic or clairvoyant powers one may have.

See also DIVINATION, FORTUNE-TELLING

SEANCE

A seance is a meeting of people who hope to communicate in some way with the dead. The word is French for 'a sitting'.

The most common kind of seance is led by a medium, through whom spirits speak or manifest paranormal phenomena. In these two cases the medium will go into trance first. Communication can happen without the medium first achieving a trance-like state, however. Sometimes she may simply 'listen' to voices from the spirits, and then repeat the content of them, or the messages may be conveyed through AUTOMATIC WRITING — the medium writing with no conscious control over her hand. Sometimes the table tilts, or is rapped by an unseen presence, indicating 'yes' or 'no' to the questions asked.

Seances, typically, are small scale. The participants sit round a table, and perhaps hold hands. Lighting is dim, and the atmosphere is hushed. Most mediums need a sympathetic audience, and perform less well under research conditions, or in bigger gatherings. Some mediums, such as Doris STOKES, are able to conduct mass seances in large halls, and need no special atmosphere in order to make contact with the dead.

Seances can be conducted without mediums. Usually, when there is no special person acting as focus for spirit messages, a OUIJA BOARD is used. Or letters are arranged round a table, and all participants put one finger on a glass. Messages are spelt out by the glass moving to the appropriate letters.

See also MEDIUMS

Above: *Seances in Victorian times were considered the province of scientists and philosophers as well as dedicated Spiritualists.*

135

SEX AND THE SUPERNATURAL

In the 17th century Incubus often took the blame for hard-to-explain pregnancies, while many cases of possession and ecstatic religious visions would today be diagnosed as psycho-sexual hysteria.

Whether rigidly controlled by hysterical puritanism or elevated to a supernatural force, sex has always played a vital role in religion, magic, mysticism and the occult. The very power of sexual passion, the helplessness of a person caught up in its violent surge, has caused it to be worshipped as a force of both good and evil. In early civilizations, as well as in so-called primitive societies today, survival — meaning a good harvest, an abundant supply of livestock, and plenty of children — is at the root of all magical and religious fertility rites. Until the 19th century belief in the magical power of sex was the reason why European peasants copulated with their wives in newly sown fields, and in Chinese philosophy the interaction of Yin and Yang, the male and female polarities, is believed to be the harmonizing force of the whole universe. Our own culture also gives sex a spiritual or mystical dimension. As, for example, in the Church of England wedding ceremony when the bridegroom says to the bride, 'With my body I thee worship.'

Sex devils

Looking into folklore we encounter two very powerful sex devils INCUBUS AND SUCCUBUS. Incubus vented his uncontrollable lust on innocent sleeping women, while Succubus enslaved vulnerable men. Popular belief had it that they assumed alluring human shape, often identical to someone the victim knew well. This belief was often extremely convenient. In the 15th century the Bishop Silvanus successfully answered a charge of seducing a pretty young nun by insisted the evil had been committed by an incubus who had taken his form. In the 17th century a high-ranking noble woman gave birth to a child during her spouse's four-year absence from home. A scandal was averted when she publicly announced that her husband had visited and impregnated her in a dream. She was believed — officially, at least. Many unmarried mothers, including a fair

Below: *In the past the power of sex was given a physical form: the incubus ravished innocent women.*

number of nuns, had reason to be grateful to an incubus. Rape by a sex devil saved their reputations, while young men used an incubus to avoid paternity obligations. Ancient civilizations had their sex devils too. There was the Assyrian Lili, a rapacious nymphomaniac who roamed the night searching for men to ravish, the Teutonic Lorelei and the Greek Sirens who lured men to their ruin. Male counterparts were satyrs, fauns and the rutting goat-God Pan.

It is the devil himself, though, who most embodies the fierce power of unbridled sensuality, the animal brutishness of physical lust. These qualities are venerated in black witchcraft where they are worshipped through sexual union with him either in human or animal form. It is alleged that the devil himself flagellates errant witches and is the ringmaster of all their orgies.

Religious Phenomena

The devil was also protagonist of the numerous outbreaks of possession that started in the early 14th century and reached a peak in French convents during the 16th and 17th centuries. In this state — characterized by wild thrashing and arching of the body, uncontroll-able jerking of the limbs and torrid outpourings of filth — virtuous young women would confess to blasphemy, cannibalism and all manner of perverted sexual acts and couplings. To exorcists and investigating Church bodies this clearly orgasmic behaviour was interpreted as evil possession by Lucifer and his demons of an innocent soul. Nowadays such behaviour is seen to be an hysterical manifestation of severe sexual repression. Guazzo, a 17th-century Italian authority on witchcraft seems to have glimpsed this possibility when he observed that possession seemed to 'especially afflict those bound by vows of virginity'. Other religious phenomena have also come under sceptical examination by modern minds as, for example, the visions and voices of St Catherine of Siena. Devout from the time she was a tiny child, Catherine pledged herself to lifelong virginity when she was 12 years old. Guilt at having for a brief time been tempted to take a husband led to her later frequently whipping herself until the blood ran. Her catatonic fits and ecstatic visions, one in which she saw herself betrothed in a solemn ceremony to Christ himself, are now seen as extreme manifestations of hysteria.

SORCERY

Like WITCHCRAFT, sorcery is a term without a standard, universal definition, but perhaps it is best defined as the working of evil by one person against another by magical means or with the help of the Devil.

Accusations of sorcery have been investigated mainly in the contexts of tribal Africa and Polynesia and of the European witch hunts. They have been explained as a reaction to socially unsettled times, as in Europe after the calamity of the Black Death and the agonies of the Reformation and the wars of religion, or as the result of a tendency of the human mind to seek an explanation for misfortune by blaming the active malevolence of another person. A man whose crops did not prosper or whose wife was barren or who had a mysterious ailment would declare that he was the victim of witchcraft or sorcery. The person accused might be a more successful neighbour or, in Africa, a jealous younger wife; in Europe it might well have been an elderly person living in some isolation from the community.

Witch-hunting was conducted at least as much by the mob as by officially constituted courts. Among the former, a common test was that of immersion. The suspected witch was bound and thrown into water. If she sank she was innocent; if she floated she was proved guilty, for witches were supposed to be supernaturally light.

In medieval Europe there was another possible explanation for outbreaks of accusations of witchcraft and sorcery in that for a long period the Inquisition was able to confiscate the possessions of those who were found guilty, and witch-finders were paid by results.

It has been shown that in the German diocese of Bamberg there were on average 100 executions for witchcraft and sorcery every year from 1626 to 1629. In 1630 confiscation of the property of condemned witches was abolished by Imperial Edict. By 1631 the execution rate had fallen to nothing.

See also BLACK MAGIC, WITCH-CRAFT

Above: *Sorcerers believed they could harness considerable powers to wreak evil.*

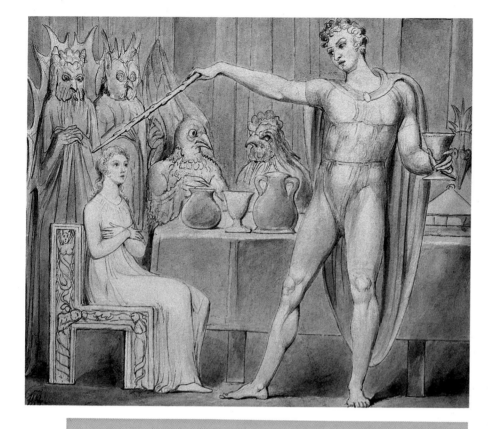

Above: *Magic books contained spells for all purposes; enchanting another could be done by words, rituals or potions. (Comus Holding the Lady Spellbound by William Blake)*

SPELLS

The word spell comes from an old Teutonic word meaning a recital or tale, but by the 16th century it had come to mean a set of words thought to have magical power, a verbal formula like an incantation. It will quite often be in verse, it may use arcane language, and it will sometimes start with a recital of the names of the supernatural powers that the user of the spell is trying to summon. A spell may be seen as the verbal equivalent of a charm or talisman.

SPIRIT GUIDES

The belief that human beings have spirit guides following their progress from birth to the grave is widespread in all cultures. All mediums are in contact with at least one guide, or control, whose task is to protect, counsel and regulate the influx of spirit communications from the other side. But it is not only mediums who are able to establish this sort of relationship. Psychically gifted individuals of all ages make friendships with their spirit guides that are often stronger and more 'real' than any of their other friendships. Child prodigies often insist that their gifts come from an invisible companion.

There are secretaries, factory workers, housewives, who also benefit from the advice of their spirit guides. Jung, the great psychoanalyst and thinker, claimed to have received all his most valuable teaching from several spirit sages with whom he continued to have important conversations for most of his life.

Even the creative workings of the mind are thought by some to be the result of spirit intervention, a supernatural power to enrich human life. Many are the writers and poets who have at times felt this to be true. Blake, for example, claimed that he was able to praise one of his major poems without embarrassment because, 'I dare not pretend to be other than secretary'.

See also MEDIUMS

SPIRIT PHOTOGRAPHY

Since there have been cameras people have tried to capture and preserve the images of ghosts or spirits on film. Unfortunately these elusive beings rarely leave their trace on conventional film, and few photographs stand up to testing.

All the photographers who made their names in the late 19th/early 20th centuries by photographing spirits were eventually exposed as fakes. Usually the negatives had been tampered with in such a way as to enhance the ghost-like effect. That all the photographs were fraudulent has never been suggested, but like some mediums, these photographers seemed to feel the need to make their results more dramatic.

Some photographs of ectoplasmic outpourings have been verified as exact and untampered with, but these are considered to be distinct from actual spirit photographs. Some amateur photographers have captured inexplicable images on film that may or may not be spirits.

There has been a far more bizarre development in a quite different use of film in psychic research. Certain 'photographers' are able to affect film through thought alone, imprinting images telepathically simply by staring at the camera. The most famous example is Ted Serios, who, under the guidance and rigorous test conditions imposed by Dr Jules Eisenbud, produced extraordinary photographic images in ways that no one has yet been able to understand.

SPIRITUALISM

Two little American girls were responsible for the origin of modern spiritualism, which rapidly spread on both sides of the Atlantic to become a religion. Hannen Swaffer, a famous convert, was certain that his newspaper boss, Lord Northcliffe, had survived on the other side.

Spiritualism is a religious cult. It is based on the belief of survival after death, for which Spiritualists accept the proof gathered at seances, where the dead communicate, directly or indirectly, through a medium. It is not specifically Christian (though many Spiritualists are Christian) but in its beliefs it more closely resembles Christianity than any other religion.

That said, the various Spiritualist groups around the world often differ in their beliefs, as there is no single specific creed. Similarly, there is no Spiritualist bible — although there are suggested readings, all of which are messages 'from the other side' received and written by a medium in trance. The most widely read of these is a book called *Spirit Teachings*, automatically written by Rev W Stainton Moses. Almost all Spiritualists, whatever else they may believe, also accept the Seven Principles, received through the medium Emma Hardinge-Britten. These are: the fatherhood of God; the brotherhood of man; the communion of spirits and the ministry of angels; the continuous existence of the human soul; personal responsibility; compensation and retribution hereafter for all the good and evil deeds done on earth; and eternal progress open to every human soul.

But Spiritualism has not always been a religion.

Its modern origins are precisely dated and placed. It started on 31 March 1848 in Hydesville, a small hamlet in New York State. That was when the first documented spirit communication took place, through the mediumship of two little girls Margaretta and Kate Fox. For three months after moving into their new house, the Fox family had been disturbed by noises that kept them awake all night. On 31 March, for the first time, they challenged the origin of the sounds. Mrs Fox made a statement describing what happened.

It was very early when we went to bed on this night — hardly dark. I had been so broken of rest I was almost sick — I had just lain down when it commenced as usual — the children, who slept in the other bed in the room, heard the rapping and tried to make similar sounds by snapping their fingers.

Mrs Fox asked the disembodied noise the ages of her children. He rapped out all seven correctly, then paused and rapped out the age of her child who had died.

I then asked, 'Is this a human being that answers my questions correctly?'

There was no rap.

I asked, 'Is it a spirit? If it is, make two raps.'

Two sounds were given as soon as the request was made.

It was discovered that someone had been murdered in the Fox house, and it was believed that they were communicating with his spirit. But they soon found that it was only through the Fox sisters that communication could be made. Indeed, unusual phenomena accompanied the girls wherever they went, and around them the first Spiritualist circle was formed. Soon after this, 'spirit rapping' became a craze that spread quickly through the United States. Spiritualism was born — but it was not yet a religion, more a scientific enquiry. For it was believed that a method had been discovered for finally verifying whether there was life after death — and what that life was like.

Above: *Mediums like Mrs Piper confirmed belief in Spiritualism.* Below: *Seances began to have religious overtones.*

The Spiritualist movement was introduced to Britain in 1852, and had an instant following. 'Men of Science' were interested because it opened up a new avenue of exploration that was otherwise ignored by conventional science. Many atheists and agnostics were attracted to the movement, because while making no claims for the existence of God, it seemed to offer irrefutable proof for the continuing existence after death.

Spiritualism as a Religion

Slowly, on both sides of the Atlantic, this 'scientific' movement veered towards religion. Those non-religious people who had become involved because of a quest for knowledge remained because there was something emotionally satisfactory as well as intellectually appealing about the movement. Soon Spiritualist meetings began to develop a ritual which included hymn singing and Bible reading, which were supposed to create the right atmosphere to allow good and noble spirits through and chase away any evil spirits.

Evidence from mediums in the form of automatic writing that exalted God brought many people round to the belief that seances were religious experiences or divinely inspired. Indeed, during a sitting of the great medium D D Home, when the people present cheered his abilities, a spirit voice was heard to say, 'You should rather give praise to God!'

Converts

By the 1870s many Spiritualist groups were calling themselves churches, and the movement continued to grow, reaching its peak between the two World Wars.

Many were the people converted to this new religion from the eminent (such as the respected scientist Oliver Lodge), the famous (Sherlock Holmes's creator Sir Arthur Conan Doyle) and the sceptics (investigative reporter Hannen Swaffer of the *People* newspaper). All of them received evidence of the survival of people they had loved or known well. In the case of the reporter, he felt he had received proof of the survival of his deceased boss, Lord Northcliffe. In dramatic proof of his conversion he organized a public Spiritualist meeting, and went on to become very active in the movement.

Since the Second World War the movement has declined somewhat. There seems to be less of a general urge to prove the survival of the personality after death, and physical and mental mediums alike have come in for much criticism. Intensive investigation into mediumship has raised some unanswered questions about the origins of apparent spirit activity. Physical mediums — such as the Fox sisters — who produce raps and other physical phenomena, have largely disappeared, replaced by psychics who believe that the phenomena are under their own mental control. It has been suggested that many mental mediums produce information and ideas from their own subconscious, or gathered by telepathy from their sitters. But there is still a large number of cases that seem to argue for the existence of life after death, and while this positive proof continues to be offered Spiritualism will flourish.

See also MEDIUMS

Right: *Spiritualists allow parapsychologists to investigate spirit phenomena, but they are poles apart in beliefs.*

SPONTANEOUS PSI EXPERIENCES

John Donne's psi experience revealed to him that his child was stillborn; an American woman's that her husband had been poisoned. But not all psi experiences bring bad news — one woman found a stolen car through this phenomenon.

'Psi' is the term used to cover all the various kinds of psychic phenomena. A spontaneous psi experience is, as the name suggests, a psychic happening that occurs without warning or conscious effort.

Spontaneous psi experiences can be divided roughly into two types. Those that involve ESP — that is, purely psychological phenomena usually just experienced by one person, and those that have a physical manifestation, so can be verified by others.

Of the ESP-related phenomena, some kind of clairvoyant knowledge is probably the most common. This can range from foreknowledge of one's own or someone else's death, to pieces of information that are far more mundane. An example of this was told by a woman whose mother had had her new car stolen. That night the daughter dreamed she saw the car in a very specific location. So vivid was the dream that she persuaded her husband to drive her to the spot the next morning to check it out. Indeed, exactly as she had dreamed, the car was there. But the fact that made the dream essentially *clairvoyant* was that there were witnesses to attest that the car had only been left in that spot minutes before the woman arrived with her husband.

Telepathy, Intuition and Dreams
Telepathy is another common example of spontaneous psi experience — usually happening at times of crisis, and connecting the minds of two loved ones.

The stories of people knowing that they 'must' rush home, with a real sense of urgency and panic, and finding that a member of the family is in distress are very common. Slightly less common, but surely an extension of the same telepathic 'reaching out', are instances when the person in distress actually seems to manifest.

One of the best documented of these cases is the experience of John Donne, the 16th-century poet and dean of St

Paul's Cathedral. He was on a diplomatic mission to France while his wife was about to give birth. One evening two friends arrived to see Donne and found him in a dreadful state. He told them, 'I have seen my wife pass twice through this room with her hair hanging about her shoulders and a dead child in her arms.'

Donne's friends, of course, were convinced he had been dreaming, but he knew that his vision was experienced while awake. The next day he sent a messenger to find out how his wife was. The news came back that she was dangerously ill — having delivered a stillborn baby at the exact time that her husband had seen her apparition.

Other spontaneous psi experiences take the form of flashes of intuition, when you just 'know' something to be correct without any dramatic accompanying experiences. One such instance was reported by some staff members of an American hospital during the Second World War. They had the unpleasant

Above: *John Donne had a vision of his wife at exactly the time she gave birth to a stillborn baby.*

141

Above: *William Blake had psi experiences throughout his life, which he expressed in his art.*

showed that the largest proportion (27 per cent) were concerned with crises in the immediate family. The next highest category consisted of non-crisis cases that were nonetheless important, involving the dreamers themselves. Oddly enough, 13 per cent of 'dreams that came true' involved strangers, many of which were about crises, but over half of which concerned things of no great importance.

Moving Objects

The less common kinds of spontaneous psi experiences involve PSYCHO-KINESIS, the moving of objects without using natural means. The best known examples of this kind are poltergeist activity. In the past these 'noisy spirits' were believed to be ghosts or malevolent forces bent on wreaking havoc. Furniture would be moved, ornaments smashed, doors and windows opened and closed and people be hurled across the room. But more recently it has been recognized that in certain cases the poltergeist activity centres around a disturbed adolescent. Nowadays it is believed that it is unharnessed psychic energy unconsciously emanating from the child which causes the phenomena. In these cases the occurrences are truly spontaneous as the child is rarely aware of being the cause of them — and indeed, may be as frightened as anyone by what is happening. Other spontaneous psychokinetic phenomena tend to be 'one-offs'. As with all spontaneous psi experiences they most often occur at a time of stress. The most common example of this sort is a picture of someone falling from the wall, or off a shelf, at the time of death. The question in these cases has been: was the picture caused to fall by the person who died, or by the witness? One theory suggests that the death is communicated to the 'target' by telepathy and, although not registered by the conscious mind, the shock in the recipient activates a psychokinetic response, which causes the picture to fall.

These spontaneous psi experiences are far from uncommon. Most people have had such an experience themselves, or know someone who has. It is for this reason that even rational people are prepared to look at evidence from psychical researchers with an open mind — for all around us strange and inexplicable things are happening every day.

duty of having to tell a young wife, who had just given birth, that her soldier husband had died of a heart attack while serving in the army in France. She immediately replied, 'It wasn't a heart attack, he was poisoned.' Later she said, 'I honestly did not know I was going to say it. It was as if someone else had said it for me. I insisted that they check with Washington. They did and I was right. He had been poisoned. I never knew why they first said it was a heart attack.'

At least half the spontaneous psi experiences reported are precognitive dreams, as with the woman who was guided to the stolen car. Fairly often the details are so clear and numerous that it is almost like a telepathically delivered photograph. Other dreams are less complete, or wrongly interpreted at the time, but with hindsight it can be seen that they too have passed on information that could not have been gathered in the usual way.

One major survey of clairvoyant dreams, which examined 2878 cases,

See also ESP, DREAMS, OUT-OF-BODY EXPERIENCES, PSYCHO-KINESIS, TELEPATHY

STOKES, DORIS

She was punished as a child for reporting that she had seen a ghost; she was reprimanded by her spirit guide for cheating; but despite these early setbacks, Doris Stokes has become one of the most effective mediums working today.

'You're a twin, aren't you love? Your sister — ever such a pretty girl — is here. She says you ought to tell your mother about — who is it? John? George? No, don't tell me . . . They'll say I'm fishing. No it's George and, oh dear, I don't know whether I should say things like this in public but you're not married to him are you . . . anyway, your sister Jean, isn't it, says that she thinks your new green velvet curtains are smashing . . .' Doris Fisher Stokes had just reduced a hardened Fleet Street journalist to tears at a demonstration of her psychic powers given for 200 members of the press. As always, it was the trivial — in this case the curtains — that was the ultimate proof to the 'subject' that Doris wasn't cheating. With a great deal of time and effort she could have done her homework about everyone likely to be present and trotted out an impressive list of names and dates. But no one knew about the curtains, and the journalist involved thought them too trivial to have mentioned to anyone at the meeting. The medium had delivered her message — and it hit the spot. Even to sceptics present it really seemed that she was, as she says, the recipient of messages from beyond the grave. Time and time again Doris has proved her extraordinary powers and continues to do so.

She claims, 'I'm nothing special. Please don't get the wrong impression. I'm just the same as you are.' Certainly there is nothing spooky about this motherly woman, the daughter of a blacksmith. Her very down-to-earth qualities make her the unlikeliest spiritualist medium, but at the same time add enormously to the effect of her work.

She has always been psychic. As a child she was punished for saying that she saw a neighbour walking by the side of a covered stretcher — which carried his dead body. Her mother simply did not believe in Doris's talent, but her father was himself a gifted medium. It was after his death that her own powers began to develop in earnest.

Why Doris Stopped Cheating

She waxes hilarious as she tells the story of her early years. She got mixed up with well-meaning eccentrics and charlatans — one of whom told her to 'keep your feet on the ground to "earth the power".' 'I felt like a human light bulb', she says engagingly. She is also one of the few practising mediums to admit that she has cheated in the past. She knew she had real powers but wanted to maintain a smooth 'performance' and was terrified that her inspiration would dry up, so she arrived for a meeting early and listened to the conversations of the audience and made notes of the names of their loved ones with whom they hoped to make contact. Everything went wrong for Doris: she couldn't find the notes, made a hash of extemporizing and — worst of all — was told by her spirit guide Ramononov to confess publicly then and there that she had cheated. She did, and it was the last time. These days if nothing 'comes through' for a while, she says so.

She is *clairaudient* — that is, she hears rather than sees the dead, although she has seen the departed, including her own father, as solid and normal as when they were alive. It was her dead father who appeared to her during the Second World War to tell her that her husband John, who was feared dead, was 'not with us and on Christmas Day you will have proof of this'. It was on that day that she learnt that John was a prisoner of war and not dead as feared.

It was as a guest on Australian television's Don Lane Show in the 1970s that she first achieved fame. Her 'direct hits' with members of the studio audience ensured that she became a household name in Australia — and very rapidly in New Zealand. In the USA she was visited by a murder victim ('I was a bit annoyed because it was my coffee break, but poor thing, he was keen for the police to find his body . . .). At that point no one even knew that a murder had been committed and the police were understandably sceptical. In the end, however, the body was found, in the boot of a white Rolls Royce as Doris had said, in the place she had described.

In Britain Doris packs them in in huge auditoriums such as London's Dominion theatre. To an observer the atmosphere created by such a gathering of largely grief-stricken people can be very disturbing. But Doris is in herself a calming presence, rock-like in her be-liefs, and quite amazing in the extent of her talent. But like all good mediums she is the first to admit that 'It isn't me. They just come and talk to me and I pass the messages on, that's all. A lot of people think I'm potty. Well I might be, but not about this. This is real.'

At one session for the staff of a magazine on the paranormal, Doris not only unerringly homed in on the girl who had secretly been set up as the test 'target' (at the last minute), but then proceeded to give her extraordinarily detailed information from 'the other side'. She gave family names, some of them unusual, nicknames, details of illnesses suffered by aunts in America (subsequently proved to be correct) and at one point baffled those present (who knew the target very well) by describing a boy of six who claimed to be the girl's son, who was 'well and happy and he forgives you'. The girl burst into tears — it emerged that she had had an abortion six years before, and had known at the time that the aborted child was a boy. She had never mentioned this to any of her colleagues.

Watching Doris cocking her head to catch perhaps indistinct voices from the dead, it seems the most natural thing in the world. To her it is, and her work has brought comfort and belief to a vast, and very grateful, audience.

See also MEDIUMS

STONEHENGE

During Victorian times it was fashionable to drive out to the peaceful Salisbury Plain in the west of England and have a picnic in the shadow of the ruins of a giant stone building. Those of a sentimental nature might then take a hammer and chip off a piece of one of the 162 stone blocks to take away as a souvenir. Fortunately this practice was banned, and Stonehenge, which has survived nearly five millennia, still stands exposed to the elements.

The name derives from the Old English stān, a stone, and one of two words: either 'hencg', a hinge, or 'hen(c)gen', a gallows. Both of these are quite acceptable, for the lintels are hinged onto the upright stones, while early gallows consisted of two uprights with a crossbeam between them. Whichever is the true derivation, we have the evidence that it had an established name before the Norman conquest, something which none of the other great stone circles had.

From the 17th century onwards a persistent fallacy has infiltrated itself into the common consciousness — that Stonehenge was built by the Druids as a temple for sun-worship, and that ritual human sacrifice took place there, most particularly on the slabs known as the Slaughter Stone and the Altar Stone. This idea is entirely contradicted by archaeological evidence, which shows that the great stone structure was built over a long period of time, its beginnings estimated around 3000 BC, the final phase being accomplished between 1550 and 1100 BC, long before the Druids came on the scene.

It is an astonishing piece of work for Stone Age and Bronze Age peoples to have undertaken, not only because the stones were transported over long distances (the bluest ones came from the Preseli Mountains in Wales) but because of the extreme precision of the alignments of the structure. Professor Gerald Hawkins, in his book *Stonehenge Decoded*, makes a fascinating, if flawed, case for Stonehenge being a massive 'Neolithic computer'.

There are, for example, discoveries made by archaeologists that the 56 'Aubrey holes' which encircle Stonehenge's central structure were used in calculations to determine the date of the eclipses of the moon. Since the eclipse is related to a cycle of 18.61 years, three of those cycles, to the nearest whole number, make a total of 56. John Michell has also made some very interesting contributions to the debate, demonstrating

how the outer circle of stones symbolize 'the major dimensions of the earth', including the polar radius and the meridian circumference.

Every age reflects its own concerns in the way it interprets the world around it. When the prevailing spirit of the age expressed itself in religion, Stonehenge was seen as a temple, and there was speculation as to the nature of the rites it witnessed. In our own space age, there is a drive to see Stonehenge as a vast and mysteriously accurate machine, a computer or astronomical observatory. But although it is possible we shall never know the full truth, what is beyond dispute is that this monument has exerted a fascination over thousands of years, and never more so than now.

Left: *Will we ever be able to find out the real truth behind these stones, around which so many myths and theories have grown?*

TAROT

Tarot cards are best known as a fortune-telling device, but they were not conceived or designed for this purpose. Contained in the pictures, symbols and numbers are universal truths, knowledge and wisdom, given a form that transcends language barriers.

They are said to have been first used by the gypsies, though the exact origin of the cards is not known.

There are two main theories about how the Tarot cards came into being, both of which have the quality of legend rather than fact. One is that they originated in Egypt at the time when the temple libraries were being destroyed. Priests devised the cards as a way of recording the sum of all their learning.

To ensure that it would be propagated rather than lost, they gave the pack to a passing gypsy telling him that it could be used for gain in games of chance. They felt that by this means it would be copied and widely used, and although mainly misunderstood, the secrets and knowledge and wisdom would be there.

The second theory is similar. It maintains that the cards were inscribed by the Waldenses, a Christian sect situated on the borders of France and Italy who were persecuted for their unorthodox interpretation of the Bible. It is said that the major arcana was used by its priests as a teaching aid that could not be challenged by enemies of the sect. This theory is given credence by the fact that the oldest surviving set of Tarot cards dates from the 14th century, when pressure against the Waldenses was at its greatest.

There are 78 cards divided into four suits of 14 cards — wands, cups, swords and pentacles, and 22 trump cards called the major arcana.

The four suits represent, among other things, fire, water, air and earth. Each suit has four court cards: king, queen, knight and page. The king stands for the essential self, the queen for the soul; the knight denotes action, and the page symbolizes the physical body.

The pictures on the Tarot cards do not have to be drawn in a standard way, indeed many different versions of the pack exist. However certain symbols are always incorporated, and the concept behind each picture in the major arcana is always the same.

Every single card has a meaning, but when used as a fortune-telling device usually only the 22 cards of the major arcana are used. These are numbered 0–21. Nought is the fool. Each card is rich in symbolism, and entire books have been written about their meaning.

Students of the cards offer their own explanations according to the fall of the cards and whether they are presented the right way up or reversed. They are also intended to stimulate the imagination, or unconscious, of the reader.

See also CARD READING

TAURUS

Taurus, the Bull, the second sign of the Zodiac, is an Earth sign, ruling those born between 21 April and 21 May.

The pull of the earth is the strongest element shaping the Taurean character. Taureans love simple pleasures, enjoying cooking, eating, crafts, gardening and everything to do with the natural world. They are patient, modest, steady, reliable people who are not ambitious, but believe in the benefits of hard work. What they put into the soil of life, they know they can expect to harvest later. They reap the benefits in terms of real wealth and satisfaction, rather than just money. Some have deep faith in religion.

They are not easily disheartened by problems, knowing that methodical perseverance will pay off in the end. They are very generous, kind, honest, protective, good-tempered and loyal. Venus rules Taureans, lifting them from the toils of the earth to the heights of cultural enjoyment from time to time. They are often good singers, musicians, painters or dancers and certainly appreciate these talents in others. Venus also makes them extremely sensitive, so that they follow their hearts, not their heads. They hate disagreements and try to create harmony in every aspect of their lives.

Sometimes, however, a Taurean can be as stubborn as an ox, sticking to conservative ideas and outdated methods of working. When they are in this frame of mind, mere reason and common sense will not prevail. Their love of food and drink can get out of hand, leading to weight and health problems. They may

also sometimes become slow, lazy, selfish, envious and mean with money, lacking the ability to plan ahead.

Taureans excel in agriculture, whether they choose to work with animals or grow crops, as well as any building work, from labouring right through to architecture. Painting and decorating suit them, as does work connected with fashion or jewellery, music, poetry and art. They have wonderful memories and an admirable ability to concentrate, so they do well in business dealings and academic life. Their love of method makes them ideal as administrators, too. Some even manage to combine business with pleasure by working with food and drink as tasters, testers or gourmets.

Compatible with those born under VIRGO and CAPRICORN, Taureans are loyal, reliable friends or lovers. They are attracted to real beauty rather than superficial glamour, and make devoted, humble lovers. They enjoy frequent, uncomplicated sex as well as other sensual pleasures such as good food. When they slip into slow, thoughtful moods all they need is a little encouragement to revive their spirits.

Physically Taureans may slightly resemble the bull that symbolizes them, tending to be sturdy and a little plump, with a thick neck, round head and strong shoulders. They often move slowly and heavily. Dark wavy hair, blue or brown eyes, rosy cheeks and straight teeth are also typically Taurean.

Weak points are the neck, throat, taste buds, thyroid gland, ears, jaw, tonsils, jugular vein, larynx and the back of the head. They should beware of throat infections, goitres, laryngitis, tonsillitis, diphtheria and overweight.

Above: *Margot Fonteyn, in common with other Taureans, loves the arts, and is herself a consummate performer.*

TEA-LEAF READING

Tea-leaf reading is a method of telling fortunes by looking at the pattern formed by the leaves once a cup of tea has been finished.

If it is a dying art, this must be because the quality of tea and the habits of tea-drinkers have changed so much in recent years. Finer leaves are used to speed up brewing time. A strainer is used so that no tea leaves gather in the cup. And more and more nowadays, leaf tea has been replaced by tea-bags.

For a good reading, the 'old-fashioned' large leaf tea should be used.

After drinking the tea, the subject swirls the dregs around three times, and turns the cup upside-down in the saucer. He or she then taps the base of the cup three times. The fortune-teller can then pick up the cup and read the message.

This is one branch of the art of geomancy: the reading of messages according to the fall of certain natural materials, such as earth, sands, pebbles and shells. The theory is that the patterns are not formed by chance. Many correspond to actual objects or recognized symbols, and according to their shapes are able to reveal something about the future.

As in all the fortune-telling arts, it is not just a question of knowing and

Above: *Tea leaves are often read by non-professional mediums, who use this as a focus of their psi powers.*

understanding the symbols. The true clairvoyant uses the leaf-patterns to focus and bring out his or her psychic ability to see into the future.

TELEKINESIS

Telekinesis, an expression of mind over matter, is the movement of solid bodies from one place to the other by mental influence or willpower alone and without any physical intervention. The flinging of furniture or crockery in poltergeist cases, or the flight of a particular object into the hand or mouth, are prime examples of telekinetic activity. The phenomena of objects materializing in closed rooms is called Teleportation or Apportation.

See also MIND-OVER-MATTER, PSYCHOKINESIS

TELEPATHY

Telepathy is the ability to transmit or receive messages between minds without using conventional means. Usually only one of the subjects is aware of the process — and that tends to be the receiver, who sees or hears the other person, or who suddenly has a strong feeling (usually about a crisis) that in retrospect turns out to be telepathically caused. In test situations one subject attempts to send a message to another — though when successes have been claimed it is difficult to judge whether it was the power of the sender, or the ability of the receiver that scored the hit.

Few ordinary people make claims to have successfully sent a message to another. Certainly, in true-life situations telepathic communications seem to result from a burst of very strong emotion that activates whatever part of the brain it is that can send messages. It is almost never consciously done, the anguish of the moment taking up all conscious thought. Perhaps the mere desire to send a message is not a sufficiently strong motivating force.

One woman reported a particularly vivid case of telepathy during the Second World War. Her family received a telegram saying that her brother had been killed in action. She went to her own bedroom to grieve, and when she emerged she said, 'I "saw" my brother coming up the stairs. He said, "Shirley, don't cry. I'm all right," and then when he got to the head of the stairs, he vanished.' The next day another telegram arrived saying that the young man was, in fact, all right. Later he told the family that he didn't know that he had been reported killed, but at that time he had lost his unit, and was in a miserable state. He was thinking about his family and hoping that they could be reassured that he was all right.

Parapsychologists have had good results with telepathy tests, even with unselected volunteers who have had no reason to believe they have particular powers. Tests have had to be developed that rule out the possibility of clairvoyance — the clear seeing of objects or events. A true telepathy test consists only of a thought, idea or picture being sent to another mind, without the visual aid of a picture or concrete object. The problem is that as the subjects are unaware of how they gain their results, the test findings vary from day to day, even with the same person under the same conditions. The other problem is that the desire to exclude other kinds of PSI, and classify each as if it were a totally separate ability, results in tests that are narrow and unexciting — and perhaps actually hampers research if the abilities are more interconnected than researchers would find convenient.

One exciting finding emerging from the telepathy tests so far carried out is that young people perform consistently better than older subjects. This adds weight to the theory that we are each born with a telepathic facility that eventually atrophies through lack of use.

The circumstantial evidence for telepathy is very strong and well-documented — 'crisis' communications suggest that it is a psychic ability with a purpose, but once confined to the laboratory it loses its motivating force, and therefore a lot of its power.

See also ESP, PARAPSYCHOLOGY

Above: *The trance state can be produced in a number of ways: ecstatic dancing is used all over the world.*

TRANCE

A trance is described as a state of suspended consciousness, of hypnosis, catalepsy or ecstasy; a state suggesting that the soul has passed out of the body for a time. Such a state may occur spontaneously or accidentally or may be induced, for example, by drugs or by prolonged rhythmical dancing. In supernatural terms the idea of the body's being temporarily vacated by the soul leads to the idea that it can be temporarily occupied by an external spirit. Such an idea underlies that of the oracle, in which the deity speaks through a priest or priestess, and of the medium, who has the ability to will a trance state in which he or she is possessed by the spirits of the dead. The trance is also central to the spiritual experiences of Yoga, in shamanistic religion, and in voodoo.

See also HYPNOSIS, MAGIC, MEDIUMS

UFOs

Are 'flying saucers' spacecraft from an alien planet or human hallucinations brought about by geophysical situations? And who are the sinister 'Men in Black' reported to have warned off witnesses? Is it significant that the first UFO sighting took place soon after the explosion of the first atom bomb?

The power of the silver screen is indisputably great, but although Stephen Spielberg's 1977 film *Close Encounters of the Third Kind* stimulated enormous public interest in the subject of Unidentified Flying Objects, it would also be true to insist that the film built upon an existing foundation of mass awareness. If the title is intriguing, it might be best to see what a Close Encounter of the First Kind is. A classification drawn up by Jenny Randles and Peter Warrington includes the following categories. Close Encounters of the First Kind (CE1): Any phenomenon causing transient effects on the witness, the environment or both (e.g. time loss, radio interference etc.). CE2: Any phenomenon causing effects similar to those of CE1 but which are semi-permanent and observable by others who did not experience the phenomenon. CE3: Phenomena which have animate entities of some kind in association with them. CE4: Events which cause a witness to suffer temporary or permanent reality distortion or which cause long-lasting change in a witness after the initial event.

This system of classification, and the

Below: The photographer claimed that he talked to nine people from this UFO when it landed.

fact that the United Nations, the US Air Force, the British House of Lords, among other bodies, recognize that there is something worthy of research, argues an established subject of scientific interest. How long has it been in existence?

The First 'Flying Saucers'
The term 'flying saucer' was coined in 1947 after a pilot, Kenneth Arnold, spotted nine discs in the air which were clearly not aircraft. His story received such widespread publicity that the US Air Force set up an investigation, but reported shortly after that Mr Arnold must have been hallucinating.

Looking back earlier than 1947 we find various reports of unexplained objects and lights in the sky, the most striking being one by a Russian painter, Roerich, whose party, while crossing the Himalayas in August 1926, observed a big shining oval which sped through the sky, made a turn of 90° and disappeared behind a mountain peak.

While the USAF was looking into the Kenneth Arnold story, other individuals were also acting upon it. In 1952, not long after the Arnold incident, Desmond Leslie wrote a book, *Flying Saucers Have Landed*, to which was appended an account of a meeting which had taken place between George Adamski and a young fair-haired Venusian in the Californian desert. The book caused a sensation and attracted the attention of Brinsley Le Poer Trench, later to become Lord Clancarty. From the meeting *Flying Saucer Review* was born.

Adamski came to Europe in 1959 and, apart from having an audience with Queen Juliana of the Netherlands, met a Swiss woman, Lou Zinsstag, who was a cousin of Carl Jung. Through her Jung became interested in the subject and published *Flying Saucers, A Modern Myth of Things Seen in the Sky*, although he never agreed to meet Adamski. This may have been as well because Adamski's claims grew ever wilder and he lost all credibility towards the end of his life. Nevertheless, as so often happens his reputation took an upturn after his death and the bizarre stories of his later years were explained away as being false messages transmitted to him by a different, less benevolent group of space people, or evidence of intervention by the CIA or other secret agency.

When Le Poer Trench inherited his title he raised the UFO question in the House of Lords, and in 1979 persuaded the chamber to hold a debate on the issue, the success of which encouraged him to form an All-Party UFO Study Group. A year or so previously Sir Eric Gairy, once Governor of Grenada, had persuaded the UN to hold a UFO debate, after his sighting of an object in 1975, and we learn that former President Idi Amin had been similarly fortunate on the shores of Lake Victoria, and interpreted it as a portent of 'good luck to Uganda'. To round off this bevy of distinguished ufologists, it should be noted that ex-President Jimmy Carter reported having spotted a UFO some years before his election, and pledged to make public any official records of the phenomenon. This never happened.

UFO Theories

What are the various theories about the UFO phenomenon? Even the sceptical Patrick Moore admits that it would be 'the height of conceit' to think that ours is the only planet on which life exists. Donald Keyhoe, a name which crops up in all UFO literature, pointed out that the first sighting took place soon after the first atom bomb explosion. He maintains space creatures have been studying us for centuries. Some believe that the craft are hostile. This is the idea behind H G Wells's *War of the Worlds*, Orson Welles's radio broadcast of which caused nationwide panic in the US. Others, however, such as Le Poer Trench, say there are two types — the one benevolent, the other group newer and more sinister. The situation is further confused by a host of reports of Men in Black who arrive to warn off witnesses. Are they aliens or government men charged to keep the whole affair secret?

One way of amplifying our knowledge of the situation would be to look for any pattern in the appearances of these spacecraft, if such they be. We knew that they are often seen at crossing points of ley lines and thus, arguably, near ancient sacred sites. They are also seen near aeroplanes. There is a 1975 report of a UFO being spotted over the Japanese air base of Hya Kuri.

An interesting study reveals the link between geological features and a high incidence of UFO reports. We know that increased electromagnetic activity (such as is produced by storms, earthquakes etc), can affect animals and human mental states, so it is possible that geophysical situations may bring on hallucinations and 'induced dreams'. It is also possible that seismic stress may release ionized gases which produce luminous effects that are visible.

This last point leads us on to numerous sorts of mistaken identification. At least 90 per cent of all properly investigated UFO sightings can be explained as misidentification of something perfectly normal, such as stars and planets, especially Venus, meteors, clouds, mirages, birds, satellites and many more.

Modern scientific methods have been able to shed some light in the darkness; the computer has opened up new ways of checking dubious photographs by breaking each picture down into nearly a quarter of a million tiny pixels (picture cells). This technique of analysis by Computer Eye has been operated on a large scale by the American group Ground Saucer Watch. The machine can enhance or decrease the value of each pixel on a 'grey scale' and can thus reveal hitherto unsuspected information on a photograph or display it in a new and striking way.

Even such high-tech methods, however, cannot resolve the knottier problems, such as the photographs taken in 1950 by Mr and Mrs Trent, a couple from Oregon, US. These have been analysed exhaustively, but while researchers still disagree as to their authenticity, the highly sceptical Condon report drawn up by the US Air Force concludes that the evidence did not positively rule out a hoax — scant recognition, but still more than was given to most 'sightings'.

Until now we have examined many aspects of ufology but there remains an area of study which is particularly controversial, the so-called 'new ufology'. It has its roots in Jung's book on flying saucers in which he treats the phenomenon as a space-age myth, but Dr Jacques Vallée is more often regarded as the founder of the movement, for his work *Passport to Magonia* proposes the existence of an interdimensional world or an alternative reality. Some 'new ufologists' argue that subjectivity is all-important and is not to be excluded, as would be the case in a conventional science, while others believe there is some objective reality but it is less important than the psychological cause. A third group feel there is a dichotomy between subjective and objective reality, with a grey area in between the two. There is a feeling that the world of Magonia is akin to Jung's 'collective unconscious'.

But as Dr Vallée said in his address to the UN debate on UFOs in 1978: 'We might say that something is "real" if enough people believe in it.'

Above: *This classic flying saucer was photographed over Trinidad Island by an amateur in 1958.*

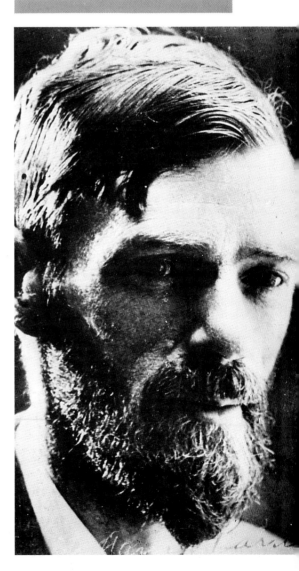

Right: *Virgoans make successful writers, as D H Lawrence triumphantly did.*

VIRGO

Virgo the Virgin, sixth sign of the Zodiac, is an Earth sign, ruling those born between 23 August and 22 September.

Virgos are said to be as independent as a cat, for however affectionate they feel towards someone they always seem to hold a small part of themselves back. They are naturally cool and quiet, preferring not to make a big show of their feelings. This doesn't make them cold, but gives them a certain reserve or shyness with other people. They are idealistic, clever, charming, intuitive, tactful, loyal, honest and artistic, with a wonderful sense of humour.

Virgos are intelligent, often doing well at school because they enjoy learning. They are quick-thinking, logical, good at problem-solving, clever with languages, methodical, precise and tidy. They also take care over their work, often preferring to work alone. They have excellent taste and are good at critical analysis, having keenly developed discriminatory powers. The sun is in Virgo as summer turns to autumn, giving Virgos great versatility. They are unpretentious, almost humble, and they like to make other people's lives easier. The help they offer is very effective, for they are practical people, thanks to the influence of the Earth in the sign.

If they are not careful, however, Virgos can gain a reputation for being overcritical of other people — not an endearing habit. They should beware of using that quick brain and linguistic ability to lash out with sarcasm, however witty. Deviousness, selfishness, meanness and a neurotic streak should also be checked. A desire to do well at work is good, but not when it leads Virgos to be officious and too fussy. If this happens, it is time for a holiday.

Virgos can become gifted writers, like D H Lawrence. Almost any career involving language, whether spoken or written, suits this sign, and they make good critics in any field. Their love of method makes Virgos good accountants, computer programmers and clerical workers. Idealism together with a practical nature and a desire to help other people mean that they make good doctors, teachers and secretaries. Their artistic abilities find a practical outlet in any work such as wood carving, engineering, carpentry, gardening or working with metals. Virgos prefer to use their skills to make useful and beautiful objects, rather than experimenting with abstract, whimsical art.

Virgos are compatible with those born under CAPRICORN and TAURUS, which are similarly practical Earth signs. They need someone who isn't put off by that aloof air, who can reach the humorous, helpful, affectionate, timid Virgo deep inside.

Physically Virgos tend to have brown curly hair, brown or sometimes blue eyes, high foreheads and pale skin. They are very upright, keeping their backs straight, but they can sometimes seem a little stiff with nerves.

Their weaknesses are the bowels, intestines, liver, abdomen, spleen and duodenum. These make them prone to digestive problems, constipation, diarrhoea, even worms, appendicitis and peritonitis, as well as nervous problems.

See also ASTROLOGY

WHITE MAGIC

White magicians usually concentrate on healing powers, but they can also produce a love potion when required, or drive away the devil.

Throughout human history and in every part of the world we find evidence of a belief in the possibility of controlling the forces of Nature by supernatural means. The belief takes an infinite variety of forms, but it rests on certain basically very similar ideas about the relationship between the human mind and the cosmos (see IMITATIVE MAGIC).

In pre-Christian or tribal societies, the practitioner of white or beneficent magic may be a person of considerable standing in the community — a shaman, a witch-doctor, a druid or a priest; in societies where the established religion frowns on magical practices (other than its own) the person believed to be gifted in this way is likely to have much humbler status, like the wise-woman of country communities.

But whether white magic is practised in tribal Africa or in the Irish or Scottish or Italian countryside the fundamental beliefs are likely to be much the same. The white magician uses his or her powers in a struggle against evil, which itself is seen as stemming from supernatural rather than natural causes; most commonly he or she is seen as a healer.

In Christian countries white magic has generally been fiercely opposed by the clergy, because of its association with paganism and its rival claim to supernatural power, but it is not unusual for white magicians to make use of what they see as the magical powers of Christian words and symbols. In this century, for example, the famous Spanish wise-woman Tia Carrica is reported to have effected some remarkable cures by drawing the sign of the cross with her finger on the foreheads of the sick, and the Holy Trinity are frequently invoked in the INCANTATIONS of magicians in European countries. Conversely, in recent years the Church of England has begun to adopt a more tolerant attitude to faith healers, who may be seen as practising a latter-day white magic.

The white magician may have acquired his or her powers by means of study and initiation at the hands of a more senior practitioner, but more often he or she is seen as having a special, inborn gift (in Celtic countries he might be the seventh son of a seventh son). There is plentiful evidence both from European and non-European contexts that, whatever the methods used, and whether they are called witch-doctors or healers or Cunning Men, white magicians frequently do have remarkable psychic powers. Just as the concentrated and focused power of the CURSE may cause actual bodily harm, so perhaps the concentrated and focused good-will of the trained or gifted white magician may actually heal. At the same time, the white magician may be a Wounded Healer: which means that the magician's special powers manifest themselves in some form of mental or physical deformity or handicap.

White Magic's Contribution to Modern Medicine

The methods of white magic are immensely varied: they include amulets and charms (the charm bracelet is a survival from white magical beliefs) and fetishes (see FETISH); the incantation and the SPELL; magic symbolism; abnormal psychic states such as the TRANCE favoured by the shamans of central Asia; various methods of DIVINATION. Above all, and very commonly, they include the use of herbs, and there is no doubt at all that the belief in the magical properties of plants over many centuries and the massive trial-and-error experience resulting from it have produced a vast amount of genuinely valuable knowledge about herbal medicine. The beliefs, grounded in imitative magic, that led the country magician to associate a particular plant with a particular healing virtue, so often reflected in the popular English names for herbs — such as liverwort and heartsease — may be erroneous, but modern medicine and HOMOEOPATHY owe a great deal to the age-old association between white magic and the plant kingdom.

Although few people in the west consciously profess to practising white magic today, white magicians still survive and prosper under a variety of names in many parts of the world. And white magical beliefs and powers persist in what we nowadays describe as 'fringe medicine', in the activities of faith healers, astrologers and fortune tellers, and perhaps also in the methodology of today's psychiatrists, who use a quite different terminology but who also strive to penetrate with the healing power of the mind the inner self of the sick and troubled.

Below: 'Heart's Ease' and 'Liverwort' describe their own function in the white magician's healing spells.

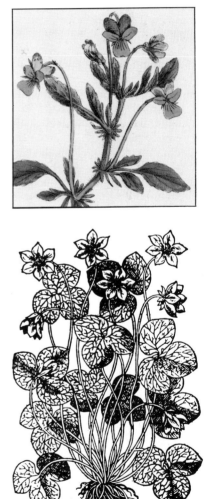

153

WITCHCRAFT

Medieval witchcraft demanded a commitment to the devil and a willingness to take part in the orgiastic witches' sabbaths. But did witchcraft only exist in the minds of the superstitious or the sexually repressed?

Witchcraft involves the doing of evil to others by supernatural means. But the term varies in meaning according to whether it is being used, for example, by anthropologists writing about tribal Africa or by historians writing about witchcraft in Europe, especially during the period of the great witch hunts from the 15th to the 17th centuries. In Europe the charge is added of Devil-worship or SATANISM and of attendance at the witches' SABBATH.

The terms 'witchcraft' and SORCERY are sometimes taken as synonymous, but anthropologists make a distinction between the two: a sorcerer is an ordinary human being who resorts to acts of evil magic; a witch, in African terms, is a witch in his or her essential nature and will very often reveal the fact by physiological signs; in Europe witchhood is not always hereditary but the witch is committed to the service of the Devil and may also be revealed by physical signs: the 'witch's teat' or 'Devil's mark'.

Tribal Witchcraft

Anthropologists, when writing about witchcraft in tribal societies, describe it almost invariably as a phenomenon of accusation; that is to say, witchcraft

accusations exist but witches in actuality do not. As with sorcery, witchcraft accusations seem to arise because of a tendency of the human mind at a certain cultural level to reject the notion of what we call 'natural causes' for occurrences of misfortune, whether it be illness, crop failure, infertility, lack of success in hunting or anything else that injures people or harms their prosperity.

Witchcraft accusations were and still are endemic in tribal societies, and they persist even in 20th century urban Africa, where people quite frequently blame witches for making them alcoholics or causing them to fail examinations. But there are also upsurges or epidemics of witchcraft accusation, and the evidence strongly suggests that these tend to occur after natural disasters, such as disease or drought, or as a result of social dislocation, as for example when tribal societies are struggling to adjust to the impact of European civilization.

European Witchcraft

Similar factors undoubtedly underlie European witchcraft, along with broadly similar popular beliefs about magic. But to these were added, in the Christian world, the Church's allegations against heretics from the earliest times until the late middle ages, including Devil-worship and all kinds of perverse and indecent practices.

From the 14th century onwards we find these allegations being made against witches. Whether they represent practices that were actually occurring or whether people were perversely attracted by the obscene rituals described by demonologists and witch-hunters in lurid detail, will probably never be known for certain. Yet another factor was Christianity's opposition to sexual pleasure for any purpose other than procreation within marriage. This must explain the very strong sexual element in practically all descriptions of European witchcraft practices, including the orgiastic dancing and promiscuous couplings of the witches' sabbath.

For a long time two quite contradictory views about European witchcraft were widely held. One was that witchcraft existed only in the superstitious minds of ignorant country people or in the tortured imaginations of sexually repressed clerics. The chief victims of the witchcraft delusion, according to this view, were lonely old women, eccentrics, or people whose personalities attracted suspicion and hostility; the

Below: Tests for witches were common. The most barbaric involved 'swimming' the witch. If she floated then she was indeed a witch. If she sank and drowned, her death proved her innocence. Other tests involved looking for the extra teat with which she fed her familiars, or 'pricking' her to find the numb spot all witches were said to possess. Retractable points were used to fake this, so that it was apparently seen to go in, but no blood was drawn and no pain was felt.

Left: *Witchcraft in some forms still flourishes today.* Below: *But the days of witchcraft being outlawed (and a Witchfinder General, such as Matthew Hopkins, being appointed) have long gone.*

'confessions' of these unfortunates were invariably extracted under torture or intimidation unless they emerged from the victims' own disturbed minds.

The contrary view was proposed in the very influential books of the historian Margaret Murray, who believed she had proved that witches did indeed exist, that they came from all classes of society including the highest, and that they were members of a cult which was nothing less than the ancient pagan religion of Western Europe.

Margaret Murray's theory is fascinating and has had a profound influence on modern witches, but the evidence of countless reports and confessions does not tend to support it: neither the witches nor their accusers ever claimed that they worshipped anything other than the Devil of Christianity, whom they saw quite explicitly as the perpetual enemy of the Christian God, and their rituals were quite deliberate parodies of Christian ritual. This is not to deny of course that there are pagan survivals in witchcraft just as there are in Christianity.

The horned figure of the Devil and the many elements of animal-worship suggested by witchcraft practices are almost certainly echoes of the religious beliefs of prehistoric Europe.

The opposite view, that there were never any witches, is also undermined by the evidence, for although many, perhaps the great majority, of the confessions were made under duress, there remain a significant number that were made freely, even boastfully. Witchcraft attracted young men and women as well

as the elderly and it was not uncommon for children to be involved in it. Notables were from time to time accused of it, the most famous perhaps being Joan of Arc, but its appeal seems mainly to have been to the poor in remote country districts.

Modern Witchcraft

Witchcraft as described above has largely died out in Europe, though instances of it have occasionally been discovered as late as the present century. Modern witches, often under the influence of Margaret Murray, would claim to be practising a revival or survival of the ancient religion, based on white magic. Their practices are likely to include ritual dancing and nudity, but exclude the indecencies and the malevolence of the late medieval witch.

ZODIAC

Astrologers represent our known solar system as a circle, with Earth at the centre, and the Sun, Moon and the planets charted round it. The Zodiac is the division of that circle into 12 segments or Houses, each taking up 30 degrees. Each House is named after a constellation of stars appearing in that section of the sky, and each has a different influence on human life. The Zodiac is the key which unlocks the meaning of the stars.

See also ASTROLOGY

BIBLIOGRAPHY

GENERAL

Curious Encounters *Loren Coleman* Faber & Faber London, Boston, 1985
The Directory of Possibilities ed. *Colin Wilson & John Grant*, Webb & Bower Exeter, 1981
Encyclopaedia of the Unexplained ed. *Richard Cavendish* Routledge & Kegan Paul, London, 1974
Encyclopaedia of Occultism and Parapsychology ed. *Leslie Shepard* 3 vols, Gale Research Co. Detroit, 1985
A Handbook of Parapsychology ed. *B B Wolman* Van Nostrand, Reinhold Co. New York
Incredible Phenomena ed. *P Brookesmith* Orbis, London, 1984
Man, Myth & Magic ed. *Richard Cavendish* 7 vols BPC Publications Ltd, London, 1970–72
Mysteries *Colin Wilson* Hodder & Stoughton, London, 1978
Natural and Supernatural: A History of the Paranormal *Brian Inglis* Hodder & Stoughton, London, 1977
The Occult *Colin Wilson* Hodder & Stoughton, London, 1971
Photographs of the Unknown *Robert Rickard & Richard Kelly* New English Library, London, 1980

INDIVIDUAL SUBJECTS

The Arts of the Alchemists *C A Burland* Weidenfeld & Nicolson, London 1967
Alchemists through the ages *A E Waite* Rudolf Steiner, Blauevelt, NY, 1970
The Projection of the Astral Body *S Muldoon & W Carrington* Rider, London, 1969
The Truth about Astrology *Michel Gauquelin* Basil Blackwell, Oxford, 1983
The Prediction Book of Astrology *P West & J Logan* Blandford Press, Poole, Dorset, 1983
The Evidence for the Bermuda Triangle *D Group* Aquarian Press
The Great Beast *John Symonds* Frederick Muller, London, 1951
The Tibetan Book of the Dead *W Y Evans-Wentz* Oxford University Press, 1960
Science and the Supernatural *John Taylor* Granada, London, 1980
Aleister Crowley *Charles Camwell* University Books, New York, 1962
Aleister Crowley and the Hidden God *Kenneth Grant* Muller, London, 1973
Alien Animals *Janet & Colin Bord* Panther, London, 1985
On the Track of Unknown Animals *Bernard Heuvelmans* Paladin Books, St Alban's, 1970; Hill & Wang, NY, 1965
Mysterious America *Loren Coleman* Faber & Faber Winchester, MA, 1983; Faber & Faber, London, 1984
Living Wonders *John Michell & Robert Rickard* Thames & Hudson, London, 1982
John Dee: The World of an Elizabethan Magus *Peter J French* Routledge & Kegan Paul, London, 1984
John Dee *Richard Deacon* Muller, London, 1968; Transatlantic Arts, New York, 1971
The Prediction Book of Divination *J Logan & L Hodson* Blandford Press, Poole, Dorset, 1984
The Complete Book of Dowsing and Divination *Peter Underwood* Rider, London, 1980
Lucid Dreams *Celia Green* Institute of Psychophysical Research, Oxford, 1968

Dream Telepathy *M Ullman & S Krippner with A Vaughan* Macmillan, New York, 1973
Extra-Sensory Powers *Alfred Douglas* Gollancz, London, 1976
ESP Research Today *J G Pratt* Scarecrow Press, Metuchen, NJ, 1973
Exorcism: Fact not Fiction *Martin Ebon* New American Library, New York, 1974
Flying Saucers: A Myth of Things Seen in the Skies *C G Jung* Routledge & Kegan Paul, London, 1959
Avalonian Quest *Geoffrey Ashe* Fontana, London, 1982
Apparitions *G N M Tyrrel* Duckworth, London, 1953; Macmillan, New York, 1970
Understanding Ghosts *Victoria Brandon* Gollancz, London, 1980
The Science of Homoeopathy *G Vithoulkas* Grove Press, New York, 1980
Hypnosis *David Waxman* Allen & Unwin, London, 1981
I Ching trans. *R Wilhelm, foreword C G Jung* Routledge & Kegan Paul, London, 1975
The Mediumship of Mrs Leonard *S Smith* University Books, Secaucus, NJ, 1964
Eliphas Lévi and the French Magical Revival *Christopher McIntosh* Weiser, New York, 1974
The New View Over Atlantis *John Michell* Thames & Hudson, London, 1983
The Ley Hunter's Companion *Paul Devereux & Ian Thomson* Thames & Hudson, London, 1979
The Secret Country *Janet & Colin Bord* Paladin Books, London, 1985
The Roots of Coincidence *Arthur Koestler* Hutchinson, London, 1972
Magic: An Occult Primer *David Conway* Jonathan Cape, London, 1972
The History of Magic *Eliphas Lévi* Rider, London, 1969
Magick *Aleister Crowley* Routledge, London, 1973; Wehman, Hackensack, NJ
Natural Medicine *Brian Inglis* Collins, London, 1977
Concentration & Meditation *Christmas Humphreys* Watkins, London, 1953
Mesmerism and the End of the Enlightenment in France *Robert Darnton* Harvard University Press, Cambridge, Mass., 1968
Mind Over Matter *Kit Pedler* Thames & Methuen, London, 1981
Mind-Reach *R Targ & H Puthoff* Delacorte, New York, 1977; Jonathan Cape, London, 1977
Nostradamus: Into the Twenty-first Century *Jean-Charles de Fontbrune* Hutchinson, London, 1984
Out of the Body Experiences *R Crookall* University Books, New York, 1970
The Language of the Hand *Cheiro* Corgi, London, 1968; Arc Books, NY, 1968
Phallic Worship *G Ryley Scott* Panther, London, 1970
The Life and Work of Mrs Piper *A L Piper* Kegan Paul, London, 1929
Poltergeist *Colin Wilson* New English Library, London, 1981
The Poltergeist *W Roll* Scarecrow Press, Metuchen, NJ, 1976

Beyond Belief *Brian Branston* Weidenfeld & Nicolson, London, 1974
Through the Time Barrier *Danah Zohar* Heinemann, London, 1982
Psi Search *N Bowles, F Hynds & J Maxwell* Harper & Row, New York, 1978
The Great Pyramid Decoded *P Lemusurier* Compton Russell, London, 1976
More Lives Than One? The Evidence of the Remarkable Bloxham Tapes *J Iverson* Souvenir Press, London, 1977
A Critical Examination of the Belief in a Life After Death *C J Ducasse* Charles C Thomas, Springfield, Ill., 1961
Satanism & Witchcraft *Jules Michelet* Arco Publications, London, 1958
Sex and Superstition *G L Simons* Abelard-Schuman, London, 1973
The Spiritualists *Ruth Brandon* Weidenfeld & Nicolson, London, 1983
Voices in My Ear *Doris Stokes & Linda Dearsley* Macdonald Futura, London, 1980
Stonehenge Complete *Christopher Chippindale* Thames & Hudson, London, 1983
Megalithic Science *Douglas Heggie* Thames & Hudson, London, New York, 1981
The Tarot *Mouni Sadhu* Allen & Unwin, London, 1970; Wehman, Hackensack, NJ, 1970
The Mystery of Telepathy *Joe Cooper* Constable, London, 1982
UFO Study *Jenny Randles* Robert Hale, London, 1981
The Meaning of Witchcraft *G B Gardner* Aquarian Press, London, 1959; Weiser, New York, 1959

CREDITS

Aerofilms 76R; George Alexander 134L; Ashmolean Museum of Western Art, Oxford 36B; Chris Barker 71; Bibliothèque de l'Arsenal (R. Lalance) 11; Birnback Publishing Service 97; Janet & Colin Bord 59, 67B, 93, 145; BPCC/Aldus Archive (Museo di San Marco, Florence) 14, (Academie des Beaux Arts, Paris) 43B, (Franz Boas) 45B, (Chatto & Windus) 52T, (Bretosy Miro, Barcelona) 55T, 58/9, 75, (Kunstmuseum, Wintertur) 80R, 82B, 85B, 87, (National Gallery) 99, (British Museum) 101B, (Tantra Museum, New Delhi) 115, 126/7, 128, (Kunsthaus, Zurich) 130B; Bridgeman Art Library (Musée des Beaux Arts, Lille) 64, (Birmingham City Art Gallery) 79L; British Tourist Authority 60T, 60B; Camera Press 44 inset, (John L. Hughes) 84, (John Smith) 92, (Tom Blau) 131B; Collection Viollet, Paris 135; John H. Cutten 72; Dover Press 153B; Mary Evans Picture Library 13B, 33T, 39T, 42, 45T, 51T, (Hodder & Stoughton) 56B, 61, 62/3, 63, 66B, 69B, 74B, 86, 90, 90/1, 100, 102, 105B, 112, 113, 119, 123B, 124/5, 125, 132, 134R, 150, alphabet letters; Fortean Picture Library 13T, 48B, 51B, 53, 65, 77, 118, 137, 151, 154, 155L, 155R; Hahnemann House Museum 66T; Michael Holford 21, (British Museum) 26, (Warburg Institute, London) 32B, (British Museum) 34/5 and 52B and 62T, (Guildhall Museum, London) 70, (British Museum) 81, (Gerry Clyde) 106; Huntingdon Library, San Marino, California 138; Robin Livio 133T; The Mansell Collection 36TR, 68, 79R, 80L, 94, 107B, 110B, 111C, 111R, 153T; Alan Meak 46R, 47; Muldoon & Carrington (Hutchinson Publishing Group Ltd) 17; Gerald Nason 76L; National Gallery 10, 136; National Gallery of Scotland (Joseph Noel Paton) 95; Phaidon Archives (T. P. Grange) 83; The Photo Source Ltd 34L, 44; Pictorial Press Ltd 15B, 28B, 78B, 117B; Picturepoint 129T, 129B; Popperfoto 12, 24B, 96/7, 139B, 140, 141, 142; Harry Price Library 37B, 116, 121, 139T; Psychic News 49, 56T, 57; Radio Times Hulton Picture Library 32T, 46L 148; Arthur Rakham 48C; Rex Features Ltd 25, 27B, 30, 73B, 88, 89, 107T, 143, 147B, 149, 152R; Ronan Picture Library 20, astrological signs; Denis Rolf 41T; Scala 50; Spectrum Colour Library 122; Weiner Library (Chris Barker) 16B; Wellcome Trustees 85T; Whitworth Art Gallery, University of Manchester 23; Peter Yamaoka 108/9; Chris Yates 40L.